SHAW 18

SHAW

The Annual of Bernard Shaw Studies
Volume Eighteen

Edited by

Fred D. Crawford

The Pennsylvania State University Press
University Park, Pennsylvania

bib#68138

ISBN 0-271-01779-1 ISSN 0741-5842

It is the policy of The Pennsylvania State University Press to use acid-free paper for the first printing of all clothbound books. Publications on uncoated stock satisfy the minimum requirements of American National Standard for Information Sciences—Permanence of Paper for Printed Library Materials. ANSI Z39.48–1992.

Note to contributors and subscribers. *SHAW*'s perspective is Bernard Shaw and his milieu—its personalities, works, relevance to his age and ours. As "his life, work, and friends"—the subtitle to a biography of G.B.S.—indicates, it is impossible to study the life, thought, and work of a major literary figure in a vacuum. Issues and people, economics, politics, religion, theater and literature and journalism—the entirety of the two half-centuries the life of G.B.S. spanned was his assumed province. *SHAW,* published annually, welcomes articles that either explicitly or implicitly add to or alter our understanding of Shaw and his milieu. Address all manuscript contributions (in 3 copies) to Fred D. Crawford, Department of English, Central Michigan University, Mt. Pleasant, MI 48859. Subscription correspondence should be addressed to *SHAW,* Penn State University Press, Suite C, 820 North University Drive, University Park, PA 16802. Unsolicited manuscripts are welcomed but will be returned only if return postage is provided. In matters of style *SHAW* recommends the *MLA Style Sheet* and advises referring to recent volumes of the *SHAW.*

CONTENTS

NOTICES

37th Annual Season, Shaw Festival
Niagara-on-the-Lake

The 1998 playbill of the Shaw Festival (Artistic Director, Christopher Newton) will include three plays by Bernard Shaw: *Major Barbara*, *John Bull's Other Island*, and *Passion, Poison, and Petrifaction*. Other productions include *You Can't Take It With You* (George S. Kaufman and Moss Hart), *Lady Windermere's Fan* (Oscar Wilde), *The Lady's Not for Burning* (Christopher Fry), *Joy* (John Galsworthy), *Foggy Day* (George and Ira Gershwin), *The Shop at Sly Corner* (Edward Percy), *Brothers in Arms* (Merrill Denison), and *Waterloo* (Arthur Conan Doyle).

For further information, write to Shaw Festival, Box 774, Niagara-on-the-Lake, Ontario, Canada L0S 1J0, or call 1-905-468-2172 or call (toll free) 1-800-511-SHAW [7429].

17th Annual Milwaukee Shaw Festival
17 April–2 May 1999

The Milwaukee Shaw Festival (Artistic Director, Montgomery Davis) will feature performances of Shaw's *Mrs Warren's Profession* and *The Illusion* (an adaptation of Pierre Corneille's *L'Illusion comique* by Tony Kushner).

For ticket information either call (414) 276–8842 or write to Milwaukee Chamber Theatre, Broadway Theatre Centre, 158 N. Broadway, Milwaukee, WI 53202.

Dan H. Laurence

THE SHAWS AND THE GURLYS: A GENEALOGICAL STUDY

Introduction

"I hate the Family," Bernard Shaw declared in a Fabian lecture he delivered in 1886. "I loathe the Family. I entirely detest and abominate the Family as the quintessence of Tyranny, Sentimentality, Inefficiency, Hypocrisy, and Humbug."[1] In the Fabian Society minutes book for that meeting, a week or two later, he inscribed, "This was one of Shaw's most outrageous performances."[2] It was, in fact, consistent with his technique of overstating a case startlingly to jolt and stir an audience to thought, although in this instance presumably reflecting a strong personal distaste for the querulous, back-biting, class-prejudiced, intolerant lot of snobs among whom he grew up, "addicted to talking about 'the Shaws' as if they were the Hohenzollerns or the Romanoffs or the Hapsburgs"[3] and viewing themselves as members of the *haute bourgeoisie*.

Surrounded in his early years by a hotchpotch of dysfunctional kinfolk, including a handful of eccentric Gurlys on his mother's side, it was inevitable the playwright in his maturity would limn these smug moralists in *Man and Superman*, *Getting Married*, *Fanny's First Play*, and *Heartbreak*

---

1. "Socialism and the Family," 1 October 1886. Full text published in John A. Bertolini, "Shaw's Family Values," *SHAW* 16 (1996): 145–54.

2. Fabian Society archive, Nuffield College Library, Oxford University.

3. Shaw to Col. F. C. Pratt, 21 June 1916. Special Collections, Case Library, Colgate University.

House. "The Shaws" are a specific target in *How He Lied to Her Husband,* where Aurora Bompas (*vice* Lucinda Carr Shaw) complains of her spouse's having "nothing but relatives. . . . [E]ight sisters and . . . ever so many brothers." Aurora does not mind the brothers, but "though the sisters quarrel with one another like mad all the time, yet let one of the brothers marry, and they all turn on their unfortunate sister-in-law and devote the rest of their lives with perfect unanimity to persuading [her husband] that his wife is unworthy of him."[4] Moreover, the relative ("a nasty vulgar-minded cat") most hateful to Aurora is given the name, Georgina, of a paternal aunt-by-marriage whom Shaw deeply despised.

The plays offer many vividly detailed reflections of Shaw's "devil of a childhood . . . frightful and loveless in realities,"[5] which seem to confirm Graham Greene's asseveration, "Unhappiness wonderfully aids the memory."[6] Moreover, many of Shaw's recollections spilled over into the prefaces and correspondence, to be enjoyed unadulterated or unrenovated for fictive use. Unforgettable is Uncle Barney, man of professed piety, who, anticipating Joyce's voyeuristic Leopold Bloom on Sandymount shore, reputedly sat, a Bible balanced on his knee, peering through opera glasses focused on the ladies' bathing beach at Dalkey. When Uncle Barney commenced to drape white fabrics about his room and to proclaim himself to be the Holy Ghost, he was bustled off to a mental retreat, where he tootled "Home, Sweet Home" on a flute (much like Randall the Rotter's performance of "Keep the Home Fires Burning" at the final curtain of *Heartbreak House*), and where he sought to asphyxiate himself by thrusting his head into a carpet bag, only to perish in the process from a heart seizure. Bertrand Russell, who heard this story repeated at innumerable luncheons, commented that whenever Shaw "came to his uncle who committed suicide by putting his head in a carpet-bag and then shutting it, a look of unutterable boredom used to appear on Mrs. Shaw's face, and if one were sitting next her one had to take care not to listen to Shaw."[7]

Also indelibly etched are portraits of Aunt Cecilia, his father's eldest sister, whose "conception of the family dignity was so prodigious (the family snobbery being unmitigated in her case by the family sense of humor) that she would have refused an earl because he was not a duke and so died a very ancient virgin";[8] the Reverend uncle, Walter Carroll,

4. *How He Lied to Her Husband,* in Bernard Shaw, *Collected Plays with Their Prefaces,* ed. Dan H. Laurence (London: Max Reinhardt, 1971), 2:1035.

5. Shaw to Ellen Terry, 11 June 1897, in Bernard Shaw, *Collected Letters 1874–1897,* ed. Dan H. Laurence (London: Max Reinhardt, 1965), p. 773.

6. Graham Greene, Introduction to *The Best of Saki* (New York: Viking, 1961), p. ix.

7. *Portraits from Memory* (London: G. Allen & Unwin, 1956), p. 72.

8. Preface to *Immaturity* (1930), in Bernard Shaw, *Complete Prefaces,* ed. Dan H. Laurence and Daniel J. Leary (London: Allen Lane the Penguin Press, 1993–97), 3:6.

who, mistaking a bottle of liniment for a cough mixture, gave his twelve-year-old daughter a fatal dose; his wife Emily, *née* Shaw, who, when her new sister-in-law called, was overheard to exclaim "That bitch!" to the parlormaid;[9] and the earlier-mentioned Aunt Georgina, wife of Shaw's youngest uncle, Frederick, a woman of ungovernable temper (there was insanity in her family), so opinionated and overbearing that her timorous husband at last lost patience with her and proceeded to beat her soundly with his fists.

There were Shavian tales, too, of a profusion of cousins, called "Kaffir" and "Ta," "Muffie," "Boke," "Boxer" (appropriated for General Bridgenorth in *Getting Married*), "Fippy," "Coo," and "Ho Ho." "Nicknaming," Shaw wrote to Aunt Emily Carroll's great granddaughter in 1946, "was an incorrigible family habit in the Shaw clan."[10] He maintained cordial relations through the years with a small number of Shaws of his generation, like Cousin Arthur (Aunt Georgina's eldest offspring), who in August 1883 was pressured unsuccessfully to join the Land Restoration Union and proselytize for it in Dublin, but at his cousin's behest *did* purchase a copy of Henry George's *Progress and Poverty*, although he never got beyond the first chapter. Not surprisingly, he ended as a banker. Cousin Fanny Johnston (better known as the novelist Mrs. Cashel Hoey), several months older than Shaw's mother, conspired with the latter to get her son introductions for employment in London, but was little more successful with Cousin George than he had been with Cousin Arthur. There was also association from time to time with cousin Robert Carroll, who came a few times to London and once joined Shaw as a piano duettist for several days in Osnaburgh Street when Lucinda Carr Shaw was holidaying in Broadstairs. Cousin Robbie, Shaw recalled, "had fits of fanaticism in his adolescence" and was alleged "to have attempted to fast naked in the woods for forty days";[11] he later was ordained in the Church of England.

And all the while, at home, there was in Shaw's boyhood the presence of a besotted parent, burdened with "self-reproaches and humiliations when he was not full of secret jokes," and "either biting his moustache

9. "Biographers' Blunders Corrected," in Bernard Shaw, *Sixteen Self Sketches* (London: Constable, 1949), p. 107. This anecdote was related also in a series of notes Shaw supplied to a relation: see footnote 10.

10. Holograph note (1946) on the reverse of the tenth in a series of Carroll family photographs sent to Shaw for identification by Dorothy Eagle (*née* Glasgow) of Oxford, a grandniece of cousin Emily Carroll, to whom the photos had belonged. Published by permission of Martin Eagle.

11. Ibid., on the sixth photograph. In the Shaw *Diaries 1885–1897*, ed. Stanley Weintraub (University Park: Penn State University Press, 1986), Robert Carroll's name is mistranscribed as "Robert Carl."

and whispering deepdrawn damns, or shaking with silent paroxysms of laughter." George Carr Shaw, carrying "an imperfectly wrapped-up goose under one arm and a ham in the same condition under the other . . . butting at the garden wall in the belief that he was pushing open the gate, and transforming his tall hat to a concertina in the process,"[12] so "disabled" his son by merriment that, far from wishing to secrete this family skeleton, or any others, Shaw opted to make the skeleton dance. And so, both in the Dublin years of adolescence and, later, in the plays, prefaces, criticism, and correspondence, the family tragedies of the Shaws emerged as comedy, as did those of the Gurlys, his mother's family, notably the country squire grandfather, who, when his aging hunting dog made its first mistake, "instantly shot it";[13] the sea-going, generally inebriated, Rabelaisian physician uncle who became a surrogate father to the boy; and little crookbacked Great Aunt Ellen Whitcroft, who in her wrath over the marriage to George Carr Shaw presented to Shaw's mother a fistful of grandfather Walter Bagnall Gurly's I.O.U.s as a wedding present.[14] "It was on the whole," wrote Shaw, "a healthy instinct that decided [me] to get what ribald fun was possible out of it."[15]

Shaw took small interest in the genealogical background of his family until Archibald Henderson bombarded him with questions for the biography that would appear in 1911. Through a study of the Shaw clan, *A Genealogical Account of the Highland Families of Shaw* (1877), by Alexander Mackintosh Shaw, G.B.S. traced his ancient lineage to Shaigh, third son of Macduff, Earl of Fife, whose name, Shaw informed interviewer Hayden Church, "became civilised into Shaw."[16] In William George Shaw's *Memorials of the Clan Shaw* (1871) he discovered that the Irish branch (Terenure, seat of the Shaws of Bushy Park, of which his father was a cousin once removed) had descended from the thirteenth-century Schaws at Rothiemurchius, and, later, from the Clan Chattan, in which the Shaws are listed fourth among sixteen leading septs. The Clan made great capital in the press when its illustrious son enrolled as a member of the Clan Chattan Association on 19 October 1946, despite his earlier insistence, "Of course I am a fullblooded William & Mary Irishman. . . . There are no Celts in Ireland."[17]

    12. *Sixteen Self Sketches*, p. 88; preface to *Immaturity*, in *Complete Prefaces*, 3:18–19.

    13. Preface to *The Simpleton of the Unexpected Isles* (1936), in *Complete Prefaces*, 3:237.

    14. "My Mother and Her Relatives," *Sixteen Self Sketches*, p. 12.

    15. Preface to *Immaturity*; in *Complete Prefaces*, 3:18.

    16. "I Am the Upstart Son of a Downstart," Manchester *Sunday Chronicle* (28 February 1932), p. 7:2.

    17. For articles and interviews on Shaw's membership, see the *Sunday Dispatch* (London), 25 November 1946, the *Scottish Daily Express* (Glasgow), 28 November 1946, and the *Evening Citizen* (Glasgow), 29 November 1946. The "no Celts" quotation is from Shaw to Frank Harris, 28 September 1920, in *The Playwright and the Pirate: Bernard Shaw and Frank Harris:*

The baronets of Bushy Park independently researched their history, publishing the lineage in *Burke's Peerage*, accepting the legend that the Irish Shaws entered Ireland through the British military in 1689, their ancestor William Shaw participating in the Battle of the Boyne. G.B.S. preferred to believe that his people had descended from the line of Oliver Cromwell. For at least the last two decades of his life he informed biographers (Henderson in 1931 and St. John Ervine in 1936, among others) that "Oliver Cromwell's daughter Bridget married General Fleetwood. Their daughter Frances married Captain Fennell of Cappoquin [Co. Waterford]. Their daughter Elizabeth married Daniel Markham. Their granddaughter [Mary Markham] married Robert Shaw, whose eldest son William Shaw was Shaw of Sandpits, Co. Kilkenny, my greatgrandfather or thereabouts." These Irish Shaws, said G.B.S., "were descended from Macduff the Unborn." They were, however, "also descended from everybody who was alive and fertile in these islands in the XVII century and earlier; but old Noll [Cromwell] and Macduff are my selections."[18]

Ironically, Shaw appears to have known less about contemporary relations than of earlier antecedents. Of his father's siblings who survived to adulthood, there were several he never met at all, including the uncles who departed before his birth to found dynasties in the Antipodes and the dipso aunt Fanny Greene, who lived only a few streets away from his boyhood home. Not infrequently his recollections of relatives were disordered or misconceived. When an Australian cousin, Charles Macmahon Shaw of Melbourne, wrote a book *Bernard's Brethren* (published in 1939), G.B.S. challenged Charles's veracity—"Charles, you are a liar."—in a series of marginal comments in the manuscript (which the publisher reproduced in letterpress on facing pages, rubricated). Cousin Charles, he insisted, could not have played, during an 1871 family visit to Dublin (when Charles was eight), with another little boy named Sonny, for that "boy" was fifteen at the time "and was beginning adult life as a clerk in an estate office." In the process, however, Shaw revealed confusions of his own. The only Australian relation he could recall was Charles's father, Uncle Walter, "who, being blind at the time, touched my face to ascertain its shape. He called on us for half an hour."[19] This time it was Shaw who was in error.

For decades he had been convinced, for some reason known only to himself, that he had *two* sightless uncles, the second being Uncle Robert, blinded by an accident in his youth. As late as 1939 Shaw recorded, "One

A Correspondence, ed. Stanley Weintraub (University Park: Penn State University Press, 1982), p. 161.

18. Shaw to St. John Ervine, 28 April–11 May 1936, in Bernard Shaw, *Collected Letters 1926–1950*, ed. Dan H. Laurence (London: Max Reinhardt, 1988), p. 430.

19. The notes face pp. 32 and 59.

was blind and dependent on his brothers: another became blind later, but remained independent and capable."[20] The oddity of this is that six years earlier, when G.B.S., in a reply to a letter from a Tasmanian relation, inquired about the Melbourne family of his blind Uncle Walter, he was informed that Aunt Amy Shaw, last surviving child of Uncle Edward, "says that Uncle Walter was never blind; that was your Uncle Bob who came out to Melbourne and returned almost immediately."[21] Except for the fact of Uncle Robert's blindness, brief stay in Melbourne, and marriage (possibly in Liverpool), G.B.S. knew nothing about the man beyond a statement by George Carr Shaw that at fourteen he had saved Uncle Robert from drowning, "and, to tell you the truth, I was never so sorry for anything in my life afterwards."[22]

There was, in fact, very little communication between Shaw and his relations,[23] except for a few close ones like his maternal cousin Judy Musters and his paternal cousin James Cockaigne ("Kaffir") Shaw and the latter's three offspring. Few more than two dozen letters from relations survive in the forty-nine bound volumes of incoming correspondence preserved in the British Library's Shaw archive. And the information about even the closest ones provided by Shaw to biographers and other interviewers was, more often than not, vague and inconclusive, as in a statement to Ervine that his father, when he died, was "the same sort of age" as his mother, when in actuality she was eighty-two at her death and he merely seventy at his. Nor could Shaw recall the birth date of his sister Agnes. When Benjamin Rosset collected from half a dozen biographical studies all the statements Shaw had supplied to his biographers, they added up to a mass of uncertainties. Agnes at her death in 1876, Shaw had stated variously, was "twenty," "twenty or thereabouts," "just as she came of age," or "within one or two weeks of her twenty-first birthday,"[24] all now proven to be wide of the mark. No one seems to have consulted Agnes's death registration, which evidences that she had reached twenty-

20. The passage in the preface to *Immaturity* (drafted in 1921, published in 1930) was left uncorrected when Shaw revised and reprinted the preface in *Shaw Gives Himself Away* (Newton: Gregynog Press, 1939).

21. Frederick C. Shaw, grandson of Uncle Edward, to G.B.S., written from Terenure, Swansea, 29 September 1933. Across the top of the letter G.B.S. wrote, "Blind Uncle Robert went to Melbourne and returned, hence my mistake for Walter when he called on us[.] Walter was never blind, and I never saw him." British Library Add. Mss. 50520, fols. 221–22.

22. "Who I Am, and What I Think," *Sixteen Self Sketches*, p. 48. In the original publication in *The Candid Friend*, 11 and 18 May 1901, Robert was masked as "Uncle Algernon."

23. "We were barely on speaking terms when we met, which we did only accidentally, never intentionally." (G.B.S., in *Bernard's Brethren*, facing p. 32.)

24. B. C. Rosset, *Shaw of Dublin: The Formative Years* (University Park: Penn State University Press, 1964), pp. 73–74.

one before her death. And although Rosset cited announcements in *Saunders's News-Letter* (Dublin) for the births of G.B.S. and his sister Lucy, neither he nor any other of the lazy bunch who called themselves biographers ever troubled to sit down in the National Library of Ireland or the British Newspaper Library at Colindale and search through a couple of bound volumes (a task that took, finally, a bit more than four hours) of *Saunders's* to locate a birth announcement that was sure to be there. For the founder and editor of the newspaper was the non-related George Ferdinand Shaw (1821–99), Fellow of Trinity College, whose family members in Harrington Street, just round the corner from Synge Street, were close friends of the Shaws then and for the rest of their lives. Not surprisingly, the notice was published two days earlier than in the rival *Freeman's Journal*.

Equally troubling for the genealogist seeking pedigree was the surprising number of errors and obscurations in Cousin Charles's account of his Australian siblings and cousins and a confused claim of relationship from an American, Mildred B. Shaw, relict of George Eden Shaw (1860–1925), who wrote to G.B.S. in 1943 from California (to which her husband had emigrated from Australia) in the apparent belief that her spouse had been one of Uncle Walter's offspring.[25] George Eden's parents had left Liverpool by sailing boat circa 1849; he was born in Melbourne in a year that fit nicely into the chronology; and he had two older brothers. Shaw apparently accepted the claim at its face value and even communicated some of the information to the Tasmanian cousins (unless Mildred wrote to them, too), for a few of the details turn up in a genealogical chart compiled at the time in Hobart. But Mildred spoke of the oldest brother as Roderick, mentioning he had been born in Liverpool, whereas the *Victorian Pioneers Index 1837–1888*[26] identifies Uncle Walter's firstborn as Olrick William, born in Melbourne in 1858. It does record a George Eden Shaw, born on 5 April 1860, but as the (third surviving) son of William and Emma Newling Shaw, of Collingwood (a suburb of Melbourne), who had wed in Manchester, England, in 1850. And George Eden's older brothers have been identified as Roderick Randorn (or Random: the handwriting is difficult to decipher) and Robert Arthur Henry.[27]

It would, of course, have been impossible for anyone with more than one hundred Shaw and Gurly grandparents, uncles, aunts, cousins, and

25. Mildred B. Shaw to Bernard Shaw, 27 September 1943. British Library Add. Mss. 50523, fols. 88–89.

26. This publication, compiled by the Registry of Births, Deaths and Marriages, Melbourne, was issued in 1991 on compact disk. There is a copy in the Family History Library of the Church of Latter-Day Saints, Salt Lake City.

27. I am indebted to Mr. John Scarce of the Department of Justice, Victoria, for his letter of 24 February 1997 clarifying and resolving the confused relationship.

their spouses to keep track of them. Shaw sometimes noted death years or dates in his address books, not infrequently with a question mark. He diligently filed away the correspondence from foreign branches of the family as he began to hear from cousins two and three times removed, and he graciously penned notes of reply or typed informative letters in response to queries. But the relatives he knew best were, inevitably, the ones to whom he had to provide support. As the years went by there were many of these, and Shaw never shirked responsibility. Having battened on his mother and, to a lesser degree, on his sister Lucy in his nonage, when concentration on his writing art was more important to him than mundane employment, he compensated generously after his marriage, when royalties poured in from America and Germany and when the Court Theatre experiment made him suddenly bankable. He paid his mother's rent and gave her a household allowance for herself and another for her half-sister Arabella Gillmore to live with her as companion. He sent Lucy to a German retreat for her health, paid all her medical expenses, and kept her in comfort until her death in 1920.

With the single exception of Constance Hamilton, who lived "in easy circumstances" in Pittsburgh, "having married a successful man of business,"[28] all the Gurly sisters and their offspring received financial assistance from Shaw as long as they lived, including annuities with built-in cost-of-living increases for several of the latter written into his will. When Shaw's mother found it impossible to look after Aunt Kate Gurly, a drunken harridan, in her own home, Shaw paid for Kate's accommodation in St. John's Temperance House, Dorset, and when she desired to return to Dublin shortly before her death in 1914, he paid for lodgings in Rathmines, and bore the cost of her burial. Aunt Charlotte Rogers in Carlow lived in a house on land of which Shaw was ground landlord, with a substantial allowance to cover her expenses. A professional mendicant, she tried Shaw's patience sorely, but always managed to wheedle from him extra coals, eyeglasses, or a Christmas basket, as well as travel expenses for her son's emigration and a cello that her convent-educated daughter craved. Even from her deathbed she dictated a request through one of the nurses, asking Shaw to give sympathetic consideration to the purchase of a wireless set for the old folks in the hospital. Despite wartime shortages Shaw was able, through his estate agent, to obtain a second-hand radio. "The Gurlys are tough and tenacious," he confided to the agent.[29]

---

28. Shaw to Major A. J. V. Fitzmaurice, his estate agent in Carlow, 8 August 1941. Fitzmaurice family papers.

29. Ibid. The nurse was Sister M. Agnes Kelly, whose letter of 24 November 1941 Shaw forwarded to Major Fitzmaurice.

He underwrote the £1,200 his cousin Kaffir required for the purchase of a house in Skerries to be run as a guesthouse: it was set up as a loan, but as in most such instances Shaw had no expectation of its return, which never materialized. When Kaffir's two daughters were hard up he provided them with allowances, and paid medical expenses of the ailing younger daughter for the last decade of her life, visiting her home in London frequently. It was, as he himself admitted, a prodigious expenditure. When a Dublin cousin informed him that the orphaned Constance Shaw (daughter of Aunt Georgina) was dying in a Dublin nursing home and needed further assistance, Shaw sent a check sufficient to double her pathetic income. "You must take the responsibility," he told his correspondent, "and—what is worse—the gratitude. I come to the rescue only on condition that you swear by the bones of our ancestors . . . not to let Constance, or anyone else know or suspect where this extra money comes from."[30] Learning that his cousin Emily Carroll was in straitened circumstances in Eastbourne he made a surprise gift to her of fifty guineas and a weekly allowance (for more than a dozen years until her demise), traveling down to the coast to visit her. His generosity stretched to include, as well, the abhorred Aunt Georgina, who borrowed £100 from him in 1908.

Even dead relations were accommodated. When the secretary of the General Cemetery Company wrote to say that two graves in Mt. Jerome, containing remains of the Shaws, were not being maintained by their proprietors, G.B.S. responded that he supposed he must come to the rescue, and sent a payment for cleaning, re-setting stones, and gardening care, although his father, sharing one of the graves with an older sister, a younger brother, and the latter's daughter, would, said Shaw, have been "the last man on earth to attach any importance to his grave."[31]

Whatever his feelings about Family, Shaw accepted stoically an obligation to it, while managing to be detached and impersonal. "Fortunately," as he confessed to a correspondent in 1939, "I have a heart of stone: else my relatives would have broken it long ago."[32]

30. Shaw to Florence Gamble (*née* Johnston), 30 November 1915. Bernard F. Burgunder Collection of Shaw, Carl A. Kroch Library, Cornell University.

31. There were two letters. The first, undated but c. 21 October 1929, published in the *Dublin Evening Mail* (7 November 1938), p. 4:6, contains the quoted passage. A later letter, dated 25 October 1929, accompanied Shaw's payment for the cemetery services. The second letter is in the archive of the cemetery company.

32. Shaw to Rachel Mahaffy (a daughter of John Pentland Mahaffy, late Provost of Trinity College, Dublin) of Sandymount, Dublin, 6 June 1939. National Library of Ireland.

GENEALOGY

Part One

The Shaw Family

TE·IPSUM·NOSCE

[Shaw, 1821, of Bushy Park, Dublin]

I

WILLIAM SHAW (c. 1651–1734), of Kilkenny (Scottish descent, born in Hampshire); came to Ireland in 1689 as captain of a regiment of foot, fought in the Battle of the Boyne (1690). In the entry in *Burke's Peerage* for his descendants the Shaws of Bushy Park, Dublin, he is reported to have served in Colonel John Mitchelburn's corps; but the Rev. Alexander Mackintosh Shaw, in his genealogy, records service under General Henry Ponsonby, for which, according to family tradition, he received after the campaign a grant of some of the forfeited lands in Kilkenny and a lease from Ponsonby of a portion of the demesne lands of Bessborough. He built or leased a residence at Sandpitts (Sand Pits), Co. Kilkenny, in which the family resided for three generations. He and his wife Elizabeth (?1654–1738) had four sons and a daughter.

II

RICHARD SHAW (1673–1729), of Ballinderry, Co. Tipperary; eldest son of William, predeceased his father; m. Judith BRISCOE, dau. of

Edward Briscoe of Timakilly, Co. Kilkenny, in January 1696. They
had six sons: Robert (see III), Edward, Richard, Roger, John, and
one unidentified; and three dau.: Ann, who married her cousin
William Shaw, and two unidentified, married to Richard Duckett
(Whitestown, Co. Waterford) and a Bagnell.

III

ROBERT SHAW (1698–1758), of Sandpitts; eldest son of Richard; m.
Mary MARKHAM, dau. of Bernard Markham of Fanningstown,
Co. Kilkenny, in 1736. They had six sons: William (see IV), Bernard, Thomas (of Clonmel), John, Robert (father of the first bar-
onet of Bushy Park), and George; and two dau.: Rebecca, who
married William Briscoe, and Elizabeth, who married Garrett
Wall.

IV

WILLIAM SHAW (20 August 1738—?), of Sandpitts; eldest son of Robert; m. Esther ENGLISH of Waterford, who may or may not have
been dau. of the rector of Thomastown, Co. Kilkenny, in 1768.
They had three sons: Rev. Robert (rector of St. John's, Kilkenny,
1808–33, who married Deborah Waring), Col. William (unmarried), and Bernard (see V); and three dau.: Jane, and two unidentified.

V

BERNARD SHAW (1773—3 February 1826), of Kilkenny; third son of
William; lawyer who became High Sheriff of Kilkenny, later a
Dublin notary and stockbroker. He m. Frances CARR (c. 1781/
1782—9 May 1871), dau. of the Rev. Edward Carr, rector of Kil-
macow, Co. Waterford, and Sarah (Forster), on 1 April 1802. He is
buried in St. Canice's Cathedral, Kilkenny, his wife in Mount Jerome Cemetery, Dublin, in the same grave as her son William Bernard (V, 6). Bernard Shaw's birth year was misdated 1771 in
Charles Macmahon Shaw's *Bernard's Brethren*, and Michael Holroyd in *Bernard Shaw: The Search for Love* (1988) gave his age in
1802 erroneously as thirty.

Issue:

1. SARAH ANNE (26 January 1803—9 May 1818).
2. MARTHA [?MARIA] (29 June 1804—8 November 1813).

3. CECILIA ("Ciss") (6 November 1805—10 December 1894); spinster; buried in Mount Jerome in the same grave as her brothers George Carr (V, 8) and Richard Frederick (V, 14).
4. FRANCES ("Fanny") (10 February 1807—13 December 1872); m. Arthur GREENE (c. 1809/1810—26 July 1876), Clerk of the Rules Court of Common Pleas, stepson of the celebrated Dublin hostess Charlotte Lady Greene, on 31 December 1829. They emigrated on 1 January 1830 to western Australia with her brother Edward Carr (V, 7), but returned after removing to Hobart, in Van Diemen's Land.

Issue:

    i.–ii. ARTHUR BERNARD (1831—29 April 1851) and a twin sister FRANCES SARAH ("Fanny") (1831—?[prior to 1858]). It is either a coincidence or an error that the latter's name and nickname are identical with V, 5, i.
    iii. EDWARD (of Kingstown).
    iv. ELIZABETH S. ("Bessie").
    v. CECILIA CHARLOTTE ("Cissie") (c. 1834/1835—18 June 1880); m. Samuel WALKER (19 June 1832—3 August 1911), on 9 October 1855; he became Lord Judge of Appeal and Lord Chancellor of Ireland.
    vi. EMILY.
5. CHARLOTTE JANE ("Shah") (6 January 1809—22 January 1890); m. Charles Bolton JOHNSTON (1802—15 May 1872), on 20 April 1828. He was projector and first secretary of Mount Jerome Cemetery; resided in Tudor Lodge, Ballybrack, Killiney. After his death she lived at 39 Waterloo Road, Dublin, and at 32 Morehampton Road, Donnybrook, Co. Dublin.

Issue:

    i. FRANCES SARAH ("Fanny") (14 February 1830—9 July 1908); m. (1) Adam Murray STEWART (d. 6 November 1855), on 14 February 1846; two dau. (whom she kidnapped from their paternal grandmother, into whose custody her deceased son had placed them, fleeing with them to Holland); (2) John Baptist Cashel HOEY (1828—6 January 1892), on 6 February 1858; he was a Dublin journalist and member of the Young Ireland party, also a Knight of Malta, who became agent-general in London for the state of Victoria, Australia. She converted to Roman Catholicism after marrying

him and, as "Mrs. Cashel Hoey," became a prolific novelist and journalist, the first celebrity in the family. See note at V, 4, i–ii.
ii. AGNES MARIA (1831–47).
iii. CHARLES EDWARD ("Boxer") (1832–1900). According to G.B.S.,* "he killed himself by drink."
iv. GEORGE (d. in India, a suicide).
v. RHODA CHARLOTTE (child), interred 19 January 1839.
vi. FLORENCE (5 March 1842—28 February 1921); m. Major George Francis GAMBLE (21 June 1837—22 February 1912), registrar and secretary of Mount Jerome Cemetery for forty years, after serving in the Royal Marine Light Infantry 1854–72. Author of several manuals on military commands and exercises. A grandson George A. H. Gamble, of Liverpool, attended the funeral of G.B.S. in 1950.
vii. MADELAINE HARRIET (1843—8 May 1922); spinster.
viii. DALKEITH. Described by G.B.S. as "a scamp and a drunkard," redeemed by marriage; wife unidentified.
ix. THOMAS GREGG (child), interred 24 April 1848.
6. WILLIAM BERNARD ("Barney") (12 January 1811—8 June 1874); graduate of Trinity College, Dublin, where he took holy orders; m. Caroline PURTLAND (1822—7 December 1894), of Bray Head, Co. Wicklow, on 30 October 1866. No issue. He was a merchant, at 2 Burgh Quay, Dublin, associated with Richard Verdon & Co., Flax, Hemp, Twine and Patent Rope Manufacture. His death occurred at Drs. John and Marcus Eustace's Private Lunatic Asylum for Gentlemen and Ladies, at Hampstead House, Glasnevin.
7. EDWARD CARR (6 May 1813—16 December 1885). Emigrated on 1 January 1830 to the Swan River colony (Western Australia), thence to Van Diemen's Land (which became Tasmania in 1853), where he engaged in farming on a property "Red Banks," at Great Swans Port (now Swansea), obtained after his marriage from his mother-in-law; m. (1) Anne FENTON (c. 1812/1813—11 March 1856), dau. of James Fenton of Dunlavin, Co. Wicklow, on 22 December 1835; (2) Emma

*The initials G.B.S. have been employed throughout the genealogy text to distinguish George Bernard Shaw from the plethora of relations bearing the same given names and surname.

Goodall COPE (c. 1821/1822—16 March 1882), dau. of Edward Cope of Birmingham, England, on 14 May 1857.

Issue (first marriage):

i. BERNARD (12 October 1836—5 September 1910); m. Louisa Augusta Helen DAVIES (1845—30 July 1924), of Georgetown, on 31 January 1877. He became sheriff and commissioner of police at Hobart, in 1886.

ii. JAMES FENTON (30 August 1838—4 May 1882); m. (1) Catherine ("Kate") GLASSFORD (d. October 1875), dau. of J. B. Glassford, on 27 August 1869; (2) Elizabeth ("Lizzie") BRAIN (who outlived him), on 17 April 1877. Inspector of Stock in Melbourne. His elder daughter (by his first wife), Margaret Beryl ("Greta") Fenton Shaw, who later married Dr. P. K. O'BRIEN of New South Wales, visited G.B.S. and his sister Lucy in London on 22 April 1898. She died in Switzerland in 1911.

iii. EDWARD (29 February 1840—14 February 1841).

iv. WILLIAM CHARLES (20 October 1841—19 February 1842).

v. MARTHA COATES ("Pattie") (22 June 1843—21 July 1903); m. Sir William John LYNE (6 April 1844—3 August 1913), of Apslawn, Great Swans Port, premier of New South Wales 1899–1900; member for Hume in the Commonwealth Parliament from its inception in 1901 until his death; minister for home affairs 1901–3, on 29 June 1870; resided in Albury, New South Wales.

vi. FRANCES CARR (14 May 1845—6 April 1853).

vii. FREDERICK (28 August 1847—21 August 1923); m. Jane HARBOTTLE (6 January 1846—3 June 1920), dau. of Thomas Harbottle of Hobart, on 21 July 1875.

viii. SARAH (20 December 1849—23 [?24] March 1853).

ix. ROBERT (18 May 1853—9 October 1916); m. Margaret Elizabeth BEJANT, on 12 August 1876; resided in Cairns, Queensland; he died in England.

Issue (second marriage):

x. AMY CECILIA (20 February 1859—1 October 1946); spinster.

8. GEORGE CARR (30 December 1814—19 April 1885); m. Lucinda Elizabeth ("Bessie") GURLY (6 October 1830—19 February 1913), on 17 June 1852, in St. Peter's Church (later demolished), Dublin. (See also *Part Two*, V, 4, i.) After laboring

as a clerk in an ironworks he was appointed to a post (1845–
50) in the Four Courts (Central Courts of Justice), Dublin;
later (from 7 October 1852) a partner of George Clibborn as a
corn merchant, with office and warehouse of Clibborn & Shaw
at 67 Jervis Street and a watermill (purchased in August 1857)
in Rutland Avenue, Dolphin's Barn, Dublin. Died in a lodging
at 21 Leeson Park Avenue.

Issue (all born at No. 3 Upper Synge Street, Dublin):

    i. LUCINDA FRANCES ("Lucy") (26 March 1853—27
March 1920), known professionally in the theater and
on the concert platform as Lucy Carr Shaw; m. Charles
Robert BUTTERFIELD (29 April 1852—26 June 1916),
known professionally as Cecil Burt, son of the Rev. Robert Butterfield of London, on 17 December 1887, in St.
John's Church, Charlotte St., London. No issue. Di-
vorced on 19 July 1909. She died at Champion Cottage,
Champion Hill, Camberwell, London.

    ii. ELINOR AGNES ("Yuppy"; later "Aggie") (7 July
1854—27 March 1876). Died of consumption in the
Hospital Saint Lawrence, and buried in Ventnor, Isle of
Wight. Birth date confirmed next day in *Saunders's News-
Letter* and on 10 July in *Freeman's Journal*.

    iii. GEORGE BERNARD ("Sonny"; later "G.B.S.") (26 July
1856—2 November 1950); m. Charlotte Frances ("Lot-
tie") PAYNE-TOWNSHEND (20 January 1857—12 September 1943), dau. of Horace Townsend (9 November
1824—4 February 1885) of Rosscarbery, Co. Cork, and
Mary Susanna Kirby (20 July 1830—9 September 1891),
on 1 June 1898, in the Registry Office, Henrietta St.,
London. No issue. Charlotte had one sister, Mary Stewart ("Sissy") (31 August 1858—5 April 1929); m. Captain
(later Brigadier General) Hugh Cecil Cholmondeley (1
December 1852—13 December 1941), on 24 March
1885, in St. Mark's Church, London. He remarried in
1931.

9. ROBERT (24 April 1816—?); emigrated to Australia, but returned and settled in England; m. Mary MACDERMOTT,
dau. of C. Macdermott; no known issue. As G.B.S. recorded in
1879 (see Appendix I), he was "blinded in his youth by an
effusion of water. . . ."

10. RICHARD OSBORNE (17 February 1818—14 May 1818).

11. HENRY (20 April 1819—28 January 1884); m. (1) Martha

COCKAIGNE (d. 24 March 1861), dau. of Rev. James Cockaigne, on 17 January 1844; (2) Eliza D. ("Dysy") MacMULLEN (c. 1829/1830—18 May 1888), dau. of his partner in the firm of [Robert] MacMullen, Shaw & Co., millers, on Burgh Quay, dealing in corn, flour, and cereals; m. c. 1862. He resided at 1 Waterloo Road, Dublin; became mentally unbalanced c. 1878.

Issue (first marriage) [chronology undetermined]:

i. MARY ANNE AGNES ("Gesh"), m. Dr. Lewis Arthur FLEURY (d. ?1898) probably in 1864; they emigrated to Monte Video, Uruguay, following receipt in that same year of his licentiate from the King and Queen's College of Physicians, Dublin; no known issue.

ii. Deceased son; unidentified.

iii. WILLIAM BERNARD (?"Boke").

iv. JAMES COCKAIGNE ("Kaffir"). Dates unlocated; reported as "the late" parent in a daughter's death notice in *The Times* in 1939. His wife was Mary Elizabeth (c. 1859/1860—15 March 1947). Their children, assisted financially by G.B.S. throughout their lives, were Mary Ethel (31 December 1880—16 July 1962), m. (1) Herbert Sebastian Davis (d. 28 January 1939) and (2) Rev. Gordon Reynold Walters (11 February 1878—5 May 1963) in 1944 (separated at the time of her death); Adelaide Olivia ("Aida") (c. 1884/1885—21 May 1939), S. R. N. (State Registered Nurse), spinster and chronic invalid, whose substantial medical expenses were borne by G.B.S.; and John Kisson ("Jack") (d. 22 June 1913, in his twenties).

v. FRANCES VICTORIA ("Coo") (c. 1848/1849—22 October 1897); m. Dr. William Ireland WHEELER (1844—25 November 1899), president of the Royal College of Surgeons in Ireland, 1883–84. A son was Rear-Admiral Sir William I. De Courcy Wheeler (8 May 1879—11 September 1943), also a president of the R. C. S., whose brother Capt. Horatio Francis ("Ho Ho") (c. 1887/1888—6 August 1962) founded the Bernard Shaw Society of Ireland on 26 July 1944, at G.B.S.'s birthplace.

Issue (second marriage):

vi. AMELIA ELIZABETH ("Muffie") (1863—7 April 1948), m. George Carr LETT (1870—17 December 1946), a Dublin solicitor.

vii. MARY RHODA (31 October 1865—?); m. [given name unknown] CREASY; resided in Colombo, Ceylon. G.B.S. and Charlotte Shaw visited her and her daughter Patricia ("Pat") on 22 January 1933, during a world cruise. Allegedly she was a women's lawn tennis champion (? of Ulster); but no records located.

viii. GEORGE (21 July 1868—?). Charles Shaw says in *Bernard's Brethren* that one of Henry's offspring "still lives" in Australia (c. 1937–38), but does not identify him. Elsewhere he indicates receipt of biographical assistance from George C. "Larry" Shaw of Nyngan, New South Wales, shire clerk of Bogan 1906–36, who sounds suspiciously like Henry's Antipodean son. An otherwise unidentified George Shaw visited G.B.S. in London on 14 November 1929.

12. EMILY (30 August 1821—12 September 1906); m. Rev. William George CARROLL (18 October 1821—9 October 1885), her first cousin, perpetual curate of St. Bride's, Dublin, a leader-writer for the *Freeman's Journal*, on 5 September 1848. They resided at 21 Harrington Street, Dublin. G.B.S. described him to Dorothy Eagle (in a holograph note on 26 April 1946: see Introduction, footnote 10) as "a man of conspicuous character, ability, and scholarship," and to Denis Johnston (1 April 1938: Trinity College Library, Dublin) as the first Irish Protestant clergyman to endorse the fledgling Home Rule movement and Republicanism.

Issue:

i. JOHN (16 June 1849—3 February 1850).

ii. EMILY (variously "Tah" or "Ta") (16 October 1850—8 January 1945); spinster.

iii. ANNA CECILIA PHIPPEN ("Fippy") (3 July 1852—12 December 1876); m. Rev. Richard POSTANCE (c. 1850/1851—4 February 1915) of St. Andrew's, Liverpool, on 29 June 1875; d. twelve days after birth of first child).

iv. FRANCES LUCINDA ("Grib") (5 September 1854—13 June 1867). She was poisoned accidentally by her father.

v. WILLIAM GEORGE ("Bill") (22 March 1856—1 January 1886); emigrated to Australia in 1881; taught school in Melbourne; later wrote leaders for a Sydney morning paper until his untimely death brought on by alcoholism.

vi. ROBERT PHIPPEN ("Robbie") (22 January 1858—26

October 1934); graduate of Trinity College, Dublin, 1885, M.A. 1892; in early adulthood a member of the singing chorus (tenor) of the D'Oyly Carte Opera Company; institutionalized for melancholia, 1881; later (1889) ordained in the Church of England; Vicar of Waybread, Harleston, Norfolk, 1919–23; m. Ann Elizabeth KEELING (1852—4 October 1934) on 21 June 1902; no known issue.

    vii. [Stillborn son, delivered on 19 November 1859.]

13. WALTER STEPHEN (15 November 1822—30 July 1885); emigrated to Liverpool, then to Melbourne, Australia (1852), where he was employed as a senior clerk in a government auditing office; m. Anna Charlotte ("Annie") HAYES (?1828–82), dau. of William Hayes and Carina Olric [?Olrick] of Dublin, on 19 December 1856 in Melbourne, to which she had emigrated c. 1854. Her age is uncertain, being recorded as 28 on the marriage certificate, 38 on the birth certificate of son Charles, and 56 on the death registration.

Issue:

    i. OLRICK WILLIAM (31 January 1858—?).

    ii. CARINA FRANCES (20 October 1859—?).

    iii. EDWARD JOSEPH (16 August 1861—?).

    iv. CHARLES MACMAHON (13 February 1863—15 April 1943); author of *Bernard's Brethren* (1939), a study of the Shaw family; branch manager of the Bank of Australasia, later (1923–36) manager of the Metropolitan Golf Club, Melbourne. His wife Frances Charlotte ("Fanny") (maiden name unknown) died on 13 November 1937. He met G.B.S. at lunch in Whitehall Court on 6 January 1938.

    v. WALTER BERNARD (30 September 1864—d. between 1937 and 1946); surveyor, later an editor of *Australian Mining and Engineering Review*; resided in Perth.

    vi. STANLEY LOW (24 June 1866—?), resided in Rangoon, Burma, in 1892; then settled in London. G.B.S. lost touch with him before 1902.

    vii. BERNARD CECIL (30 May 1868—?), citrus grower in Safety Bay, Western Australia; informed G.B.S. on 19 August 1946 (BL Add. Mss. 50526, fol. 169) that at 78 he was the "last survivor" among his siblings.

?viii. [The Tasmanian genealogy records *two* daughters, unidentified. Charles Shaw, in *Bernard's Brethren*, speaks of a sister (Carina) as being "one girl amongst six adoring brothers" when their family visited the Henry Shaws in Dublin (1871). It is possible that a second daughter died in infancy or remained home with her mother (who did not make the journey to Ireland), being too young to travel.]

14. RICHARD FREDERICK (called Frederick or "Fred") (24 January 1824—1 January 1900), chief of staff, Irish Valuation Office, Dublin; m. Georgina Louisa Simmons WATERS (c. 1829/1830—11 September 1911), dau. of George Waters, on 6 December 1855; legally separated; in late years she resided in London. He later "became harmlessly dotty" (G.B.S. in *Bernard's Brethren*) "and died in the family mental retreat, . . . where his brother William had also passed over."

Issue:

    i. CONSTANCE EMILY (1856—9 January 1916); spinster; buried in the same grave as her father and George Carr Shaw.

    ii. ARTHUR WELLINGTON BOLTON (c. 1861/1862—3 April 1939), bank official; died at 7 Mount Street Crescent, Dublin. His son, Dr. Arthur Frederick Bernard Shaw (17 August 1888—3 June 1947), noted pathologist of the Royal Victoria Infirmary, Newcastle-on-Tyne, met G.B.S. in Newcastle on 25 April 1921; his daughter, Edith Cecilia Mayne, of Chambly Canton, Quebec, Canada, corresponded with G.B.S. in 1949–50, sending family photos.

    iii. HORACE F. C.; member of the Irish Land Commission; resided at 120 Shelbourne Road, Dublin.

15. [Stillborn infant, delivered on 1 June 1825.]

Part Two

The Gurly Family

I

JAMES GOURLAY (or GOURLY) (d. 1691), of Wexford, probably a native of Cumberland who removed to Chester in 1688. Died in Ireland, buried in Wexford on 28 July.

II

JOHN GOURLAY (or GOURLY) (d. 1746), son of James.

III

JAMES GURLEY (?1706/1707—2 August 1801), son of John, youngest of five siblings; m. (given name unknown) RATHBURNE; they had two sons, Rathbone and Thomas.

IV

THOMAS GURLEY (1730—21 April 1796), of Tullow Street, Carlow, second son of James, attorney-at-law and Justice of the Peace; m. Elizabeth TENCH, dau. of Capt. Joshua Tench and Frances RICHARDS of Wexford, on 11 October 1756; nine children.

V

THOMAS GURLEY (1760—14 April 1816), of Belville (Belleville), eldest child of Thomas of Carlow; solicitor and registrar of Leighlin diocese; m. Elizabeth McDONAGH (1760—31 December 1821).

Issue included:

1. HANNAH (c. 1787/1788—13 April 1872), convert to Roman Catholicism; a novice at Maryboro Convent (1824) and, as Mother M. Augustine, re-founded a Presentation Convent at Stradbally, Co. Laois, January 1860.
2. SARAH (1790—?); m. William BOX; three dau.
3. THOMAS (1792—?), emigrated to Canada; employed by H. M. Customs in Kingston, Ontario; dau. Mary and son Walter.
4. WALTER BAGNALL (BAGENAL) GURLY (1800—20 December 1885); a country gentleman raised in Carlow, who moved west to Kinlough, Cong, Co. Mayo, c. 1855, then to Oughterard, Co. Galway, in 1858; m. (1) Lucinda WHITCROFT (1802—14 January 1839), dau. of Squire John Hamilton Whitcroft (1768—23 March 1843), of Highfield Manor, Whitechurch, Rathfarnham, a cotton manufacturer, landowner, and pawnbroker, and Lucinda DAVIS of Dublin, on 29 December 1829; (2) Elizabeth Anne ("Nanny") CLARKE (c. 1829/1830—24 August 1892), dau. of Simeon Clarke, a miller, on 25 May 1852.

Issue (first marriage):

i. LUCINDA ELIZABETH ("Bessie") (6 October 1830—
19 February 1913); raised by her aunt Ellen Whitcroft
(?1804—5 January 1862), spinster, in Killiney and at
Palmerston Place, Dublin, and aided by her uncle John
Hamilton Whitcroft (1805—13 November 1877), whose
second wife Catherine ("Aunt Kate") Price (m. October
1846; d. November 1878) was the only relation of that
generation for whom G.B.S. and his sister showed any
attachment (G.B.S. corresponded with her from London
and Lucy returned to Ireland to attend her funeral); m.
George Carr SHAW on 17 June 1852; abandoned him
and moved to London on 17 June 1873. Her last residence was "High Lawn," 8 Park Village West, London.

Issue: see *Part One*, V, 8, i–iii.

ii. WALTER JOHN (1831—30 August 1899); m. (in the
United States) Emily Jane WALTON (1838—10 January
1884), an English widow; no issue. He was a physician
(licentiate of the Royal College of Surgeons, 1863), prac-
ticing at 200 High Road, Leyton, Essex, after long service as a ship's doctor for the Inman Line. He held a
second medical degree from Trinity College, 1876.

Issue (second marriage):

[The first child was born in Carlow; the next two in Kinlough, Cong, Co. Mayo; the last three in Oughterard,
Co. Galway.]

iii. CATHERINE CLARKE ("Kate") (4 April 1853—15
March 1914); spinster, hunchbacked as a result of a fall
from a horse in her childhood. Michael Holroyd, in *Bernard Shaw: The Search for Love* (1988), questioned her le-
gitimacy, asserting she was born nearly two months
before her parents' nuptials in May 1852; but the register (Book 7, p. 6) of St. Mary's, Carlow, records birth
year as 1853. Although a convert to Roman Catholicism
in her last years, she was buried in the Protestant Mount
Jerome Cemetery, Dublin.

iv. ARABELLA SOPHIA ("Moila") (bapt. 17 August
1856—28 February 1941); m. John Duke GILLMORE
(d. 1904), clerk of the Union (poorhouse), Oughterard;

she resided with her half-sister Lucinda Shaw from 1898 until the latter's death in 1913; later became companion to G.B.S.'s former inamorata, Mrs. Jane ("Jenny") Patterson, and her executrix and heir in 1924. Her father misidentified as Robert Gurly in baptismal register.

Issue:

(1) WALTER DUKE (19 March 1884—7 August 1902); killed in a fall from a precipice at Chable sur Martigny, Switzerland, during a holiday excursion paid for by G.B.S. and Charlotte Shaw; interred in Lausanne.

(2) GEORGINA JANE ("Judy") (21 June 1885—4 November 1974); m. Harold Chaworth MUSTERS (?1871—25 May 1942), on 20 August 1912; G.B.S.'s first fulltime secretary, 1907–12; resided in Egypt 1912–25, where her husband worked for the Eastern Telegraph Company; in her late years she resided in Folkestone and Farnham.

v. GEORGINA HENRIETTA ("Georgie") (bapt. 29 March 1858—2 August 1911); spinster. Two years younger than G.B.S., she was the favorite of all his aunts: he referred to her as "young Georgie" to distinguish her from Aunt Georgina Shaw (V, 14). Her father misidentified as Robert Gurly in baptismal register.

vi. CHARLOTTE OLIVIA (17 July 1860—24 November 1941); m. Edward ROGERS (27 September 1859—?), a clerk to Carlow County Council, on 28 February 1894. After her husband's death she removed from Athy Road to Hay Market, Carlow. G.B.S. visited Carlow only once, on 1 October 1910 for an overnight stay; there is no evidence that he visited the aunt he had never met.

Issue:

(1) EAMES BAGENAL (1895—10 April 1980); emigrated to the United States in July 1913, first residing in St. Louis, then at 1249 Yale Street, Santa Monica, California. G.B.S. recorded in his address book a son, Edward Knight Rogers ("Ned"), born 24 July 1918. Eames and his wife Hazel [?KNIGHT] visited G.B.S. at the Santa Monica dock on 28 March 1933, when the Shaws rejoined their ship after visiting the Metro-Goldwyn-Mayer

studios, Eames expending his last fifty cents for gasoline for his flivver but never letting on that they were broke (letter to his mother, 9 September 1933, which she passed on to G.B.S.: British Library Add. Mss. 50520, fols. 218–20).

(2) GEORGINA ELIZABETH ("Georgie"; later "Gina") (30 May 1902—19 July 1977); m. Edward Norman MEREDITH, 30 October 1923. Resided at 34 Barrow Street, Dublin, later at 26 Old Finglas Road, Glasnevin.

vii. CONSTANCE ANN ("Nannie") (2 August 1862—17 June 1944); m. William Walter HAMILTON (October ?1849 ?1853—28 May 1940). Her age modified to 34 in the 1900 census, 38 in 1910, 45 in 1920; and 69 in cemetery registration, 1944. His birth year is given as 1845 on gravestone, but recorded as 1849 in 1900 census, and age given as 87 in cemetery registration, 1940. According to the 1900 census he emigrated in 1869 and she in 1882; his emigration year becomes 1874 (and he is listed as Naturalized) in 1910; both are listed in 1920 as Aliens who arrived in 1884. In 1900 their birthplace is recorded as Ireland; from 1920 onward this is altered to England. Their Pittsburgh residence originally was at 5311 Fifth Avenue, then at 5434 Howe Street, where he also owned a livery stable (at No. 5307). Subsequently they moved to 921 Bellefonte Street, and accumulated considerable Pittsburgh property. G.B.S. never met his aunt.

Issue:

(1) WILLIAM WALTER, JR. (22 October 1890—19 March 1941); served in World War I as a corporal, inducted on 9 August 1918 (he corresponded with G.B.S. while overseas); unmarried.

(2) JOHN ALEXANDER (13 May 1891—25 December 1918); m. Anita (maiden name unknown). A son, John A. Hamilton, Jr., was still living, in Greensburg, Pa., at 83, in February 1997.

(3) PERCIVAL GURLY (3 October 1892—21 October 1892).

(4) JANETTE (6 November 1893: premature birth, lived only three hours).

(5) VIRGINIA C. (?Constance) (12 October 1894—23

March 1901). The remains of (3), (4), and (5) were transferred from single graves to a newly acquired family plot on 29 March 1901.

(6) DOROTHY JANE (15 May 1897—17 October 1992); m. [Rudolph] Richard Edmund HEINATZ (c. 1893/1894—12 April 1979), son of O. R. and Marie Heinatz, on 18 September 1920.

(7) MARY ELIZABETH (1 June 1899—3 December 1957); m. William Clark HAGAN (1888—5 December 1963), son of F. S. and Ida Hagan, on 10 June 1920.

(8) ROBERT GEORGE (16 February 1903—11 June 1976); m. Elizabeth R. (maiden name unknown) (1905—18 March 1991).

(9) THOMAS EDWARD (4 April 1904—4 November 1965); m. Margaret STEWART, who allegedly was still living in a Pittsburgh nursing home (not located) in February 1997.

(10) ALBERT DOUGLAS (3 February 1906—1 September 1947); m. Sarah Elizabeth HANNAN (22 January 1905—28 December 1971); served in World War II as a technician (T/5, then equivalent to corporal) in the 47th Station Hospital in the Pacific Theatre of Operations; inducted on 24 September 1942. He visited G.B.S. in 1927, while majoring in Economics at the University of Pittsburgh, and corresponded with him in 1928. After learning of the death of Charlotte Shaw he sent G.B.S. a message of condolence from the South Pacific on 24 October 1943.

viii. FLORENCE BEATRICE (31 July 1866—?); died young, although recorded as alive in the 23 September 1876 will of Dr. Walter John Gurly.

ix. [Son: died in infancy; chronology undetermined.]

5. MARY (spinster); last of Thomas Gurley's issue.

Appendix I

[In 1879 Bernard Shaw drafted on two leaves of stationery (British Library Add. Mss. 50710B, fols. 2a, b, 3a) a veiled history of alcoholism and dipsomania in the Shaw family, sending a copy to his friend Dr. J. Kingston Barton on 25 October 1879, as recorded on the reverse of the second leaf. A transcription by Dr. Stanley Rypins was published in the Shaw Diaries *(1986), edited by Stanley Weintraub (pp. 27–29); but as this text contained a considerable number of misreadings by Rypins, a corrected text is published here. Shaw's references to his relations are not always chronologically accurate.]*

Instance of voluntary abandonment of brandy drinking. An Irish family consisted of seven brothers and four sisters. The father [Bernard Shaw, Shaw's grandfather: *Part One*, V], a man of weak character, who was constantly fuddled, died young, of heart disease. The mother [Shaw's grandmother, Frances Carr Shaw: V] died in possession of all her faculties, in her eighty ninth year, of a bronchial attack. Two of the sons were unknown to me [Edward Carr Shaw: V, 7; and Walter Stephen Shaw: V, 13]. One of these, was, I believe, a consistent abstainer; the other drank, but, considering his extraction, was a comparatively sober man. A third [Robert Shaw: V, 9], blinded in his youth by an effusion of water, never had an opportunity of drinking. A fourth [Henry Shaw: V, 11] was perfectly temperate, drinking wine only, and that very moderately. He was the most prosperous of the family; but on experiencing reverses late in life, exhibited severe nervous prostration. The remaining three were dipsomaniacs. The eldest [William Bernard Shaw: V, 6], from his college days, was an excessive smoker and a drunkard. Frequently he was drunk early in the morning. With a few short intervals of abstinence, which apparently only proved the hopelessness of his case, he lived befuddled until he was past fifty. He then relinquished alcohol and tobacco simultaneously, and never relapsed, although he survived [for] ten years. Not long before his death, he married for the first time. Shortly afterwards, he became religiously mad[,] refused to speak, was confined in an asylum, and died of heart disease in the act of attempting to strangle himself. He had no children.

His youngest brother [Richard Frederick Shaw: V, 14], when of middle age, began to indulge in bouts of drinking. He, I believe, had delirium tremens at least once. He held a government appointment, and received several warnings in consequence of his conduct. At last he conquered the habit and has since been free from it. He married a woman several members of whose family were insane. She was abstemious, but her temper was hysterically evident. Their eldest son has already taken the pledge & broken it. When the other brother [George Carr Shaw, Shaw's father: V, 8] married, he was already a habitual drunkard. In society he drank porter, champagne, whisky, anything he could get, sometimes swallowing stout enough to make him sick. Subsequently, when he had no opportunity of drinking except in taverns, he only took brandy. He smoked regularly and immoderately. His appetite was good; but he suffered from diarrhea at intervals. Although he was never sober, he was seldom utterly drunk. He made efforts to reform himself, and on one occasion succeeded in abstaining for sixteen months; but these efforts always ended in a relapse. On one or two occasions, he disappeared for a few days and returned with his watch, clothes &c damaged & every symptom of an uncontrolled excess; but ordinarily he came home in the evening, fuddled, eat [old style, pronounced "et"] his dinner, had a nap, and then kept going out for drams until he went to bed. He never drank or kept drink in the house. Eventually he had a fit, and shortly, but—to the best of my recollection—not immediately afterwards, he stopped drinking; and for more than ten years has been so rigid a tee[to]taller that those who know him find it difficult to realise what he formerly was. He continued to smoke, possibly more than before, but not to an extent which any but a very light smoker would consider excessive. The intermittent diarrhea still remains. Like many other members of the family he was eccentric in his demeanour. If any unpleasant reflection occurred to him, he, if in a room, rubbed his hands rapidly together and ground his teeth. If in the street, he took a short run. I have seen him, when drunk, seize a small article on the mantelpiece and dash it upon the hearthstone, or kick a newspaper into the air; but though he was very unstable, he never used the slightest violence to any person. Apart from being ordinarily a well disposed man, his timidity probably made forbearance habitual to him.

These three men were alike in being unconvivial dramdrinkers. They avoided observation whilst drinking, were eloquent on the misery of intemperance, and considered even the most ordinary indulgence in wine as dangerous and disgraceful. They were quite free from the kindred vices and neither gambled nor followed women. Their excesses rendered them wretched. They appreciated music[,] books, & acting, but had not the energy to cultivate these tasks, and never took the initiative in visiting any place of entertainment. They were extremely deficient in will, but shewed no obliquity of moral sense, except that they carefully dissimulated their disease, and allowed those who did not know them intimately to believe that they abhorred drink (which was perhaps true) and were teetotall (which was false). They were easily fuddled, and no medium was possible to them between total abstinence & excess. They all, when well advanced in life and apparently confirmed beyond hope in their habits, gave up drinking at once and for ever. Had they been idle men of independent means, they would probably have killed themselves long before this period.

Of the four sisters, one, the eldest of the family [Cecilia Shaw: V, 3], is a maiden lady. She has always been temperate. The second [Emily Carroll: V, 12] exceeded in nothing but snuff. She married a clergyman, an ill tempered, but quite sober man. Their eldest son is a reformed drunkard.* The third [Charlotte Johnston: V, 5], was also free from the family failing. She married an equally irreproachable man, who died of lung disease of many years standing. She had three sons. The eldest killed himself by drink. The next shortened the process by suicide. The youngest was a scamp and a drunkard, but on marrying, recovered himself. The fourth sister [Frances Greene: V, 4] drank secretly for a long time, but eventually gave way to it completely, and died. Her husband towards the end of his life was often fuddled. One of their daughters [not identified], a married lady, is said to be developing dipsomania; but others, though I think it probable, I have no assurance of.

*Since relapsed & gone to New Zealand [Australia]. His younger brother [Robert] fell into melancholia last year, & is now in an asylum. (1882). [G.B.S.]

Appendix II

Members of the Shaw family who inscribed their names as Dublin Freemen in the city's Roll of Freedom:

Bernard Shaw: Freeman by right of "Grace Especial," on 23 April 1804.

George Carr Shaw, of Roundtown, Co. Dublin: Freeman by right of "Birth," on 18 October 1841.

Henry Shaw, of Synge Street, Dublin. Freeman by right of "Birth," on 28 April 1845.

Richard F. Shaw, of 43 Cullenswood Avenue, Dublin. Freeman by right of "Birth," on 13 March 1854.

George Bernard Shaw, of Ayot St. Lawrence, Welwyn, Herts. Freeman by right of "Birth," conferred on him "in absentia" by the Dublin City Council at its meeting of 4 March 1946. He inscribed his name, "G. Bernard Shaw," in the roll book when it was brought to him at Ayot St. Lawrence on 28 August 1946.

Principal Sources of Information

The Shaw Family

Alexander Mackintosh Shaw, *A Genealogical Account of the Highland Families of Shaw* (1877): section on the Irish branch. "Genealogical Chart of the Shaw Family of Counties Tipperary, Kilkenny and Dublin, together with other Lineal Ancestors of George Bernard Shaw," an insert in Archibald Henderson, *Bernard Shaw: His Life and Works* (1911), compiled by Rev. William Ball Wright and prepared by the Grafton Genealogical Press, New York. *Burke's Peerage*. Records of the Tasmanian branch of the Shaw family, provided by Marion (Mrs. Charles) Shaw, "Red Banks," Swansea, Tasmania, Australia. Registry of Births, Deaths and Marriages, Melbourne, Victoria. Genealogical Section, State Public Library of Victoria, Melbourne. National Archive, Canberra, Australia. Probate Office, Somerset House, London. General Register Office, St. Catherine's House, London. (On 1 April 1997 the General Register Office and the Census Records Department of the Public Records Office were transferred to the Family Records Centre, 1 Myddelton Street, London EC1R 1UW.) Imperial War Museum, London. Shaw's diaries 1885–97 and engagements diaries 1904–50, British Library of Political and Economic Science, London School of Economics. Shaw's address books, miscellaneous notebooks, and incoming correspondence, British Library. Holograph memorandum for Dr. J. K. Barton on alcoholism in the Shaw family: British Library, Add. Mss. 50710B. Records Office, Joyce House, Dublin. *Thom's City Directories*. National Archives, Dublin. Interment records and tombstone inscriptions, General Cemetery Company (Mt. Jerome Cemetery), Dublin. Carroll family records, photographs, and Shaw correspondence, provided by Dorothy Eagle in 1969; now in the possession of her sons Roger (North Wales, United Kingdom) and Martin (County Cork, Republic of Ireland). *Crockford's Clerical Directory*. Shaw correspondence, Harry Ransom Humanities Research Center, University of Texas at Austin. Shaw address book (c. 1930–42), Bernard F. Burgunder Collection of Shaw, Division of Rare and Manuscript Collections, Cornell University Libraries. Charles Macmahon Shaw, *Bernard's Brethren* (1939). B. C. Rosset, *Shaw of Dublin* (1964). St. John Ervine, *Bernard Shaw: His Life, Work and Friends* (1956). Archibald Henderson, *Bernard Shaw: Man of the Century* (1956). Bernard Shaw, *Sixteen Self Sketches* (1949). Bernard Shaw, prefaces to *Immaturity* (1930) and *London Music in 1888–89*; reprinted in *Complete Prefaces*, Vol. 3 (1997).

The Gurly Family

Registers of St. Mary's Church, Carlow, and of Cong parish, Co. Mayo (now housed in the Representative Church Body Library, Dublin), and of Kilcummin parish, Oughterard. Interviews with Georgina (Judy) Musters, 1958–71. Carlow Heritage Society records, Carlow. Correspondence with Eames Rogers. General Register Office, St. Catherine's House, London. Probate Office, Somerset House, London. Record Office, Joyce House, Dublin. Registers of the Church of the Ascension, Pittsburgh, Pa. Allegheny County Register of Wills, Pittsburgh. Interment records, Homewood Cemetery, Pittsburgh. U.S. census records for Pittsburgh. Bernard O'Neill, "Shaw's Six Step-Aunts," *Carloviana* (Carlow), December 1956, pp. 8–12. Notes on "The Whitcrofts" and "the Gurley Family of Wexford and Carlow" supplied by St. John Ervine in 1951 to Georgina Musters. Ervine's letter concerning the Whitcrofts, *Irish Times*, 15 May 1951. Richard Lucas, *A General Directory of the Kingdom of Ireland, or Merchants' and Traders' Most Useful Companion* (Dublin, 1778).

Acknowledgments

In addition to my gratitude to the individuals and institutions recorded in the foregoing source credits, I wish to acknowledge with deepest gratitude the unwonted generosity of Professor A. M. Gibbs of Macquarie University, Sydney, New South Wales, who flew to Tasmania on my behalf for a meeting with the present generations of Shaws, to obtain documentary and photographic evidence relating to Uncle Edward and his descendants; and then made a second journey, to Melbourne, to gather whatever information he could find for Uncle Walter's branch of the family. Generosity of time and energy must also be gratefully noted with thanks to T. F. Evans, who traveled to Shropshire to photograph the graves of Charlotte Shaw's relations; Miss W. Thirkettle, Assistant Archivist of the Manx National Heritage, Douglas, Isle of Man, who located and photocopied Rev. Robert Carroll's baptismal certificate and ordination papers; Ruth Newberry, who searched church and census records, and visited the Homewood Cemetery, in Pittsburgh, to obtain information from tombstones and interment records; and Marilyn Evert of Homewood Cemetery, who generously searched twice through the archives. For valuable services in filling in the gaps, a paean to Ron Abrahams, Fred D. Crawford, Martin Eagle, the Fitzmaurice Estate Agency (Carlow), Nicholas Grene, Maureen Halligan, Daniel J. Leary, Frances McCarthy (Chairperson of the Dublin Shaw Society and Custodian of the Shaw Birthplace), Michael Purcell of the Carlow Heritage Society, Marion Shaw, Ann Simmons of Archbishop Marsh's Library, Dublin, Wendy Fish of the Wellcome Institute for the History of Medicine, London, Joan B. Malley of the Church of the Ascension, Pittsburgh, Dr. Susan Hood, Assistant Archivist, of the Representative Church Body Library, Church of Ireland, Dublin, and Sister M. Baptist Meany, Archivist, Presentation Mission House, Lucan, Co. Dublin.

Extracts from Shaw's correspondence and other papers are published by permission of the Society of Authors on behalf of the Estate of Bernard Shaw; I am especially indebted to the late Roma Woodnutt, Estates Manager. Extracts are published also by kind permission of the Bernard F. Burgunder Collection of Shaw, Division of Rare and Manuscript Collections, Cornell University Library; of the Richard Weiner Collection of Shaw, Special Collections (with thanks to curator Carl Peterson), Case Library, Colgate University; and of the National Library of Ireland.

Dedicated to the memory of
JOHN O'DONOVAN (1921–1985),
Dublin's indefatigable researcher, to whom all
Shavians (aware or not) are deeply indebted.

Michel W. Pharand

THE SIREN ON THE ROCK: BERNARD SHAW VS. SARAH BERNHARDT

On a morning at the end of May 1879, "the Divine Sarah" and the fifty-odd members of the Comédie-Française landed at Folkestone and were greeted by thousands of cheering admirers. Among them were Johnston Forbes Robertson, who handed Sarah a gardenia, and Oscar Wilde, who scattered an armful of lilies at her feet. In eighteen performances during the next two months, Bernhardt would conquer London in *Phèdre*, *L'Étrangère*, *Le Sphinx*, *Zaïre*, *Andromaque*, *Ruy Blas*, and *Hernani*. Meanwhile, pursuing a less-than-successful career as a writer, Bernard Shaw was living at home with his mother and writing *Immaturity*, a first novel begun a few months earlier on 5 March. Sarah Henriette Rosine Bernhardt (née Bernard, 1844–1923) was thirty-four and at the height of her fame on her first visit to England, but twenty-two-year-old Shaw was still fourteen years from the premiere of his first play and eight years from his first critique of a Bernhardt performance. Eventually Shaw gave up novels and poured his energy into a stream of letters, speeches, reviews, pamphlets, and plays. Sarah continued to portray on stage the decadent *femmes fatales* that created her legend: Théodora, Phèdre, Cléopâtre, Tosca, Médée, and Marguerite Gauthier, to name a few. "She lived to mesmerize," we are told, "to dazzle, to lure the public into the mysteries of sensuality and poetic illusion. He [Shaw] was the rock of truth; she the siren on the rock."[1]

Although Bernhardt had been trained as a classical actress, by the time

Shaw saw the siren in her element she was well-versed in the so-called "late Romantic" style of acting, "where it was enough that a performer simply intoxicate with a display of emotional force."[2] It was enough to intoxicate twenty-three-year-old D. H. Lawrence who, in 1908, after seeing Bernhardt as Marguerite Gauthier in *La Dame aux camélias* in Nottingham, described the sixty-three-year-old actress as "the incarnation of wild emotion . . . the primeval passions of woman . . . I could love such a woman myself, love her to madness; all for the pure wild passion of it."[3] Such was Bernhardt's charisma that playwrights wrote dramas with her in mind, as did Wilde with his French *Salomé*—in which she never appeared, thanks to the intervention of the Lord Chamberlain—and Victorien Sardou (1831–1908), the most famous French dramatist of his age, with *Fédora* and *La Tosca*. Her repertoire became an idiosyncratic mixture of commissioned works, popular plays, and classics such as *Phèdre,* whose second act—in which Phèdre confesses her incestuous love to Hippolyte—was often played separately.

But it was Sardou more than any dramatist who helped make Sarah Bernhardt the most famous actress of the Comédie-Française. In a paper read on 5 February 1889 entitled "Acting, by One Who Does Not Believe in It," Shaw gives an amusing account of their highly profitable collaboration: "He [Sardou] deliberately took that part of Madame Bernhardt's nature which she shares with any tigress, and he exploited that to the utmost farthingsworth. Finding that it paid, he did it again."[4] And often in the very same way: Most of Sardou's heroines were women "torn between uncontrollable impulses of power-hungry aggression and passive subservience" who fell in love with men they either sacrificed or destroyed (Stokes, p. 36). Even though many French critics saw that Sardou's melodramas and those of his fellow playwrights were often of little merit—calling these Bernhardt vehicles "mediocre" or "feeble"—she managed to remain "a specialist in theatrical deaths" who "died each time in a different way, to the great admiration of the audience."[5]

However, after a few years of Théodora and Tosca, the critics complained that Bernhardt had become vulgarized. Yet why, Shaw asked, did they not immediately protest against *Théodora* "as a vile degradation of the actress, of the stage, of the drama, and of the playgoing public?" (Dukore, p. 103). Quite simply because of popular demand: The stereotype of the nineteenth-century *femme féroce* was at the height of its vogue in the 1880s, and Bernhardt "found it advantageous to make a specialty of the role."[6] From her opening performance at the Gaiety Theater on 2 June 1879, she took London by storm. Critic Francïsque Sarcey wrote back to Paris, "Nothing can give any idea of the craze Sarah is exciting. It's a mania."[7]

The adulation of the masses did not prevent Shaw from finding Bernhardt irksome. Her emotionalism exemplified everything he despised in bad acting, especially bad French acting. In a pseudonymous essay in the *Star* of 1 February 1889 entitled "Royalty Theater . . . French v. English Histrionics," he took issue with what Arthur Bingham Walkley had called "that Gallic system of histrionics which holds illusion and naturalness subservient to perfect elocution and consummate finish of style." Shaw pointed out that "the French actor is no actor at all, but only that horrible speaking automaton, an elocutionist, and that his proceedings on the stage represent not life, but that empty simulacrum called a style." French actors, he concluded, were "galvanized" by stage formalities (Dukore, pp. 90–91). "The Divine Sarah" displayed in one performance after another that "wild emotion" the young D. H. Lawrence had witnessed. Her histrionics went against all of Shaw's dramaturgical principles: self-control, natural delivery, realistic portrayals of life. One French critic explained her appeal this way: "Though intoxicated, she remains lucid in her intoxication. She is frenzied, but yet within the bounds of logic, style and clarity" (quoted in Horville, p. 43). Nonetheless, for Shaw her intoxication always overshadowed the three classic Gallic characteristics. "Disliking French drama of most periods," writes one critic, "Shaw was predisposed to dislike French acting of almost every kind" (Stokes, p. 57).

Thus Bernhardt's flamboyant stage presence and typically French acting style became responsible both for her widespread appeal and for some of Shaw's most colorful passages of theater criticism. As Doña Sol in *Hernani* in 1879, Bernhardt would suddenly switch from despair and hatred to resignation and content in an entirely believable manner. Such shifts in mood, combined with an *ostinato* delivery and spasmodic bodily movements, were to become the foundation of her success (Stokes, p. 35). They also became Shaw's perennial Bernhardt hobbyhorse. The critic, he stated in "On the Living and the Dead" (in *Saturday Review*, 25 December 1897), "is the policeman of dramatic art; and it is his express business to denounce its delinquencies" (Dukore, p. 969). But as we shall see, Shaw's denunciations had little effect on Bernhardt's acting or on her immense popularity both in France and in England.

Shaw's earliest mention of Bernhardt in print was a passing reference in *Our Corner* (August 1885) to her role in Sardou's *Théodora* (Dukore, p. 35). The following year, in his 13 October art review in the *World* of a Hanover Gallery opening, he called attention to "the Bastien Lepage portrait of Sarah Bernhardt, with its vaunted cut-steel frame,"[8] a work of 1879, the year of her first visit to London. Nine months later, Shaw recorded in his diary for 18 July 1887, "First night Sarah Bernhardt's engagement at the Lyceum. Sardou's *Theodora*."[9] The next day his first full-length critique of a Bernhardt performance appeared as an unsigned review in the *Manchester Guardian*, entitled "From Our London Correspondent." "The great actress met all the demands made on her by M. Sardou's play with consummate ease and mastery," he wrote, "the enthusiasm of the audience growing steadily from her reception to the fall of the curtain."[10]

Shaw's early praise was short-lived: This was the beginning of a long and eloquent antipathy, during which he saw Bernhardt perform in at least thirteen plays. In order of composition, these were Victor Hugo, *Hernani* (1830); Alfred de Musset, *Lorenzaccio* (1834); Alexandre Dumas, fils, *La Dame aux camélias* (1852); Henri Meilhac and Ludovic Halévy, *Frou Frou* (1869); Jules Barbier, *Jeanne d'Arc* (1873); Victorien Sardou, *Fédora* (1882); Sardou, *Théodora* (1884); Sardou, *La Tosca* (1887); Hermann Sudermann, *Heimat* (1893); Maurice Maeterlinck, *Pelléas et Mélisande* (1893); Sardou, *Gismonda* (1894); Edmond Rostand, *La Princesse lointaine* (1895); and Rostand, *L'Aiglon* (1900).

Many of these works infuriated Shaw by their lavish *mises-en-scène* and, especially, by Bernhardt's virtuoso acting. The latter consisted of "the continual repetition of movements, gestures and expressions from a variety of stage positions" (Stokes, p. 43), and emphasized what Reynaldo Hahn called "feline suppleness" and Jules Lemaître "the windings of a snake" (quoted in Stokes, p. 44). These sinewy, statuesque poses were described by Théodore de Banville as a model for "a Greek statue, wishing to symbolise Poetry." Edmond Rostand went so far as to dub Bernhardt "the queen of posture." This posturing, combined with an abruptness of gesture that one contemporary critic called "a kind of feverishness and hyperaesthesia," fueled Shaw's fiery comments (quoted in Horville, pp. 45, 47, 57).

By the time Shaw saw her again on 11 July 1892 in *Frou Frou*, Bernhardt was forty-eight, "well past her prime," he believed, "and relied on paint and cleverness" (*Diaries*, p. 834). To his exasperation, she also relied on that combination of exaggerated elocution and formulaic acting that made her performances as predictable as the "well-made plays" themselves. She could also be arrogant, and Shaw reported in 1894 that in the Albert Hall, Bernhardt was audible but unintelligible—mostly because of her French accent—and that after polite applause, "she conveyed to us very plainly by the manner of her withdrawal that she considered us a parcel of imbeciles."[11]

No matter how much she irritated Shaw, Bernhardt, more than any male or female performer of any nationality, remained a touchstone in his advice to actresses or in discussions about acting (and overacting). In the *Saturday Review* of 30 March 1895, he complained that in Ibsen's *Rosmersholm*, Marthe Mellot played Rebecca West "in the manner of Sarah Bernhardt, the least appropriate of all manners for the part," exploiting "the explosive, hysterical, wasteful passion which makes nothing but a scene," with "a tearing finish in the Bernhardt style" (Dukore, p. 297). To Janet Achurch on 23 April 1895, Shaw praised Bernhardt's ability to move an audience, as when an actress must speak her part "with a pathetic intensity that makes you forget that the actual words do not mean anything pathetic at all, affecting the public as Sarah Bernhardt affects people who do not know a word of French, or Duse people who do not know a word of Italian."[12] And about Achurch's performance in *The Wild Duck*, he wrote on 20 May 1897, "It is clear that you are not going to act any more: it is all Sara [*sic*] Bernhardt now—no brains, no pains, none of the distinction and freshness of thoughtful, self controlled work, nothing but letting yourself go and giving in to 'em hot and strong . . ." (*Letters 1874–1897*, pp. 765–66). He even told Ellen Terry—Bernhardt's good friend and constant admirer—on 4 July 1897 that Bernhardt had "reduced her business to the most mechanical routine possible" and was nothing more than "a worn out hack tragedienne" (*Letters 1874–1897*, p. 780).

Bernhardt's melodramatic mannerisms were only part of what Shaw could not stomach. As a singer, amateur organist, and professional music critic, he was especially offended by her legendary "golden voice," an unfortunate phrase coined by Victor Hugo at the banquet celebrating the hundredth performance of *Ruy Blas* (Horville, p. 60). Bernhardt's voice was in fact very melodious, but it could also become strident and declamatory. It was also rather thin, forcing her "to play in a minor key, which grated when it needed to go into the upper register" (Horville, p. 61). None of this affected the young Sigmund Freud, who saw Bernhardt in Paris in 1885 in *Théodora:* "After the first words of her lovely, vibrant voice I felt I had known her for years" (quoted in Gold and Fizdale, p. 4). Shaw himself referred to Bernhardt in 1889 as an "internationally musical speaker of the highest class" (*Shaw's Music*, 1: 849), but remarked the following year that as Jules Barbier's Joan of Arc, with music by Charles Gounod, she "intones her lines and poses like a saint" and "sends the lines out in a plaintive stream of melody throughout which only a fine ear can catch the false ring. You would almost swear that they meant something and that she was in earnest" (*Shaw's Music*, 2: 22).

Although some French contemporaries, like Théodore de Banville, thought Bernhardt spoke verse "as the nightingale sings, as the wind sighs, as the stream murmurs," others agreed with Shaw and reported that her voice often sounded "strangled . . . raucous, and . . . ineffectual," "too violent and jerky," and "strident" (quoted in Horville, pp. 60, 61). "Able only with difficulty to make use of differences of range," writes one critic, "she skillfully exploited flexibility and variations of tone. By this means she was able to give her phrasing smoothness and a flowing quality. . . . Apt at bringing out the lyricism of the verse, her delivery could easily become monotonous, falling into a tedious chanting" (Horville, pp. 61–62).

Shaw was continually haunted by this "tedious chanting." Following a representation of Sardou's *Gismonda*, his 1 June 1895 *Saturday Review* critique, "Sardoodledom," attacks "that 'voix céleste' stop" that she keeps always pulled out "like a sentimental New England villager with an American organ" in a performance that was "vulgar and commercial, . . . hackneyed and old-fashioned" (Dukore, pp. 356–57). Writing to Florence Farr on 6 June 1902, Shaw complained that Bernhardt's "abominable 'golden voice,' which has always made me sick, is cantilation, or, to use the customary word, intoning."[13] And that October, he wrote that Ada Rehan's voice, "compared to Sarah Bernhardt's *voix d'or*, has been as all the sounds of the woodland to the chinking of twenty-franc pieces" (Dukore, p. 913). Shaw was only satisfied when he could *not* hear Bernhardt: After seeing the silent film *Elisabeth, Reine d'Angleterre* (1912), he wrote to Ellen Terry in 1915 and called it "very fine, and much better without that voix d'or that always set my teeth on edge than with it."[14]

If Bernhardt's acting was so unmusical, predictable and hyperdramatic, how could she entrance her audiences—both French and foreign—for so long? In two ways: by sheer force of personality and by giving the public exactly what it wanted. In his article of 15 June 1895 entitled "Duse and Bernhardt"—which Bernard Dukore calls "by common consent . . . the best criticism of acting in the English language" (p. xxxii)—Shaw contrasts the French actress to the equally famous Italian star, Eleonora Duse (1859–1924) in their roles as Magda in Hermann Sudermann's *Heimat*. While Shaw could pardon Bernhardt's overpainted face because of its unashamed and artful execution ("Her lips are like a newly painted pillar box"), he deplored "the childishly egotistical character of her acting, which is not the art of making you think more highly or feel more deeply, but the art of making you admire her, pity her, champion her, weep with her, laugh at her jokes . . . and applaud her wildly when the curtain falls," of "cajoling you, harrowing you, exciting you—on the whole, fooling you. . . . She does not enter into the leading character: she substitutes herself for it." This was far from Shaw's ideal of the thinking actor, but the crowds loved her, even though, as Shaw mocked, Bernhardt's "stock of attitudes and facial effects could be catalogued as easily as her stock of dramatic ideas: the counting would hardly go beyond the fingers of both hands" (Dukore, pp. 367–68, 369). And Shaw was right: Her bewitching personality enveloped a role to the extent that, as one contemporary French drama critic observed, she ended up "playing herself all the time" (quoted in Horville, p. 42). Médée or Cléopâtre, Phèdre or Andromaque, Théodora or Tosca: all of them were Sarah.

What appalled Shaw was that the secret of Bernhardt's success was her appeal to the emotions, her performances nothing more than explosions of feeling. The following year, he wrote that compared with Duse, Bernhardt was nothing but "a hackneyed provincial melodramatic actress" (Dukore, p. 555). In fact, some believe it was Shaw more than any other critic "who led future generations to think of Sarah as a moneygrubbing queen of melodrama and Duse as an otherworldly priestess of high art" (Gold and Fizdale, pp. 255–56).

Shaw's descriptions are indeed pen portraits of the "queen of melodrama" in full Dionysian mode. In his 22 June 1895 review of *La Princesse lointaine* by Rostand, he described her evocatively: tearing through her lines "at the utmost pitch and power of her voice, she shews no further sense of what she is saying, and is unable to recover herself when, in the final speech, the feeling changes" and she "finally rushes off the stage in a forced frenzy." He suggested that her "ranting" be "replaced by a genuine study and interpretation of the passages which are sacrificed to it." He concluded with his usual stab at her voice, remarking that the critic "who finds melody in one sustained note would find exquisite curves in a packing case" (Dukore, pp. 375–77). On this last point, one French critic remarked of the same play that "she doubtless thought that it would be impossible to over-use the drawling singsong" (quoted in Horville, p. 62). Two years later, in his 26 June 1897 review of Musset's *Lorenzaccio*, Shaw summed up Bernhardt's stage antics as a combination of "golden voice," "celebrated smile," "businesslike and competent" acting, and "tearing a passion to tatters," a routine "which is refurbished every year with fresh scenery, fresh dialogue, and a fresh author, whilst remaining itself invariable" (Dukore, p. 884). Very different is Anatole France's review of the same play in Paris the previous year, which praises Bernhardt's "sureness of gesture, the tragic beauty of her pose and glance, the increased power in the timbre of her voice, and the suppleness and breadth of her diction"—all of which Shaw routinely condemned in his reviews of Bernhardt on stage (quoted in Gold and Fizdale, p. 261).

It is a tribute to Bernhardt's charisma that even the arch-realist Shaw could not help falling under the siren's spell on occasion. Despite her histrionics, stiff acting, and monotone voice, Shaw suggested to his French translator Augustin Hamon, in a letter of 4 December 1906, that Bernhardt "ought to play" Mrs. Warren (*Letters 1898–1910*, p. 664). Moreover, as one who took an interest in all aspects of the theater, Shaw acknowledged Bernhardt's shrewdness. To Ellen Terry, he wrote on 15 May 1903 that Bernhardt's "plan of always keeping her stage full of the prettiest women she can find is a very worldly-wise one" (*Letters 1898–1910*, p. 325). And to actress Gertrude Kingston on 6 July 1917, he wrote that "no single success can keep up a theater unless it be that of a man who can play the big Hamlet Macbeth repertory which has no female equivalent. It has been tried again and again; and the only apparent solid result is Sarah, who always built herself in with the prettiest women and strongest men she could lay her hands on."[15] But these are rare exceptions to Shaw's generally adversarial stance.

In fact, Shaw remained adversarial even at Bernhardt's death, his final comments a short and rather mixed tribute published in the Manchester *Sunday Chronicle* of 1 April 1923, ambiguously entitled "Handicaps of a Queen of Tragedy." Shaw admits that he had been touched "by her Pelléas as she never touched me in any other part." On the other hand, "She was not an author's actress. The only character she gave to the stage was her own. . . . She never got into the skin of her parts: she simply exploited them, prefering her own skin, sometimes with good reason." He goes on to recall the first time he saw her, forty years earlier in *Hernani* (Dukore, 1386–87). Although he left no record of his views on that performance, he had written in his 26 June 1897 review of *Lorenzaccio* about "the fascination which, as Dona Sol, she once gave to Hernani" (Dukore, p. 884). Here he mentions "an unforgettable moment in the last act" that, he emphasizes, had reappeared in every play as "a mechanical rant." He even takes a last jibe at her voice, writing that the "famous voix d'or was produced by intoning like an effeminate Oxford curate." While admitting that "she improved with age, becoming much jollier and more sensible," Shaw finishes with a left-handed compliment: "Only a clever, resolute, self-centred woman could have imposed 'the Divine Sarah' on Europe and America . . ." (Dukore, pp. 1386–87).

Shaw may have been somewhat disingenuous in his memorial epitaph because, according to one critic, he was "coerced" into writing it (Stokes, p. 58). Perhaps, too, Bernhardt had "imposed" herself unwittingly on Shaw, despite his claim that if Bernhardt "had any other part in the great dramatic development that took place in her time, it did not reach us here" (Dukore, p. 1386). On the contrary, Martin Meisel points out that *Saint Joan,* as a play written for a woman star, "is a direct continuation of the line of the most 'legitimate' women-plays of the nineteenth century, historical, tragic, and rhetorical, elevated in diction and sentiment,[16] all of which describes the plays that Bernhardt's productions made famous. Moreover, she may have been part of the impetus behind Shaw's *Saint Joan:* In her journal (on 19 May 1923), Lady Gregory writes that "G.B.S. says he chose Joan of Arc because of Bernhardt and others having played so many parts turning on sexual attraction he wanted to give Joan as a heroine absolutely without that side."[17] One wonders what Bernhardt would have done with—or, rather, "to"—Shaw's *Sainte Jeanne* had she lived to displace the meek, waif-like (and hugely popular) Ludmilla Pitoëff from the stage. Most likely she would have played Jeanne as the woman she once described as "a frail being led by a divine soul. An invisible angel supported her arm which carried the heavy sword. It is the legend that interests us."[18] It was exactly the opposite for Shaw. Moreover, Bernhardt's tears, writes one critic, "were almost as famous as her voice."[19] She may even have out-emotionalized Ludmilla.

Although his opinion of Bernhardt's acting was generally very low, Shaw was not alone in recognizing her shortcomings. Even some French critics deplored in their national stage heroine the same flaws that Shaw exposed in the British press. One of these was the novelist and playwright Romain Rolland (1866–1944), who considered the romantic dramas of Dumas fils, Sardou, and Rostand a threat to his "théâtre populaire" and Bernhardt as the one performer who exerted a definitive influence on the success of his fellow dramatists. Like Shaw, Rolland objected to Bernhardt's gaudiness and mechanical acting, in one instance outdoing Shaw's use of epithets in describing her. Writing in 1904, he named her as the one who best characterized "ce néo-romantisme byzantinisé,—où américanisé,—raidi, figé, sans jeunesse, sans vigeur, surchargé d'ornements, de bijoux vrais ou faux, morne sous son fracas, blafard dans son éclat" [this Byzantinized, or Americanized, neo-Romanticism: stiff, rigid, without youth, without vigor, weighed down with ornaments, with jewels real or fake, bleak beneath its bluster, pallid in its glitter].[20]

It is interesting that Shaw's and Rolland's descriptions of Bernhardt's shortcomings are at odds with what she herself wrote in a short chapter entitled "Naturalism" in her book, *The Art of Theatre*. In it she urges the artist to "exhibit the feelings that are supposed to animate him, in the manner they are exhibited in real life by average men amongst his contemporaries." After what Shaw had seen (and written) of Bernhardt's acting, he would doubtless have been astonished to read that "You must avoid stiff and chronic poses in order to fit into the innumerable vicissitudes of existence. . . . Nothing is more distasteful than to act according to a formula that is constantly repeated" (*Art,* pp. 98–100). It was that very "formula" that propelled Bernhardt and her playwrights to stardom.

In keeping with her views on naturalism in acting—and despite the "romantic" nature of her personality and of her stage characterizations—is Bernhardt's idea of the theater as a didactic medium for an intellectual audience. While excoriating her acting style, Shaw would have found it difficult to disagree with Bernhardt's conception of the theater as a place for "the intellectual education of the masses," as "a perennial and effective form of instruction," and as "the most direct speaking-trumpet of new philosophical, social, religious and moral ideas." Like Shaw, she thought of the theater as an institution that invites the public "to think, to understand, and to extract from what happens on the stage something other than a vulgar pleasure of the eyes" (*Art,* pp. 181, 175, 179, 180). Bernhardt's views echo closely Shaw's famous definition of the theater (in "The Author's Apology" for his *Saturday Review* criticisms, Preface to *Dramatic Opinions and Essays* of October 1906) as "a factory of thought, a prompter of conscience, an elucidator of social conduct" (Dukore, p. 1134). Despite all the emotionalism and spectacle of her performances, it seems that Bernhardt and Shaw were thinking along the same theoretical lines.

In light of her interest in realistic acting and didactic drama, it is not surprising that of all her famous contemporaries—Sardou, Augier, Rostand, Dumas fils—the one playwright Bernhardt held in highest esteem was the one that Shaw himself considered the greatest of all living French dramatists: the second-rate Eugène Brieux (1858–1932), an ardent socialist about whom Shaw wrote a long panegyric and some of whose plays Charlotte Shaw translated into English.[21] Bernhardt praised Brieux's "bold, penetrating, and luminous plays," his "philosophical, moral, or social doctrines," in which "society is vigorously scourged, and the blemishes of social hypocrisy are laid bare" (*Art,* pp. 180–81). Yet Bernhardt never appeared in a work by Brieux. His realistic dramas were designed to illustrate controversial issues of the day, such as venereal disease, birth control, the dowry system, prostitution, and divorce. They were not written to showcase a *prima donna* who could portray famous historical or mythical tragic figures in plays that featured "blackmail, treason, torture, suicide, murder and *lots* of adultery."[22]

Such plays made Bernhardt not only infamous but also the richest and most important French actress of her time, the first modern female superstar. She became an internationally recognized tragedienne of Sophocles and Racine as well as the heroine (and often the hero) of the most popular dramas and melodramas of the day, a contribution to French culture honored with the medal of the Légion d'Honneur in 1913 and a requiem mass in Westminster Cathedral.

One critic asks, "Where would Sarah be if we had only the testimony of Bernard Shaw?" (Trewin, p. 126). Sarah would be safe upon the pedestal raised by many other famous English and Irish writers. Maurice Baring, her most fervent English admirer, thought her voice "so soft, so melting, so perfectly clean-cut that one never lost a syllable" (Salmon, p. 119). A. B. Walkley was "spellbound" by Phèdre's "low, wailing melody" (Salmon, p. 128). James Agate, a devoted worshipper, believed that "those who remember her acting at its best will marvel at the panegyrist's ineffectual poverty" (Salmon, p. 120). W. B. Yeats, a devotee of verse drama, saw in Bernhardt "an endorsement of the ideal of rhythmic delivery and minimal movement that . . . he had been reaching towards with the production of his own plays" (Stokes, p. 58). Oscar Wilde, a Bernhardt fanatic, praised "the superb elocution of the French—so clean, so cadenced, and so musical" (quoted in Stokes, p. 57). Shaw's was not the only dissenting Anglo-Saxon voice—Matthew Arnold and Henry James shared some of his reservations—but it was certainly the loudest and most sustained.

Paradoxically, Bernhardt enjoyed the same renown and controversial reputation as her Irish nemesis. Both were caricatured as well as apotheosized by the press. Both possessed an often exaggerated sense of their amazing capabilities. Both took an active part in the staging, casting, and production of their plays. And both were adept at self-promotion and garnered enormous profits from the theater. "Was she really a great actress," Sir John Gielgud queries, "or merely a great star personality with a genius for publicity and showmanship?" (quoted in Emboden, p. 9). We need only replace "she" with "he" and "actress" with "playwright" to discover a question that has been asked of Shaw more than of any dramatist in history.

But the similarities end there: Sarah Bernhardt was simply too "French" for Shaw, a man "more dedicated to Anglo-Saxon matter than to Gallic manner" (Gold and Fizdale, p. 258), to making a point rather than creating an effect. Although she became an international cult figure, the French siren never succeeded in luring the Irishman "into the mysteries of sensuality and poetic illusion." Shaw was too solid a "rock of truth," and Bernhardt's song, as we have seen, did not enchant him.[23]

Notes

1. Arthur Gold and Robert Fizdale, *The Divine Sarah: A Life of Sarah Bernhardt* (New York: Knopf, 1991), p. 3. Subsequent references to Gold and Fizdale appear parenthetically in the text.

2. John Stokes, "Sarah Bernhardt," in John Stokes, Michael R. Booth, and Susan Bassnett, *Bernhardt, Terry, Duse: The Actress in Her Time* (Cambridge, Cambridge University Press, 1988), p. 35. Subsequent references to Stokes appear parenthetically in the text.

3. *The Letters of D. H. Lawrence, Vol. I: 1901–13*, ed. James T. Boulton (Cambridge: Cambridge University Press, 1979), p. 58.

4. Bernard Shaw, "Acting, by One Who Does Not Believe in It; or The Place of The Stage in The Fool's Paradise of Art," in Bernard F. Dukore, ed., *Bernard Shaw: The Drama Observed*, 4 vols. (University Park: Penn State University Press, 1993), p. 103. Subsequent references to Dukore appear parenthetically in the text.

5. Robert Horville, "The Stage Techniques of Sarah Bernhardt," translated by Eric Salmon, in Eric Salmon, ed., *Bernhardt and the Theatre of Her Time* (Westport, Conn., and London: Greenwood Press, 1984), pp. 37, 40. Subsequent references to Horville appear parenthetically in the text.

6. Maurice Valency, *The Cart and the Trumpet: The Plays of George Bernard Shaw* (New York: Oxford University Press, 1973), p. 84.

7. Quoted in J. C. Trewin, "Bernhardt on the London Stage," in Eric Salmon, ed.,

Bernhardt and the Theatre of Her Time, p. 116. Subsequent references to Trewin appear parenthetically in the text.

8. *Bernard Shaw on the London Art Scene, 1885–1950,* ed. Stanley Weintraub (University Park and London: Penn State University Press, 1989), p. 123. A color reproduction of the portrait by Jules Bastien-Lepage (1848–84) is found in Joanna Richardson, *Sarah Bernhardt and Her World* (New York: G. P. Putnam's Sons, 1977), p. 52.

9. *Bernard Shaw, The Diaries 1885–1897,* 2 vols., ed. Stanley Weintraub (University Park and London: Penn State University Press, 1986), p. 295. Subsequent references to the *Diaries* appear parenthetically in the text.

10. Bernard Shaw (unsigned), "From Our London Correspondent," *Manchester Guardian* (19 July 1887), p. 5 (item C337 of *Bernard Shaw: A Bibliography,* 2 vols., ed. Dan H. Laurence [Oxford: Clarendon, 1983], p. 542). I am grateful to Bernard F. Dukore for providing a copy of this review.

11. *Shaw's Music: The Complete Musical Criticism,* 3 vols., ed. Dan H. Laurence (New York: Dodd, Mead, 1981), 3:328. Subsequent references to *Shaw's Music* appear parenthetically in the text.

12. Bernard Shaw, *Collected Letters 1874–1897,* ed. Dan H. Laurence (New York: Dodd, Mead, 1965), p. 529. Subsequent references to *Letters 1874–1897* appear parenthetically in the text.

13. Bernard Shaw, *Collected Letters 1898–1910,* ed. Dan H. Laurence (New York: Dodd, Mead, 1972), p. 274. Subsequent references to *Letters 1898–1910* appear parenthetically in the text.

14. Bernard Shaw, *Collected Letters 1911–1925,* ed. Dan H. Laurence (New York: Viking, 1985), p. 283.

15. *Bernard Shaw: Theatrics,* ed. Dan H. Laurence (Toronto: University of Toronto Press, 1995), p. 139.

16. Martin Meisel, *Shaw and the Nineteenth-Century Theater* (Princeton: Princeton University Press, 1984), p. 366, n. 21.

17. Dan H. Laurence and Nicholas Grene, *Shaw, Lady Gregory and the Abbey: A Correspondence and a Record* (Gerrards Cross: Colin Smythe, 1993), p. 167.

18. Sarah Bernhardt, *The Art of the Theatre,* trans. H. J. Stenning (London: Geoffrey Bles, 1924), p. 124. Subsequent references to *Art* appear parenthetically in the text.

19. William Emboden, *Sarah Bernhardt* (New York: Macmillan, 1975), p. 91.

20. Romain Rolland, *Le théâtre du peuple: essai d'esthétique d'un théâtre nouveau* (Paris: Hachette, 1913), p. 31.

21. Cf. "Preface to Three Plays by Brieux" (written 1909, published 1911) in Dukore, pp. 1188–1222. See also my "Eugène Brieux and Bernard Shaw: Iconoclasts of Social Reform," *SHAW* 8 (1988): 97–104.

22. Richard Findlater, "Bernhardt and the British Player Queens: A Venture into Comparative Theatrical Mythology," in Eric Salmon, ed., *Bernhardt and the Theatre of Her Time,* p. 94, author's emphasis.

23. Shaw may also have been impervious to Bernhardt's charms for personal reasons. According to Dan Laurence, when he spoke with Shaw's cousin and first fulltime secretary, "Judy" Musters, at Folkestone on 23 June 1963, she recalled Shaw's remark that one of the reasons he probably did not like Bernhardt was that she resembled his aunt Georgina Shaw, whom he detested. Georgina separated from her husband (Shaw's youngest uncle, Richard Frederick Shaw) and moved to London, where she often visited Shaw's mother. I am grateful to Dan Laurence for providing this information and for alerting me to a comment by Hesketh Pearson in *G.B.S.: A Full Length Portrait* (New York and London: Harper & Brothers, 1942): "It is perhaps only fair to mention that Shaw confessed that his criticisms of the divine Sarah were worthless. 'I could never do her justice or believe in her impersonations because she was so like my aunt Georgina.' As with several of his funniest sallies, this was a simple statement of fact" (p. 149).

Stanley Weintraub

EUGENE O'NEILL:
THE SHAVIAN DIMENSION

Sitting in the offices of the Theatre Guild while being interviewed by a *New York Times* reporter, Eugene O'Neill suddenly looked up at a drawing on the wall and smiled. "I wish they'd take that down," he said; "the old gentleman seems to be laughing at me."[1] The year was 1931, and the picture was a portrait of Shaw. O'Neill was only five years from winning the Nobel Prize for Literature, the only American playwright, still, to have earned the prize.

Shaw had been there, for O'Neill, at the beginning, and in the play that he was already contemplating, his gentle satire *Ah, Wilderness!* (1933). The impressionable boy of seventeen at the heart of the play, Richard Miller, O'Neill's nostalgic mirror of himself in the early 1900s, is surreptitiously reading Shaw. Soon, O'Neill's wife Carlotta would be writing to her husband's editor, Saxe Commins, "Gene has asked me to ask you if you can send him the dates of the publications of Shaw's *earlier* plays—*before & around* 1907."[2] O'Neill wanted to have them on young Richard's bedroom shelves and wanted to make sure he was committing no anachronism.

At the close of the 1930s, when he was working on a more deeply autobiographical play, about his father, Irish-American actor James O'Neill, and his mother, who paid the price for her husband's fame, Shaw's books would also be in the small bookcase in the Tyrone summer home in *Long Day's Journey into Night* (1939–40). Here the O'Neill figure, Edmund Tyrone, would be older. The play is set in 1912.

It was not the invented Richard Miller, but his original, O'Neill himself, who at eighteen encountered Shaw in 1907. Eugene must have heard about Shaw much earlier, at home, for a friend of the elder O'Neill, Jimmie Durkin, wrote to G.B.S. in 1909 that "while I am a stranger to you, your writings have endeared me to you as an old acquaintance," for James O'Neill "has discussed you and your work with me for hours, with much enjoyment to the both of us."[3] Two years before that, in 1907, young Eugene had seen the great Russian actress Alla Nazimova as *Hedda Gabler,* an Ibsen play that focused his ambitions. To the editor of a Norwegian-American newspaper he recalled going back "again and again for ten successive nights. . . . It gave me my first conception of a modern theatre where truth might live."[4]

Eager to learn more about Ibsen, O'Neill sought out Benjamin R. Tucker's "Unique Bookshop" in Manhattan. It was the ideal venue in which to learn about Shaw as well as Ibsen, for Tucker, as editor of *Liberty,* an American anarchist journal, had published, in 1895, Shaw's "open letter" rejoinder, written at Tucker's request, to Max Nordau's philistine polemic *Entartung,* translated as *Degeneration.* Shaw took no fee for "A Degenerate's View of Nordau," a sardonic 13,000–word demolition of Nordau's claim that contemporary artists (and their art) were either sick or lunatic, and Tucker happily published a double number of *Liberty* to fit in all of Shaw's observations about the social utility of the arts, then sent free copies to every paper in America for which he had an address. (With some revisions it would become, in 1908, *The Sanity of Art.* Shaw would let Tucker publish the 104–page New York edition, which it is unlikely that O'Neill would miss in the Unique Bookshop.)

Tucker got O'Neill to start with Shaw's *Quintessence of Ibsenism* (1891). O'Neill already knew about Shaw: *Mrs Warren's Profession* had been closed by the police for alleged indecency, and the entire cast had spent the night in a New York jail. As, "wildly excited," Eugene read *Quintessence,* he marked in red ink everything that impressed him, or that he agreed with, and ended with a book that was underscored on every page. He carried the book about with him in his pocket, and his disdain increased for his father's sort of theater, in which, Eugene later said, "Virtue always triumphed and vice always got its just deserts. . . . A man was either a hero or a villain, and a woman was either virtuous or vile."[5] In his last year at boarding school O'Neill armed himself with quotations from Shaw to fit every argument and convinced himself that the falsity of much of popular art only reflected the corruption and hypocrisy in society.

He went, too, to Shaw's plays, also available at Tucker's bookshop, and read them all, reinforcing his feeling that glib, happy endings, romantic rather than ironic, had no realistic relation to life. He absorbed the early Shaw so completely, an O'Neill biographer (Doris Alexander) contends, "that years later, when he created the character of Captain Brant in *Mourning Becomes Electra,* he would make him almost an exact duplicate of Shaw's Captain Brassbound [in the 1899 play *Captain Brassbound's Conversion*] without even being conscious of the plagiarism."[6] The play he first identified himself with, however, was *Candida* (1895), in particular the eighteen-year-old aspiring poet, Eugene Marchbanks. The coincidence of names intensified his passion for the play. In a romantic exchange with one young woman, O'Neill implored, "I make the poet's plea in *Candida*."

Later, when she examined the play for an explanation, she found more than the coincidence in names. Like O'Neill, Shaw's poet was shy, awkward, and had a "haunted, tormented expression."[7] She read the "auction" scene late in the play in which Candida Morell asks her husband and the young poet, more ironically than both realize, what they are willing to bid for her love. The husband, who would be lost without her, proudly claims that he will defend her and her quality of life, while the poet who desperately worships her offers "My weakness. My desolation. My heart's need."

"That's a good bid, Eugene," says Candida, but she realizes that his world is not hers and that her husband, not Marchbanks, would fall apart without her. She sends the poet off. Marchbanks, expecting it, announces melodramatically, "Out, then, into the night with me!" O'Neill's autobiographical Richard, not quite seventeen, quotes that line when his mother rebukes him for reading "indecent" books, among them *Candida*. At the door, he adds, contemptuously, the enigmatic final comment in Shaw's stage directions for the play: *"They do not know the secret in the poet's heart."*[8]

In the bland, middle-class house in *Ah, Wilderness!* the "shy, dreamy, defiant" Richard conceals on his shelves Carlyle's *The French Revolution* and Wilde's *Ballad of Reading Gaol,* the plays of Ibsen, the poems of Swinburne, the *Rubaiyat,* and two books, his mother charges, "by that Bernard Shaw."

"The greatest playwright alive today!" retorts Richard.

One of the books, Essie Miller goes on, "was so vile they wouldn't even let it play in New York!" The other, she informs Mr. Miller, "had a long title I couldn't make head or tail of, only it wasn't a play."

"The Quintessence of Ibsenism," says Richard proudly.

As the third scene of Act IV opens, Nat Miller is leafing through the pile of books confiscated by his wife from their son's bedroom. Miller *"chuckles at something he reads,"* then observes to Mrs. Miller, "That Shaw's a comical cuss—even if his ideas are so crazy they oughtn't allow them to be printed. And Swinburne's got a fine swing to his poetry—if he'd only choose some other subjects besides loose women."

"I can see," she says (*"teasingly,"* O'Neill notes), "where you're becoming corrupted by those books, too—pretending to read them out of duty to Richard, when your nose has been glued to the page!"

Although the Millers want Richard to go to Yale, his future is undefined when the curtain comes down. The real Eugene, searching for what he called "real life," would drop out of Princeton and go off as a merchant seaman, then experience a physical breakdown that confined him to a tuberculosis sanatorium. His enforced leisure to read convinced O'Neill that he wanted to be a playwright like his theater idols. On his recovery in 1913, when he was already twenty-four, he studied playwriting at Harvard for a year and saw his early attempts performed by an amateur group on Cape Cod—the Provincetown Players, which after moving to New York became the stage on which O'Neill learned how plays actually worked. Most were autobiographical, as is typical of apprentice writers, and his growing pains appear in them, as well as his reading and his encounters as a seaman on deck, below deck, and in sleazy ports.

He seemed unable to escape his early encounters with Ibsen and Shaw. In an early play, *Fog*, his Poet—with a capital *P*—is a Marchbanks figure. Another, *A Wife for a Life*, reaches for Shavian domestic comedy. In *Now I Ask You*, the recently married Lucy Ashleigh, his heroine, sounds like a Chekhov character, quotes Strindberg, acts like Hedda Gabler, and is fascinated by a young artist who tries to seduce her with echoes of *Candida*. Gabriel and Lucy closely parallel the third act of Shaw's play, with Gabriel drawing his chair close to hers and offering to "come into your life and take you away, to the mountain tops, to the castles in the air, to the haunt of brave dreams where life is free, and joyous, and noble. . . . Can't you read the secret in my heart? Don't you hear the song my soul has been singing ever since I first looked into your eyes?"[9] Her husband walks in, as did Candida's, and is immediately demoralized by what he erroneously thinks has already happened.

Just as derivative is *Servitude*,[10] another 1914 work beginning when Nora slams the door in *A Doll's House* and continuing as a sort of *Candida*, with the interloper this time a Nora rather than a Marchbanks. A play with Shaw-like dialogue about the role of women in marriage, it features a preachy playwright of advanced ideas, much like the Rev. James Mavor Morell in *Candida*, whom women also swoon over, and a young married woman, Ethel Frazer, who has left her husband to live by David Roylston's radical code of self-realization.

Seeking out the playwright to reassure herself that she is on the right path to self-realization, she is infatuated with him. Then she realizes that he is just another selfish husband exploiting a devoted wife who has submerged her own aspirations in coddling him. And it ends as does *Candida* with the departure of the third party and the reconciliation of husband and wife. "Mentally I am your creation," Mrs. Frazer tells Roylston, confronting him with the living result of his stage moralizing. "I demand that you restore my peace of mind by justifying me to myself." And he attempts to do so, asserting cynically that a comfortable marriage sustains his literary creativity. "My work comes first. As long as my home life gives free scope for my creative faculty I will demand nothing further from it. . . . I accept my domestic bliss at its surface value and save my analytical eye for the creations of my brain." Love, he contends, "is the world upside down."

When his wife is forced to face the reality of her role as servant, Mrs. Frazer commiserates with her, "How unhappy you must have been!" But she is startled by the paradox of Alice Roylston's response, "Unhappy! . . . How little you know. I have been happy in serving him, happy in the knowledge that I have had my little part in helping him to success, happy to be able to shield and protect him." In a reversal of *Candida*, O'Neill has Mrs. Roylston willing to leave her husband to Ethel Frazer if that will contribute to his professional success, and he is awakened to his unsavory real self. Like Morell with Candida, he kneels beside his wife and begs forgiveness.

But she claims, restating the paradox of her answer to Mrs. Frazer, "This *was* my happiness." And her husband, in O'Neill's stage directions, *"bends down and kisses her reverently."* The young playwright, unsure whether to be satiric or sentimental, has it both ways.

In *The Quintessence of Ibenism*, Shaw had referred to the ideal audience at a modern production juxtaposing distancing with empathy as "guilty creatures at a play." In O'Neill's *Servitude* both sexes were not spared from that recognition of guilt, yet O'Neill had not yet found his own voice. It would take the unsparing gloom of his 1920s tragedies to accomplish that. And in the years before them he would see, in New York, not only Shavian "treats," as he put it, like *Pygmalion*, but the repertoire of the Irish Players of Dublin, which included plays like those of Synge, which O'Neill would mirror. In the 1920s he saw *Heartbreak House* and *Saint Joan*, done by the new production group, the Theatre Guild, which would also perform O'Neill's plays. That conjunction made it all the more likely that Shaw would learn about O'Neill, and when G.B.S. would try to help out his devoted biographer Archibald Henderson by producing (in 1924) a pseudo-dialogue published as *Table-Talk of G.B.S.*, he made his earliest references to O'Neill.

"I have seen a couple of his plays," Shaw said, "and read some others. They depend to some extent on false acting. For example, when Jean Cadell played *Diff'rent* in London, and played it so well that she made the woman absolutely real, the result was too painful to be bearable. . . . O'Neill's dramatic gift and sense of the stage are unquestionable; but as far as I know his work he is still only a Fantee[11] Shakespeare, peopling his tales with Calibans. I wonder what he would make of a civilized comedy like Moliere's *Misanthrope.*"[12]

Shaw had not known that while O'Neill was reaching for Shakespearean tragedy he was also trying to write a Shavian comedy, attempting an
anachronistic historical satire in the style of *Caesar and Cleopatra*. Critics
have thematically associated *Marco Millions,* begun in 1923, with the publication of Sinclair Lewis's novel *Babbitt,* an evisceration of the go-getting
businessman of the 1920, yet Shaw has his own glib businessman in the
Roman rug merchant Apollodorus. *Caesar and Cleopatra* itself, written in
1898–99, seems, like O'Neill's play, never intended to be actable in its
entirety. Both are too long, and even O'Neill's later version cries for deep
cuts. While Shaw's own later script, revised in 1912, begins with a Prologue spoken by an Egyptian god that recognizes the existence of a contemporary audience and warns spectators uneasy in their seats not to
presume to applaud him, O'Neill shifts his anachronistic equivalent to
the Epilogue, in which Marco Polo is found rising with the audience in
the theater. O'Neill's first text, much cut in 1927,[13] he knew would be
overly long, but he confessed to a colleague, Kenneth Macgowan, "I'm
letting the sky be the limit and putting every fancy in."

Glimpsing but not perceiving the close connections, O'Neill biographer
Louis Shaeffer wrote, "While the central idea has possibilities, O'Neill was
not the man to develop them. In the hands, say, of Shaw, the story could
have been thoughtful, witty comedy along the lines of *Caesar and Cleopatra;* but O'Neill, though he had a sardonic sense of humor, and an Irishman's flair for comic exaggeration, was too slow on his feet for the kind
of verbal Ping-Pong his story required."

Perhaps the basic flaw is O'Neill's concept of Marco Polo[14] as banal and
superficial, entirely a thoughtless go-getter after quick wealth. The
thoughtful people, the Khan and his beautiful granddaughter, Princess
Kukachin, who loves Marco because she misunderstands him, are given
relatively minor roles. Although she is in effect the Cleopatra to Marco
Polo's Caesar, she is not given enough depth, and the bittersweet romance has no balance. At the close, Marco returns to Italy laden with
wealth, ready to marry his long-waiting, now middle-aged, virgin, while
Kukachin, having lost the will to live, dwindles into premature death.
Her passivity is meant to contrast ironically to Marco's irrepressible ebul-
lience, while the paradox at the close of Shaw's play is that Caesar, also
abandoning a pretty—if imperious—young thing to return to Italy
(Rome rather than Venice) is knowingly returning to assassination plots
and a grim end to glory, leaving an ambitious rather than lovesick Cleopatra to rule with a younger lover he is sending in his place, Marc Antony.

For a reader coming from the script of *Caesar and Cleopatra,* the Shavian
resonances in O'Neill's satire are striking, especially in the uncut, earlier
version. There are echoes of Shaw's straitlaced, proud Britannus in Marco's cellmate Rusticiano, who rejects Marco's rather cynical advice about

authorship with "I shall write as becomes a gentleman." Marco himself is a young man of severe, unsentimental objectivity—in that respect a young Julius Caesar. "Facts, statistics, useful data in general," he explains, "—a book that'll do good, that's what I want to write." When Rusticiano insists, huffily, about his own book, "I am writing it for Art, not for money," he reveals his Apollodorus side, Shaw having exploited his rug merchant to satirize the Art-for-Art's sake aspirants of the 1890s.

Shaw was so pleased by the results of his deliberate collision of the present with the past that he added notes to the published play to elaborate on some of his anachronisms. O'Neill is content to let the clash of times in dialogue and in stage directions reverberate in the reader or listener without any gloss. His satirical lines, largely given to or addressed to Marco, are on business ethics, religious hypocrisy, Western obtuseness, national jingoism. "Never forget," Marco's uncle, Maffeo Polo, tells him patriotically, "that by the blessing of God you were born in the finest little old spot on God's green footstool!" As if that had not sounded Irish enough, O'Neill has Marco tell his father a story he claims he heard "from an idol-polisher in Tibet": "It seems an Irishman got drunk in Tangut and wandered into a temple where he mistook one of the female statues for a real woman and. . . ." He then goes off into a comic pantomime that embarrasses his father and uncle. "Dolt!" scolds Nicolo.

Shaw's favorite anachronism in *Caesar and Cleopatra* is a steam-operated crane that hauls supplies to the top of the lighthouse in Alexandria—"a machine with boiling water in it which I do not understand," says Britannus. "It is not of British design."[15] O'Neill's apparent equivalent is a conveyor belt on the Khan's wharf at Zaiton, but he gives it, ironically, only the appearance of powered machinery:

> *In the right, is a warehouse, from a door in which an endless chain of half-naked slaves, their necks, waists, and right ankles linked up by chains, form an endless chain which revolves mechanically as it were, on sprocket wheels in the interiors of the shed and the junk. As each individual link passes out of the shed it carries a bale on its head, moves with mechanical precision across the wharf, disappears into the junk, reappears a moment later having dumped its load and moves back into the shed. The whole process is a man power replica of the endless chain engines with bucket scoops that dredge, load coal, sand, etc. By the side of the shed, a foreman sits with a drum and gong with which he marks a perfect time for the slaves, a four beat rhythm, three beats of the drum, the fourth a bang on the gong as one slave at each end loads and unloads. The effect is very like the noise of a machine.*

Marco strikingly echoes, too, other Shaw plays. When Kublai Khan and Marco discuss the possibility of the soul's immortality, the prosaic Venetian responds, mirroring the recognition of death by Adam and Eve in the corpse of a deer in Shaw's just-produced *Back to Methuselah*, that if humans had no soul, "nothing" would follow when one died: "you'd be dead—just like an animal." And at the close, when Marco finally returns to Venice, his now dowdy but patient betrothed, Donata, gushes, hurrying to kiss him—as Raina does in *Arms and the Man* when Sergius Saranoff returns from his war—"My hero!" (Soon after O'Neill began going to the theater, "My Hero" became a popular song, from the unauthorized musicalization of *Arms and the Man, The Chocolate Soldier*. By 1910 it was a long-running hit in New York.) And echoing the beginning of the fourth act of *Caesar and Cleopatra* itself, the tempestuous (although fragile) Princess Kukachin, like the young Cleopatra, makes demands of her servants with the warning, supposedly typical of mistress-slave relationships, "—or I shall order you beaten!"

Marco's cheap acceptance of his Western religion is rejected by the Khan much as he rejects Eastern alternatives of "drown[ing] in dream until you become a dream." He mocks his own theologian, Chu Yin, with a sardonic response that mirrors Don Juan in Shaw's *Man and Superman* repudiating the Devil's vain sentimentality. "I have found no new faith in your Way," scoffs Kublai Khan, "and I have lost the old faith in mine. I no longer believe in my significance nor in man's. That we should imagine a meaning for ourselves beyond the obvious one of gorging our greedy pride . . . is for me only a final proof of idiot vanity. No, man does not yet deserve a soul. He is still the least human species of ape and because he is the only house-broken one we call him civilized—but we shouldn't be cheated by our own make-believe."

A science adviser to the Khan describes Marco, in a term that suggests Andrew Undershaft's religious self-definition in *Major Barbara*, as a "mystic idealist." (Undershaft would reject idealism, but claims to be "a confirmed mystic.") But when a competing adviser scorns Marco as a materialist, the scientist scoffs that Marco "knows nothing of Matter, not even his own body, of which he is piously ashamed, and he worships a grey-whiskered Ghost with a bad temper whose address is a golden street somewhere in the sky." The lines are even more scathing about orthodox faith than Shaw's, and the references to human prudishness about the body may reflect Shaw's dialogue in *Man and Superman* as well as its intellectual successor, *Back to Methuselah*. Shaw's Caesar even teases Britannus about painting his body blue (with woad), the early Briton explaining in his own defense that "though our enemies may strip us of our clothes and our lives, they cannot strip us of our respectability."

A direct echo of *Major Barbara* appears in Act V, when Marco demonstrates his invention of artillery to the Khan, revealing a cannon from which a lead ball is shot out to knock a breach in a wall of blocks. In *Major*

Barbara, Undershaft the armorer and super-Capitalist demonstrates his new cannon, mangling a group of life-sized models of soldiers. And he observes cynically that efficient weapons "make war on war" by turning human rivalry into such awesome destruction that their very existence will usher in an era of peace. "War," O'Neill's Marco explains with the facile persuasiveness of a traveling salesman, "is a waste of labor and material which eats into the dividends of life. . . . Then why war, I asked myself? Why not a lasting peace with profit? But isn't war a natural resource of our human natures, poisoned at birth by the justice of God with original sin? How are you going to end it? . . . There's only one workable way and that's to lick everybody else in the world. A tough proposition, you object? Not any more! This little invention you see before you makes conquering easy." And he uses the powder that the Chinese heretofore had used only for harmless fireworks displays to power his cannon.

"You see?" he points out enthusiastically when his father, Nicolo, retrieves the deadly lead ball. "Now just picture to yourself this little ball magnified. . . . The destruction of property and loss of life would be tremendous! No one could resist you! You'd conquer the world into one great peace-loving, hard-working brotherhood of man!"

The nihilist in O'Neill sees no meaning in such a universe, but Shaw more hopefully creates a debate on the subject in the *Don Juan in Hell* interlude in *Man and Superman.* "Has the colossal mechanism no purpose?" Juan asks. "None, my friend," says the Devil. "You think, because you have a purpose, Nature must have one. You might as well expect it to have fingers and toes because you have them." O'Neill's Kublai Khan concedes no purpose and uses the fading of the youthful beauty of Kukachin, and her inevitable unhappiness, even misery, with or without Marco Polo, as evidence that life is "insane." "Why is all this?" he asks Chu Yin. "What purpose can it serve? My hideous intuition is that the very essence of life may be merely an infinite, crazy energy which creates and destroys without [any] other purpose than to pass infinite time. . . ."

Possibly struck by how Shaw dramatically managed Caesar's leavetaking at the close, with Cleopatra arriving dressed entirely in black in contrast to the colorful crowd of others in the scene, O'Neill stages the departure of Princess Kukachin almost as a direct echo. In his stage directions, *"A cry of adoration goes up from the crowd as with one movement they prostrate themselves as the Princess comes down from the cabin dressed in a robe of silver and stands at the rail looking down."* In what O'Neill describes as "a long, ululating whisper" they cry out, "Farewell—farewell—farewell. . . ."

Even Marco Polo is moved. Caesar, earlier, has had to suppress his own emotions at the close of Shaw's play.

At the end of *Marco Millions,* O'Neill seems to return to *The Quintessence of Ibenism* and Shaw's excoriation of Duty as one of the worst sins visited upon humanity. All of Marco's dubious accomplishments, he boasts, have come from his fidelity to Duty. *"Squirming"*—O'Neill writes—*"onto a high moral plane,"* Marco explains to the Venetians who welcome him on his return, wealth-laden, "I was true to a trust that was placed in me. I had a job to do and I did it, that's all there was to it. I acted as a man of honesty and integrity ought to act, for, thank God, my moral sense of duty has always proved stronger than any temptation."

"Yes," Rusticiano says, *"a bit slyly ironic,"* "you are a good man." The scene fades to a final one in which the Khan receives the body of his adored Kukachin, shipped home from Persia. The lights come up for the Epilogue, an ironic twist upon Shaw's Prologue:

> *The play is over. The lights come up brilliantly in the theatre. In an aisle seat in the first row a man gets up, conceals a yawn in his palm, stretches his legs as if they had become cramped by too long an evening, takes his hat from under the seat and starts to file slowly out with the others in the audience. But, although there is nothing out of the ordinary in his actions, his appearance excites general comment and surprise for he is dressed as a Venetian merchant of the later 13th century. In fact, it is none other than MARCO POLO himself looking a bit sleepy, a trifle puzzled and not a little irritated as his thoughts, in spite of himself, cling for a passing moment to the play just ended. He appears quite unaware of being unusual and walks in the crowd without self-consciousness, very much as one of them. Arrived at the lobby, his face begins to clear of all disturbing memories of what had transpired on the stage. The noise, the lights of the street, all recall him at once to himself. Impatiently he waits for his car, casting a glance here and there at faces in the groups around him, his eyes impersonally speculative, his bearing stolid with the dignity of one who is sure of his place in the world. His car, a luxurious Pierce-Arrow limousine, draws up at the curb. He gets in briskly, the door is slammed, the car edges away into the traffic and POLO, with a satisfied sigh at the comfort of it all, comes back to life.*

By the early 1920s, O'Neill appeared to find his own voice, a somber and realistic one that earned him an enthusiastic reception in the U.S. And Shaw was reading, and even seeing, O'Neill's early productions. He had already been produced abroad, Shaw writing that by 1923 he had already seen O'Neill on the stage "once or twice." If he recognized any Shavian reverberations, he kept them to himself, but there were, except in the more mordant plays, hints of Shaw, and when O'Neill's urge toward satire returned, more would emerge, for he continued to keep up with Shaw's plays. (It may have had nothing to do with Shaw, but even one of O'Neill's homes, a house on Sea Island, Georgia, would have a study for the playwright that recalled the interior setting of *Heartbreak House,* a captain's quarters on an old sailing ship.)

O'Neill had hoped for a lavish production of *Marco Millions,* but even in the prosperous mid–1920s the staging of its many scenes seemed too costly. One producer, Gilbert Miller, claimed that he could not find what O'Neill described as a "romantic, handsome hero"—a casting that would have undermined the satire in order to sell tickets. (Shaw had experienced similar problems in staging *Caesar and Cleopatra,* delaying its first commercial production seven years, into 1906—and that occurred in Berlin, a year before productions in London and New York.) O'Neill went back to writing another play that would distress theater managers, the overly long *Strange Interlude.* He saw precedents for long plays in Shaw. *Man and Superman* was now being done complete. Its first full production in London had been in 1925, as O'Neill was beginning his new play, and Shaw's five-play cycle, *Back to Methuselah,* had been daringly done in both London and New York over two evenings. "Strange Interlude, which occupied an afternoon and an evening with an interval for dinner," Shaw joked to London publisher Baliol Holloway, "was such a success that the Theatre Guild begged me to write my next play in eight acts."[16]

Strange Interlude was based not only on a story that O'Neill had heard in Provincetown in 1923, but also, biographer Louis Sheaffer claims, on *Man and Superman,* another work that exceeded traditional commercial length. O'Neill's Nina Leeds is by Sheaffer's reckoning his Everywoman just as Shaw's Ann Whitefield is his embodiment of feminine vitality assisted by the unscrupulousness necessary to work her genetic will. "If women were as fastidious as men, morally or physically," Shaw wrote sardonically in his preface, "there would be an end to the race." Her purpose, says John Tanner, the man she intends to make her husband, to his supposed rival, Octavius, "is neither her happiness nor yours, but Nature's. Vitality in a woman is a blind fury of creation. She sacrifices herself to it: do you think she will hesitate to sacrifice you?"

Although Shaw's play, despite the kind of dialogue described in Restoration drama as a "duel of sex" and the subplot of a not-quite-concealed pregnancy, is ironic in tone in comparison with O'Neill's preoccupation with coupling and its results, other echoes from Shaw's plays reverberate through *Strange Interlude.* Nina's first lover, who dies in World War I, is named Gordon *Shaw.* An early aviator, he parallels John Tanner, who, a dozen years before the war and immediately before the Wright brothers' first flight, is an early automobilist.

A later aspirant for the affections of Nina Leeds (O'Neill's parallel to Ann Whitefield) is Charles Marsden. However much based upon two O'Neill friends, both artists and both with little or no interest in women, Marsden seems also to be Shaw's Octavius Robinson, John Tanner's ap-

parent rival for Ann. Yet Robinson's misunderstanding that Ann loves
him results from Tanner's pushing him in Ann's path to deflect her pursuit of Tanner himself. Ann knows better. "Men like that," she confides
to Tanner, "always live in comfortable bachelor quarters with broken
hearts, and are adored by their landladies." Octavius, a genteel poet,
sighs, rather than lusts, after Ann. O'Neill's equivalent to Tanner on the
other hand—Darrell—is also Nina's second lover, succeeding the man
she marries (Sam Evans) after Gordon Shaw's death. Edmund Darrell, in
O'Neill's complicated sexual roundabout, regards himself, as does Tanner, "as too knowing about the nature and wiles of Woman to suc-
cumb"—not because, like Shaw's smug hero, he has read all the relevant
philosophers and scientists on sex, but because, as a physician, he considers himself "immune to love through his scientific understanding of its
real sexual nature." Both men, Louis Sheaffer observes, are "overpow-
ered" by what Shaw and his protagonist label the "Life Force"—the "universal creative energy" for which human beings are only the agents.
Darrell is swept by it into Nina's arms as Tanner is drawn to Ann. The
Life Force "enchants" him, John Tanner claims: "I have the whole world
in my arms when I clasp you." But to both women it makes little difference what higher motive is involved.

   Rehearsals for the marathon Theatre Guild productions of both the
nine-act *Strange Interlude* and the lengthy (but now shortened) *Marco Millions* went on almost concurrently late in 1927. Alfred Lunt, then playing
the rogue artist in Shaw's *Doctor's Dilemma* to his wife's Jennifer (who
would be Louis Dubedat's widow by the end of the play) was to be Marco
Polo, and O'Neill went to see the Shaw play to size up Lunt.[17]

   Unfortunately for *Marco Millions,* Lunt, who disliked the play as well as
his burlesque role, was cast in it and performed without enthusiasm. The
sardonic contrasts between Western materialism and Eastern idealism
seemed unsubtle, the artistry artificial. O'Neill was operating in the
wrong dimension for him. The play was only a tepid success. He returned, next, to the tragic mode in which he felt more comfortable. Again
his play would be overly long, taking up both a matinee and an evening
performance, a classic Greek trilogy under a single title, *Mourning Becomes
Electra.* Setting his equivalent to the Agamemnon story during the American Civil War, his link to Homeric Troy, O'Neill created a melodrama
fueled by the Oedipal passions of son for mother and daughter for father,
then brother for sister. The adulteries within the Mannon family include
that of Captain Adam Brant, who is the Aegisthus to Christine Mannon's
Clytemnestra. Even here, however, O'Neill seemed unable to escape
Shaw. Captain Brant, insists Doris Alexander, becomes a completely different personality in O'Neill's second draft of the play than he had been
in the first.

A complete new character, she asserts, "walked into his play and blended so fully with his fated family that O'Neill never saw himself that his Captain Brant was really . . . Shaw's Captain Brassbound stepped intact out of *Captain Brassbound's Conversion*." O'Neill had read Shaw's play about justice and revenge in the volume *Three Plays for Puritans* (1901) and had seen it performed while he was at Harvard. Shaw's sea captain is embittered by passion for revenge against his uncle, now an English judge, whom he charges "with the death of my mother and the theft of my inheritance." In O'Neill's play, Captain Brant accuses his cousin Ezra Mannon, "and does so out of the same feeling of guilt he had in Shaw's play because he had not been 'very fond' of his mother or 'very good' to her." Brassbound's mother had, he reveals, "a violent temper," while Brant confides that his mother had been "very strict" with him, even beating him, while she petted and spoiled his cousin Ezra. "In both plays," Doris Alexander contends, "Captain Brassbound-Brant hides his own guilt by accusing his uncle-cousin of letting his mother die 'of sickness and starvation,' for he himself has fled from her. He is very touchy about her honor in both plays. In Shaw he springs at his uncle, crying, 'He did not spare my mother'—"That woman," he calls her—'because of her sex. I will not spare him because of his age.' In O'Neill's play Brant springs up at Lavinia's* taunt at her, crying, 'Belay, damn you!—or I'll forget you're a woman—no Mannon can insult her while I—' " There the dialogue breaks off.

Alexander concludes that O'Neill made Brant a clipper captain because Brassbound skippered a sailing vessel and that O'Neill also gave him the same romantic appearance, "more like a gambler or a poet," she writes, "than a ship captain." Although O'Neill may have taken aspects of his Brant from an historical figure, "otherwise he kept his Brassbound origin, and even took from Shaw's character the irony of [his] judging a judge. Before Brassbound took over Brant," she writes, "Ezra Mannon had been [in the first draft] only [the] 'town's leading citizen, Mayor before [the] war.' He became a former judge as well when Brassbound came into O'Neill's play."

Although the parallels seem persuasive, Alexander sees the link weaken when in *Mourning Becomes Electra* the Captain quickly falls "passionately in love, which he never would have done for Shaw."[18] Yet Brassbound does quickly fall in love, despite his attempts to resist it, with the charming but older Lady Cecily (a hint in the direction of O'Neill's mother-son incest there?), and he proposes to her. Tempted as she is, the indomitable lady traveler refuses him, and breathes, at the close, "What an escape!" Even there, O'Neill sails close to his source.

---

*Lavinia Mannon is the daughter, or Electra, figure; her brother is Orin (Orestes).

As his play was being prepared for performance, he tried to convince Maurice Wertheim of the Theatre Guild that *Mourning* "*is* a trilogy and not three separate plays" and required what he characterized as "the driving impact of a trilogy concentrated in one week—a bigger [*Strange*] *Interlude* in that sense!" However "seemingly impossible," he contended, the producers "may well lose out by [not] doing what is comparatively a commonplace stunt, done before with Shaw's *Methuselah*. . . ."[19]

Since the published text of *Strange Interlude* had sold more than a hundred thousand copies, Saxe Commins, O'Neill's editor, hoped for a similar success after the Broadway opening of the new play. To help promote the book, he planned to precede it with a brochure of short pieces about O'Neill and his work by theatrical and literary luminaries, and he solicited such notables as Thomas Mann, Bernard Shaw, Sinclair Lewis, and Sean O'Casey. Mann sent regrets, although conceding that he saw an "epic" quality in O'Neill's plays. Lewis wrote that O'Neill had "revolutionized" what had been a "rather stupid and tawdry drama." O'Casey saw O'Neill's work, gushily, as "always bearing witness to the things great and the things beautiful which have saved the Theatre from the shame of a house of ill-repute and a den of thieves. . . ." Shaw's secretary, Blanche Patch, writing for him to Commins, responded characteristically "that nothing is more revoltingly unreadable than logrolling and that he implores you to abandon the project. . . . Otherwise O'Neill will probably sue you for damages."[20]

That did not keep Shaw from the play, however. Someone told him, he wrote "Mrs. Pat" Campbell on 2 May 1932, "that you were wonderful and beautiful as O'Neill's Electra, which, as it happened, I had just read." The next day he learned that his informant "had made a slight error." Mrs. Campbell was playing the original Clytemnestra, "not O'Neill's." Just returned to the Riviera from New York, she shot back, "I found O'Neill's *Mourning Becomes Electra* horrible. [Alla] Nazimova had one fine emotional moment, worth something to see, but not [worth] all I suffered that afternoon and evening."[21]

For all his admiration of O'Neill, especially his stage handling of sexual psychology, Shaw was still ambivalent about him. A vein of Victorian Irish prudishness left him uneasy about O'Neill's more direct sexuality. In the year of the production of *Mourning* he wrote to his old friend Frank Harris, who wanted to publish a letter Shaw had written to him about personal sexual experiences but which Shaw had insisted, first, on bowdlerizing, that the biography would be an opportunity to regain a reputation sullied by money-grubbing pornographic memoirs. "This book is your chance of recovering your tall hat; and you want to throw it away for the sake of being in the fashion of O'Neill, Joyce, and George Moore."[22] Yet Shaw also wrote to English impresario Charles Cochran,

"If only someone would build you a huge Woolworth theatre (all seats sixpence) to start with O'Casey and O'Neill, and no plays by men who had ever seen a five-pound note before they were thirty or been inside a school after they were thirteen, you would be buried in Westminster Abbey."[23] Shaw did not have O'Neill's biography exactly right, but he was clearly on his side.

That became even more obvious after the rapturous reception of *Mourning*, which ran 150 performances despite expensive tickets and the deep Depression. Wits described it as "Mourning Becomes O'Neill" and "Evening Becomes Interminable," but critics and audiences perceived a grandeur in the somber play, and in 1932, the year after, when Shaw and Yeats were planning the founding of an Irish Academy of Letters that would include some associate members of Irish ancestry who were not Irish-born, Shaw recommended American-born O'Neill and Welsh-born Lawrence of Arabia. Dubliner James Joyce turned town his appointment, but O'Neill wrote to his elder son, "I regard this as an honor, whereas other Academies don't mean much to me. Anything with Yeats, Shaw, A.E., O'Casey, Flaherty, Robinson in it is good enough for me."[24]

Four years later, in November 1936, O'Neill, at forty-eight, received the Nobel Prize for Literature. Shaw told a reporter that it was "an excellent decision. I always thought this year's prize should go either to Upton Sinclair or O'Neill, so America would have received it in either case. Of course, I am very pleased."[25] (Sinclair proved too political for the Nobel Committee, then and later.) What especially pleased O'Neill, he told fellow playwright Russel Crouse, was that the Irish ambassador in Washington congratulated him for "adding, along with Shaw and Yeats, to the credit of old Ireland." What, he asked, "could be more perfect?"[26]

Thwarted in the completion of his last plays by illness—O'Neill was handicapped by the tremors of Parkinson's disease and its attendant psychological devastation—he finished little he began after 1940. One of his attempts, for which he wrote a scenario and some scenes, was "The Last Conquest,"[27] which has echoes of Shaw's *Don Juan in Hell* interlude from *Man and Superman*. It has as its principal characters Caesar, Satan, and an Everyman figure like Shaw's Don Juan who may be Christ and who, in one draft, is a statue carved by Satan. *Don Juan in Hell*, of course, has a talking statue as one of its four characters. A philosophical dialogue basically between Man and the Devil, the sketch for a play is dominated by a proud, boastful, although warm Devil who, like Shaw's, has grown bored and possesses a satiric bravado rather than a fire-and-brimstone evil, while the Man (or Christ figure), for whom he has little but contempt, seems engaged in an eternal charade of resistance to Satanic temptation and longs for solitude remote from a despised humanity. He craves crucifixion, while Satan begs to take his place or at least to suspend the events that will lead inevitably to it.

As late as 1948, O'Neill was still struggling to finish the drama, a mordant parallel to *Don Juan in Hell*. His darker vision reflected the somber O'Neill personality now even more darkened by physical deterioration. He died in November 1953, three years after Shaw. Obituaries saw no connection between the intense, tragic drama of O'Neill and the sardonic perspectives of Shaw, but O'Neill's playwriting journey had begun with Shaw, and the fading echoes of that initiation were still there at the end.

Notes

1. S. J. Wolf, "O'Neill Plots a Course for the Drama," *New York Times* (4 October 1931), Section 5, p. 6.

2. Carlotta Monterey O'Neill to Saxe Commins, [September 1932], in *"Love and Admiration and Respect": The O'Neill-Commins Correspondence*, ed. Dorothy Commins (Durham: Duke University Press, 1986), pp. 120–21. Commins responded on 20 September 1932 with a Shaw bibliography.

3. Jimmie Durkin to James O'Neill, TLS, Spokane, WA, 20 February 1905. British Library Add. Mss. 50516, fols. 228–29.

4. O'Neill to Hans Olav, 13 May 1938, in *Selected Letters of Eugene O'Neill*, ed. Travis Bogard and Jackson R. Bryer (New Haven: Yale University Press, 1988), p. 477. (Hereafter, *Letters*.)

5. Louis Sheaffer, *O'Neill: Son and Playwright* (Boston: Little, Brown, 1968), pp. 104–5 ("red ink" as well as "virtuous or vile").

6. Doris Alexander, *The Tempering of Eugene O'Neill* (New York: Harcourt, Brace, 1962), p. 96.

7. Arthur and Barbara Gelb, "O'Neill and Shaw," *Shaw Review* 5 (January 1962): 3.

8. *The Plays of Eugene O'Neill* (New York: Oxford University Press, 1988), p. 57. All O'Neill text plays, unless otherwise noted, are from the edition.

9. *Now I Ask You*, in *Ten Lost Plays* (New York: Random House, 1964), viewed as Shavian by Travis Bogard in his *Contour in Time: The Plays of Eugene O'Neill* (New York: Oxford University Press, 1988), p. 57.

10. *Servitude*, in *Ten Lost Plays*, pp. 225–303.

11. The Fantee or Fanti (first English usage 1819) are a tribe inhabiting the southern Gold Coast (now Ghana). Shaw seems to have been suggesting—perhaps with O'Neill's *The Emperor Jones* in mind—unpolished or unsophisticated writing in comparison to Shakespeare.

12. Shaw in *Table-Talk of G.B.S.*, (ostensibly) ed. by Archibald Henderson (New York: Harper, 1925), p. 93. In reality Shaw wrote the supposed conversations and permitted the hard-up Henderson to collect the royalties as editor.

13. The performance text of *Marco Millions* is in *Plays;* the earlier and longer text of *Marco's Millions* is in *The Unknown O'Neill: Unpublished or Unfamiliar Writings of Eugene O'Neill*, ed. Travis Bogard (New Haven: Yale University Press, 1988), pp. 191–307. All extracts from the first text are from this edition. Doris Alexander, TLS to SW, Venice, 22 June 1996,

observes that Bogard has apparently misread the manuscript title, which at first was *Marco Million*, after the satirical name for young Polo, *"Il Milione."* ("In Italian one gives a name to the article. Later O'Neill decided the idea would be conveyed better if he called it *Marco Millions."* Other misreadings, she notes, include, "My hideous intuition is . . ." for "My hideous suspicion is. . . ." I have silently corrected this in the text.)

14. It is more than seven hundred years since Marco Polo returned from his twenty-four years away from Venice, seventeen of them allegedly spent in China. Three years after his return from wherever he had been, he found himself locked up in a Genoese jail for nearly a year, for his part in a Venetian war with Genoa, and recounted or invented his experiences to a fellow prisoner, Rusticello (in O'Neill's play, Rusticiano). Christopher Columbus annotated his own Latin copy: the thirteenth-century original, apparently written in a heavily Latinized Old French, is lost, but Polo's claimed adventures were translated into many European languages, even Irish. What causes suspicion among later scholars is Marco Polo's obvious reliance on earlier travelers' accounts for his details, yet omitting mention of something so obvious as the Great Wall, of Chinese tea-drinking, foot-binding of females, cormorant fishing, and other facets of the interior. Possibly he never crossed into China from Mongolia, but bargained with traders for porcelain and other objects with which he returned.

15. Shaw's plays are quoted from the *Collected Plays with Their Prefaces*, ed. Dan H. Laurence (London: Max Reinhardt, 1970–74).

16. Shaw to Balliol Holloway, 12 June 1930, in *Bernard Shaw, Theatrics*, ed. Dan H. Laurence (Toronto: University of Toronto Press, 1995), pp. 186–87.

17. O'Neill to Agnes Boulton O'Neill, 27 November 1927, *Letters*, p. 266.

18. Doris Alexander, *Eugene O'Neill's Creative Struggle* (University Park: Penn State Press, 1992), p. 157.

19. O'Neill to Maurice Wertheim, 15 June 1931, in *Letters*, p. 388.

20. Quoted by Louis Sheaffer in *O'Neill: Son and Artist* (Boston: Little, Brown, 1973), p. 380. *Logrolling*, an American political term, now in disuse, referred to the exchange of votes—or favors.

21. Shaw to Mrs. Stella Patrick Campbell, 2 May and 3 May 1932, in *Bernard Shaw and Mrs. Patrick Campbell: Their Correspondence*, ed. Alan Dent (New York: Knopf, 1952), p. 348.

22. Shaw to Frank Harris, 21 April 1931, in *The Playwright and the Pirate*, ed. Stanley Weintraub (University Park: Penn State University Press, 1982), p. 254.

23. Shaw to Charles Cochran, quoted by Eileen O'Casey in *Sean* (New York: Coward-McCann, 1972), p. 108.

24. O'Neill to Eugene O'Neill, Jr., 11 November 1932, in *Letters*, p. 407.

25. *New York Times,* (13 November 1936), p. 24.

26. O'Neill to Russel Crouse, 25 November 1936, in *Letters*, p. 455.

27. "The Last Conquest" (incomplete), in *Eugene O'Neill: The Unfinished Plays*, ed. Virginia Floyd (New York: Ungar, 1988), pp. 41–57.

Bernard Shaw *(Irish Times)*

SHAW'S ADVICE TO IRISHMEN

[The following report of Shaw's Dublin lecture "Literature in Ireland" appeared in the Irish Times *on 28 October 1918 under the title "Mr. G. Bernard Shaw and Irish Literature. His Advice to Irishmen." Shaw and Charlotte were spending the last ten days of an extensive Irish holiday with Sir Horace Plunkett, who had tried, and failed, to have Shaw nominated to the Irish Convention that Shaw disparages near the end of his talk.*

Shaw's remarks on James Joyce indicate that he had already read parts of Ulysses *four years before it appeared as a book. (The* Little Review *had begun publishing extracts in March 1918.) On 11 June 1921, when he wrote to Sylvia Beach his refusal to buy a subscription edition, he commented that he had "read several fragments of Ulysses in its serial form." See* Collected Letters 1911–1925, *ed. Dan H. Laurence (New York: Viking, 1985), p. 719.*

Shaw's statement that he would assist British recruiting "because it was a magnificent way of getting Irishmen out of Ireland" came two weeks before the Armistice. He had subtitled his 1915 playlet O'Flaherty, V.C. *"A Recruiting Pamphlet."*

Shaw's text ©1998 The Trustees of the British Museum, The Governors and Guardians of the National Gallery of Ireland, and the Royal Academy of Dramatic Art. Published by permission of the Shaw Estate.—FDC]

On Saturday evening [26 October 1918], in the Little Theatre, 40 Upper Sackville Street, under the auspices of the Dublin Literary Society, Mr. George Bernard Shaw delivered a lecture on "Literature in Ireland." He said that, as a man of letters, the last place in which he desired to appear was addressing a literary society, if he could help it, for he did not know anything about literature. He did not read other people's works; he had

enough to do to read his own proofsheets. But it occasionally happened
that if he was writing a critical article, and he had to quote Mr. Wells or
some other of the literary lights of the day, he found that it was with the
greatest difficulty that he could refrain from altering the sentences. From
the moment his hand began to copy Mr. Wells' work, he wanted to write
the thing entirely differently. He admitted that he liked his own style.
The burlesque in his plays was not nonsense. He defied any man to get
more fun out of his (the speaker's) work than he had got himself. People
told him that it did not matter what he said about anything. But there
was one thing that strikes everybody who faces modern Irish literature,
and that was that Ireland only produces literature by a sort of cross-fertilisation. They had got no Irish literature until George Moore went to Paris
and began to write. In the same way they had Synge, who had done
nothing at all until he went to Paris. And now they all go to Paris. (Laughter.) There was Mr. Joyce. He gets a sort of double cross-fertilisation; he
goes there and gets his inspiration from Strindberg, a Swede. Mr. Joyce
translates Strindberg's "Inferno" (a description of his life in Paris) into
Ireland, and he proceeds to show that Dublin may be as much a hell to
him as Paris was to Strindberg.

"Most of your poetry about the Irish rising," said Mr. Shaw, "is not
Irish at all. When you come to the literature that is represented by the
Gaelic League and *Sinn Féin* in Ireland—and nobody knows the origin of
that better than I do, for the Gaelic League was invented in Bedford
Park, London—you find that never was there a more tremendous delusion than the delusion that the Gaelic League is modern Ireland. The
natural effect of it is to make the Irishman absolutely self-conscious as an
Irishman. That is a diseased state of mind. No healthy Irishman is in that
condition. We go into all the qualities of man outside his nationality and
we allege that the Irishman is a wonderful product, enormously superior
to any man on the face of the earth. (Laughter.) We have got that idea to
a particular degree, and it is all nonsense. We are an exceedingly futile
and disagreeable people. Our misfortunes are all the fruit of our own
character. I am continually telling Englishmen that they are entirely mistaken in admiring Irishmen, and that they have the worst qualities of all
the rest of the human race. I tell my English friends that I like them
better than I like my own countrymen. I regard them as grown-up children, and though occasionally some of them will kill women and children
and knock down part of a town—I am sorry it was not the worst part of
the town—still, I do not regard them as vindictive." (Laughter.) Returning to the subject of literature, Mr. Shaw said he was convinced that there
was no more Irish literature—no literature that was more Irish—than his
own works. He did not mean to say that he did not admire certain qualities in the works of Mr. Moore and Mr. Joyce. Some of it sickened him.

In Mr. Moore's latest work there was a lot that was not decent, and he did not see why it should have been written. He (Mr. Shaw) would write indecency if it justified itself, but Mr. Moore's indecency does not justify itself. He admired it as literature, but not as Irish literature. He did not admire the plays of Synge as Irish literature. The thing did not come out of Irish life; it came out of that life which a man learns a good deal about in Paris. The first criticism he would pass upon "The Playboy of the Western World" was that an Irish peasant would be disgusted and revolted by it. The main theme of the play exhibited the curious tendency that people have to admire crime; but that was not in the slightest degree peculiar to Ireland any more than it was to any other place. It was true of almost the entire human race. One could get a good deal of music out of the speech of the Irish people, and Synge had got it; nevertheless, the intellectual drawing of the thing was not Irish at all. It could not have been produced by a man who had never been out of Ireland, and who did not avail of the modern methods by which people got the culture of Paris from the reading of books. The same thing was true of the literature of the modern movement. The play that idealises Ireland is almost always a play which comes from foreign inspiration. When you come to the literature that tries to throw a glamour over Ireland, and shows her to be a delightful place, you always find that it is essentially a foreign literature, and when you come to the literature which represents Ireland to be a backward, dull place, you are unfortunately obliged to admit that it is an Irish play about Irish life. That, said Mr. Shaw, was a very serious indictment to bring against the literature of the nation, and yet he did not see his way out of it.

Criticism, especially in Dublin, took the form of derision. From his childhood he had imbibed the habit of derision. He had tried to get out of it, but he could not, quite. In spite of living in England, he found that curious cackling derision breaking out in him, and he wished that he had been born somewhere else than in Dublin. Dublin people could not quite get rid of what was a fundamental lunacy—namely, in thinking that they are Ireland. They really thought they were superior, but they had done nothing to justify it. In spite of a certain flexibility of mind, they had not justified their existence as yet. Sometimes, when the Irishman went abroad, he became a success. In America he immediately achieved success as a policeman or a ward politician. (Laughter.) He [Shaw] had said that he would help recruiting, because it was a magnificent way of getting Irishmen out of Ireland. (Laughter.) The best thing to do with an Irishman is to take him by the scruff of the neck and show him some other place, and when he came back to Ireland something might be made of him. And then every Englishman should be sent to Ireland for a certain period of his life. The climate of Ireland has such an effect upon an Englishman who spends eighteen months here that he is a changed man for the rest of his life. It would not be well for him to stay in the South of Ireland, for if he did he would lose his character altogether. (Laughter.) The Irishman had no opportunity of doing anything until he got out of Ireland. He advised those who could to go over to England by the next boat, for until they did they would not have any real understanding of what Ireland is. But he also advised them, if they have a grievance, to forget it, or at least conceal it. If they have a grievance, healthy people would say, "Serve you right." His opinion was that Ireland was too much given to making a poor mouth of it, and without sufficient reason. Up to a little time ago, he believed that the Irish had a certain religious and political genius. The Irish Convention shook that belief. The Convention should have come to a certain conclusion, and if it had the faculty of saying what it thought the majority would have issued a report, and would have affirmed its opinion. But it allowed two relatively small minorities to produce a report. The consequence was that one had to admit that the Irish Convention, to that extent, was a political failure—that somehow the Irish were not taking their politics with sufficient conviction, that the winners did not take their winnings, and that they allowed their opponents to take up whatever was lying on the table. He felt sure that after the researches of Irish literary people in Gaelic literature they would go back to English authors, and read Shakespeare and Dickens, and the works of other such preposterous persons.

Mr. Bridgman moved a vote of thanks to Mr. Shaw, and Mr. Ernest Boyd, in seconding the motion, remarked that Mr. Shaw had dodged the question of Irish literature. The literature he had been speaking about was not Irish, although it was written by Irishmen.

The vote of thanks was passed with acclamation.

Robert G. Everding

PLANTING MULBERRY:
A HISTORY OF SHAW FESTIVALS

In 1925 Shaw balked at the number of people wanting "to start Shaw theatres" and warned that "Twenty years ago, I was a priceless catch for Vedrenne & Barker. Today there is nothing left of their Shavian successes but an ancient and fishlike smell."[1] Fortunately future producers ignored Shaw's words and embarked upon festivals dedicated to his genius. This essay explores the evolution of these festivals with focus on their diverse philosophies, theatrical organizations, and economic structures; it concludes with an examination of arguments raised by festival critics.

A drama festival is defined as "performances people attend knowing why"[2] and an event with "a greater than usual number of theatrical performances under primitive conditions in an out-of-the-way place."[3] Shaw himself attended two such festivals: Stratford-upon-Avon and Bayreuth that celebrated, respectively, Shakespeare and Wagner with annual stagings of their works. Both festivals were located in bucolic, rural settings that inspired in their visitors a sense of pilgrimage and retreat.

The first stirrings to honor Shaw in like manner came appropriately in his native Ireland. In a 12 August 1916 letter, Lady Gregory proposed "to do an autumn season of G.B.S.—our Irish Shakespeare—I hope for an annual festival of him!"[4] Her plan called for a six-week festival composed of *John Bull's Other Island, The Devil's Disciple, The Doctor's Dilemma,* and *Androcles and the Lion.* Shaw was not enthusiastic about the scheme. He vetoed *The Devil's Disciple* because of his concern that it might be perceived as anti-British war propaganda and *The Doctor's Dilemma* because its success required acting talent beyond the theater's abilities. Shaw also questioned the wisdom of attempting a production of *Androcles and the Lion* on the small Abbey stage. While he recommended substituting *Candida* and *Widowers' Houses,* he preferred his wife's suggestion that the theater produce Ibsen's plays. The season opened with a September-October Shaw festival offering *John Bull's Other Island, Widowers' Houses,* and *Arms and the Man;* in spring 1917, *Man and Superman, The Inca of Perusalem,* and *The Doctor's Dilemma* were presented. Lady Gregory's hope for an annual festival never materialized.

In 1920 the Everyman Theatre (Hampstead) declared its intention to restore to the stage English dramatists silenced by the war and its demand for diverting entertainment. The theater dedicated its 1921 season to Shaw with January-June productions of the complete *Man and Superman, Major Barbara, Candida, The Doctor's Dilemma, You Never Can Tell,* and a triple bill of *The Shewing-up of Blanco Posnet, How He Lied to Her Husband,* and *The Dark Lady of the Sonnets.* The next season a "Shaw Festival" offered *Fanny's First Play, Arms and the Man, Getting Married, Misalliance, Widowers' Houses, You Never Can Tell,* and *Candida.* The festival was considered "an unqualified success and some advocated the establishment of a permanent Shaw repertory. However, the idea was rejected because of concerns that 'to adopt such a policy would have been a serious blunder. After a year or two we should exhaust the potential audience; disrupt the regular support we were trying to build; and cease experimental play selection.' "[5]

Back to Methuselah donned a festal mantle for both its world and its English premieres. In 1922 the Theatre Guild presented the work in three parts over several weeks, replete with a Shaw Festival souvenir program. For three weeks in October 1923, the Birmingham Repertory Theatre under the leadership of Sir Barry Jackson offered a "Bernard Shaw Festival" during which it presented his Metabiological Pentateuch for four cycles, each consisting of four evenings and one matinee, and followed these cycles with a brief run of *Getting Married.*

The Macdona Players also contributed to the festival concept through its 1924–31 Shaw seasons at various London playhouses. Its 1925 season, for instance, ran for five months at the Regent Theatre and offered six Shaw plays, including the first London public presentations of *Mrs Warren's Profession* and the first London staging of the entire *Man and Superman.*

These early endeavors served, however, as mere prelude to the Malvern Festival that Barry Jackson created in 1929 and dedicated to Shaw. While Malvern did not devote itself exclusively to performances of his plays, Shaw's genius permeated the festival. The premiere season was totally Shavian, consisting of *Back to Methuselah, Heartbreak House, Caesar and Cleopatra,* and the English premiere of *The Apple Cart.* Malvern produced a total of nineteen Shavian scripts (some more than once), including two world and four English premieres. Unlike Stratford or Bayreuth, however, Malvern's patron saint was in residence to visit rehearsals and mingle with visitors.

Malvern was a peaceful spa town set in the Malvern hills, blessed with good summer weather and offering a retreat setting in the tradition of Stratford or Bayreuth. Yet Jackson's vision exceeded both senior festivals in offering its patrons a total experience. At its peak there were garden parties, Sunday concerts, folk dances, visiting exhibitions, film festivals, and a marionette theater; boating on the pond, bowling on the green, putting on the course, donkey riding into the hills, swimming in the pools; theater professors' morning lectures about that evening's play and artists' informal teatime talks. Following the evening performance, one might select night swimming, ballroom dancing, or endless conversing.

The Birmingham Repertory Theatre Company (also headed by Barry Jackson) with its reputation for acting excellence provided a core ensemble with special players imported for specific roles. The company of some sixty actors included notable talents such as Cedric Hardwicke, Edith Evans, Eileen Beldon, and Scott Sunderland. Performances occurred in the newly renovated 900–seat theater with plays presented in repertory so that the season's complete offerings could be seen by the one-week visitor. The festival began as a two-week event but grew to four weeks in 1934 and thrived until the outbreak of war.

The financial responsibility was assumed by Jackson, a wealthy theatrical visionary who fortunately measured success artistically more than economically. One historian noted that "Obviously the presentation of half a dozen different plays for a season of only four weeks was an undertaking that could never pay. Each year there was a financial loss; made good by Sir Barry."[6] The losses were sizable, "as much, perhaps, as eight to ten thousand pounds annually."[7] Still, when Jackson departed after the 1937 season, he had provided the world with a festival model worthy of replication.

Malvern inspired Jasper Deeter, a professional actor who gained prominence with the Provincetown Players, to create the first American annual Shaw festival. In 1923 Deeter established a year-around professional repertory theater in the 167–seat Hedgerow Theater (converted from a snuff mill that was originally constructed in 1840) in the Moylan-Rose valley outside Philadelphia. His inaugural production was *Candida* and included in the cast Ann Harding and Morris Carnovsky; by 1934, when Deeter created his first Shaw festival, the repertory included eight Shavian scripts.

The professional company consisted of some twenty-five members who received no salary but lived and worked communally for board, lodging, clothes, and medical services. The demanding commitment included not only a rigorous six-night-a-week performance schedule with a different play presented each evening, but also extensive annual tours. Company turnover was rare during this period of economic depression because the Hedgerow offered actors steadier and more artistically challenging employment than that available on Broadway.

The Hedgerow's initial Shaw Festival ran only one week and offered six different Shavian works: *Candida, Misalliance* (without an intermission), *Arms and the Man, Androcles and the Lion, Saint Joan* (two performances), and *Heartbreak House.* That summer the festival initiated its annual practice of adding a new Shavian play to the repertory at the performance on the playwright's birthday. In 1937 the festival not only spanned four weeks but also offered audiences the unique opportunity to study Shaw's dramaturgical development through a chronological presentation of eleven plays, beginning with *Arms and the Man* (1894) and concluding with *Too True to Be Good* (1932). The 1939 festival featured the complete *Man and Superman* that began at 7:30 P.M. and concluded six hours later in time for patrons to catch the final trolley to Philadelphia.

While Deeter contemplated ending the festival after the 1939 season,[8] he retained the event for two more summers until wartime conditions necessitated its discontinuance. Facing the loss of his experienced male actors, Deeter petitioned President Roosevelt for a blanket deferment for the male members of his company because they performed "work of national importance." It is interesting that in 1940 Shaw made a similar argument in his protest over the government's refusal to exempt the Sadler's Wells Ballet company. Roosevelt rejected the request, but he intervened to approve the reclassification of three Hedgerow actors to conscientious-objector status. This action brought protests from the local draft board that argued that "the three men lived 'Bohemian type' lives which contained no religious tendencies or background."[9] Although Roosevelt's decision took effect, Deeter still lost the actors' services when they departed for civilian workcamps. A month later the courts sentenced another Hedgerow actor to two years in federal prison for refusing to report for induction.

While Malvern and Hedgerow demonstrated the artistic potential and economic viability of the Shaw festival, the next decade saw limited expansion. In 1938 a prestigious community theater, the Pasadena Playhouse (California), devoted its fourth annual Midsummer Drama Festival to "Seven from Shaw," presenting for a week each *Arms and the Man, Major Barbara, On the Rocks, Heartbreak House,* and (in three parts) *Back to Methuselah;* the festival structured its program under the title "A Cycle of Man and Civilization" to focus attention on Shaw's philosophical development and encouraged attendance by limiting the top ticket price to one dollar. In England during the war J. Baxter Somerville and Peter Hoar of the Lyric Theatre (Hammersmith) produced a mobile version of a Shaw festival when its Touring Bernard Shaw Repertory Company set out in 1942 on a fifteen-week tour of five plays featuring Ellen Pollock (Eliza, Candida, Barbara, A) and Michael Golden (Higgins, Morell, Undershaft, Z); the 1943 fourteen-week tour performed three plays and included in the company Ann Casson, Heron Carvic, and Charles Quartermaine. There were also three "Shaw seasons" offered: The Lyric Theatre (Hammersmith) reopened in 1944 with six Shaw plays; the Malvern Company under Roy Limbert did a Shaw program at Harrogate in 1948; and the Bedford Theatre (Camden Town) in 1949 under the management of Donald Wolfit offered a six-week Shaw season that staged seven scripts.

Shaw's death set in motion a second wave of festivals. In Harold Rubinstein's sketch *Bernard Shaw in Heaven* (first produced at a 1956 midnight matinee in the Court Theatre to celebrate Shaw's centenary), newly arrived Shaw is informed that "They'd have buried you in Westminster Abbey if you hadn't made that impossible. . . . The first hysteria didn't last, of course. But what a scramble to cash in on it followed! What with theatre-managers tumbling over each other to announce Shaw festivals. . . ."[10]

Basil C. Langton was among those producers, for in 1951 he announced plans for a permanent summer Shaw festival at the Rice Playhouse on the island of Martha's Vineyard (Massachusetts). Langton brought considerable expertise to the venture, having performed with both the Stratford Shakespeare Festival and the Birmingham Repertory Theatre. In 1944 he toured professionally in *Man and Superman* (Tanner), *Pygmalion* (Higgins), and *Saint Joan* (de Poulengey); he also directed more than twenty-five Shaw plays in association with the playwright and created and managed two successful theater companies.

In the summer of 1951 Langton fulfilled his intention "to make the island a haven of Shaw study and entertainment"[11] by presenting a 6 July–1 September professional season of one-week runs of *Man and Superman*, *Pygmalion*, *Heartbreak House*, *Arms and the Man*, three Broadway revivals, and one new play. He also presented a series of three lectures: "Shaw and Laughter," "Shaw and Tears," and "Shaw and the Dance," as well as a reading of *Don Juan in Hell*. Langton appeared pleased with his festival's reception, pointing out that attendance for *Heartbreak House* exceeded that for *Born Yesterday* and announcing his plans to conduct a fall tour.

The following summer he presented *The Devil's Disciple*, *Androcles and the Lion*, *Arms and the Man*, *Too True to Be Good*, a reading of *Don Juan in Hell*, and three original scripts. He added a training school because he believed that "we need a Shavian Repertory . . . where we can see the

master in action, and where students may train in the company of professional actors, skilled in the Shavian convention."[12] Sadly the festival
ceased after this summer, but Langton continued his Shavian permeation
by directing and acting in *Man and Superman* at the Olney Summer Theatre (1953) and by directing the Wellesley Group 20 Players' presenta-
tional-style production of *Saint Joan* that toured Puerto Rico (1954).

There was also a 1951 Shaw festival in London. Alec Clunes staged a
six-month festival at the Arts Theatre that presented *Arms and the Man,
Don Juan in Hell,* and eighteen Shavian one-act plays (divided into four
programs). This festival was part of a larger unofficial citywide tribute to
Shaw as some half dozen London theaters presented Shavian productions as part of the Festival of Britain. Shavian drama so inundated London that the Society of Authors imposed a temporary moratorium on
further West End productions of Shaw's works, commencing with the
blockage of a production of *Pygmalion* that sought to move from the Embassy to the Westminster Theatre.

In 1953 it appeared that Deeter might revive his annual festival, for
that summer the Hedgerow produced its ninth Shaw festival with productions of the complete *Man and Superman, Heartbreak House, Too True to
Be Good,* and *Arms and the Man.* However, the company was undergoing
a self-assessment that explored issues of subsidization, expansion, and
relocation. One casualty of this review was the annual Shaw festival.
While the company continued to perform Shavian works, the festival was
never revived. The Hedgerow closed in 1956; when it reopened in 1959,
Jasper Deeter was no longer involved with the theater.

Off-Broadway also participated in this festival frenzy. The Greenwich
Mews presented a 1955 festival composed of *The Philanderer, Village Wooing,* and selections from *Fanny's First Play* and *Buoyant Billions.* Four years
later the Provincetown Playhouse produced a summer Shaw Festival
comprising *Getting Married, Buoyant Billions, The Shewing-up of Blanco Posnet, Overruled, The Dark Lady of the Sonnets* and *Passion, Poison, and Petrifaction.* It drew little critical approbation, with one reviewer noting that
"While the intention was excellent, the company merely succeeded in
adding their poverty of talent and inadequate production resources to
plays that were already quite poor enough."[13]

Regional theaters and college campuses presented additional one-time
festivals. The Ohio Valley Summer Theatre devoted its 1951 season to a
Shaw festival that opened with the film *Pygmalion,* staged productions of
four Shaw plays, and included the cinematic version of *Caesar and Cleopatra.* The University of Minnesota dedicated its 1956–57 Arena Theatre
season to an all-Shaw program in honor of his centenary. In 1960 the
Brighton Beach Theatre (New York) did what amounted to an unofficial
Shaw festival with its August-September productions of *The Admirable*

Bashville, The Man of Destiny, Candida, Arms and the Man, and *Caesar and Cleopatra.* The University of South Florida (Tampa) held a 1963 July Shaw festival featuring repertory productions of *Misalliance, Pygmalion,* and *Androcles and the Lion.*

The 1950s was also a decade in which Shaw enjoyed frequent revival and enormous popularity as stage, musical theater, recordings, film, radio, and television appropriated his plays for their commercial ends. The stage fed this growing public awareness with a series of high-profile revivals, including *Caesar and Cleopatra* (Laurence Olivier and Vivien Leigh), *Man and Superman* (Kay Hammond and John Clements), *The Millionairess* (Katharine Hepburn), and *Saint Joan* (Uta Hagen, then Siobhan McKenna). The decade also witnessed two theatrical phenomena that captured the public imagination: Charles Laughton's concert-reading of *Don Juan in Hell* that was hailed as "one of the most exciting experiences of this and any other season"[14] and the musical *My Fair Lady* that introduced "Shaw to the largest and most cosmopolitan audience he ever enjoyed."[15] Laughton's success also initiated the recording of several Shavian productions for a growing home-listening market, while film studios produced popular renditions of *Androcles and the Lion, Saint Joan, The Doctor's Dilemma,* and *The Devil's Disciple.* Television also embraced the witty Irishman as popular series such as *Omnibus* and *The Hallmark Hall of Fame* brought shrunken versions of Shaw's plays into millions of homes. Although these commercial enterprises often reshaped and exploited Shavian drama, they enlarged Shaw's popularity to a degree that compelled literary critic Edmund Wilson to conclude that "There is now an automatic Shaw audience."[16] It was this sizable potential audience that made the creation of a permanent professional Shaw festival viable both artistically and fiscally.

One call for such a development came in 1959 from Byron Pumphrey, a member of the Shaw Society of California who, noting the growth of Shakespearean festivals, asked, "isn't it about time that some community, somewhere, accorded a like recognition to the other great English [*sic*] playwright. . . . I refer to none other than the not so bashful Bernard Shaw,"[17] and Pumphrey suggested that the Los Angeles Shaw Society create a Shavian festival. In June 1962 he reiterated his plea and insisted that "we need it, not two or three centuries hence, but now, for it is now that mankind stands in most desperate need for that comic spirit that illuminates Shaw's plays—that wonderful leavening of sanity which allows us to see, as in *Saint Joan,* the dementedness, the absurdity, the vanity, and the lust for power that makes [*sic*] a shambles of this world."[18] This time, however, Pumphrey envisioned a permanent festival located at the University of California at Santa Barbara and funded by the area's cultivated, well-to-do arts patrons; he added that the inaugural production would, of course, be *The Millionairess*. In the 1 July 1962 *Chicago Sunday Tribune*, critic Claudia Cassidy added her voice by suggesting that "Perhaps the time has come to revive the Shaw festivals . . . by taking dead aim at the literate, inquisitive audience not frightened by conversation or even by soap boxes, but quick to recognize the plays as platforms on which one of the most brilliant minds ever to use the theatre as a sounding board expounds and expostulates." While Cassidy did not anticipate the immediate establishment of a festival, she expressed her hope that one might appear in the "reassuring future."[19]

In that same year, however, a Shaw festival was created at Niagara-on-the-Lake, Ontario, Canada. Located in a beautiful lakeside area surrounded by parks and vineyards, this rural Victorian town offered a setting similar to Malvern or Moylan. The town's proximity to Toronto promised a sizable local audience, while the nearby Stratford Shakespeare Festival offered the potential for sharing an already-developed international clientele. Therefore, when resident Brian Doherty, a lawyer with a quarter of a century of theatrical experience as a playwright and producer, became concerned about a threat to Niagara-on-the-Lake's historical heritage, he saw a solution in the creation of "something like Shakespeare in Stratford." That "something" was an annual professional Shaw festival. He explained that "It's simply that Shaw was the only outstanding playwright writing in English, with the obvious exception of Shakespeare, who produced a sufficient number of plays to support a festival."[20]

Using local actors, Doherty presented a summer "Salute to Shaw" of eight weekend performances of *Candida* and *Don Juan in Hell*. The presentations occurred in the 350–seat proscenium theater in the town's Victorian court house; season revenues were $2,382, and expenses were $2,238. Buoyed by such an unqualified fiscal success, Doherty christened the following summer "The Shaw Festival" and converted his experiment into a semi-professional venture with a salaried artistic director (Andrew Allan) and several paid actors. The season expanded to three weeks and presented *You Never Can Tell, Androcles and the Lion,* and the double bill of *How He Lied to Her Husband* and *The Man of Destiny*. In 1965 the festival at Niagara-on-the-Lake (today called colloquially "The Shaw") ran six weeks, received its first Ontario Council grant, started a building fund, and introduced the first of its annual Shaw seminars.

The arrival of Barry Morse in 1966 marked a pivotal moment in the festival's professional development. In his one year as artistic director, he brought credibility and national attention by hiring established actors such as Leslie Yeo, Pat Galloway, Zoe Caldwell, and Paxton Whitehead and by matching their talents with a demanding bill of *Man and Superman, The Apple Cart,* and *Misalliance*. The season expanded to nine weeks (63 performances) and played to ninety-eight percent capacity, a significant increase over the previous season's sixty-two percent figure.

Paxton Whitehead guided the festival during the next decade with a programming philosophy that forged a festival identity, enlarged audiences, and brought fiscal stability. He extended the season gradually to fifteen weeks and scheduled as many as five plays. Script selection focused on "crowd pleasers"—Shaw's most popular plays and those of contemporaries such as Coward, Kaufman, Bennett, and Feydeau—even if that resulted in a season with only one Shaw offering. His initial season presented *Arms and the Man, Major Barbara,* and *The Circle* (Somerset Maugham). Whitehead cast these commercial vehicles with recognized celebrities such as Douglas Rain, Jessica Tandy, Stanley Holloway, Ian Richardson, Ann Casson, Kate Reid, and Carole Shelley. The need for a new theater facility motivated this commercial approach, for Whitehead realized that the festival's potential could not be realized without a new theater and that the needed funds for that facility could not be raised if deficits called in question the festival's viability. Hence he announced that "My philosophy simple is that I will not enter into a season in which there is deficit financing."[21] He noted that "our whole intent . . . was to consolidate the Shaw Festival as a fixture on the Canadian scene . . . to demonstrate the validity of an on-going Shaw Festival."[22] To achieve this end, Whitehead concentrated on improving earned income through increased ticket receipts and revenue-generating events such as winter concerts and pre- and post-season tours to Toronto, Ottawa, Winnipeg, Washington, D.C., and Philadelphia. No season overseen by Whitehead ended in a deficit. A typical Whitehead budget (1967) balanced season expenses ($147,452) with revenues from box-office receipts ($86,709), government grants ($40,450), touring ($7,639), and giving ($12,870). In 1973 The Shaw opened its new 830–seat Festival Theatre, an event that allowed Whitehead to turn to a more adventuresome programming policy. The 1974 season included productions of *The Devil's Disciple, Too True to Be Good,* and *The Admirable Bashville;* in Whitehead's final season as artistic director (1977), four of the five plays were written by Shaw.

After two years of interim leadership, the festival hired Christopher Newton, who was then the artistic director of the Vancouver Playhouse and had been an actor at The Shaw in 1964. As Lisbie Rae noted, his arrival "revolutionized the Shaw Festival, setting it on a new and more challenging course. He applied revolutionary shock tactics to sweep aside remnants of the old regime and shake up conservative elements in the festival, the town, and the audience."[23] His revolution began with significant programmatic, organizational, and fiscal changes.

With the addition of a third venue (the 350–seat Royal George Theatre), Newton embarked upon an ambitious programming expansion by increasing the number of annual offerings to ten plays, of which only three were Shavian. In his first season the non-Shavian works included scripts by Russian, Canadian, American, Hungarian, French, and German playwrights and represented a broad diversity of genres, styles, and periods. Under Whitehead's leadership the festival moved from exclusively Shavian summers to ones that included one or two works by Shaw's contemporaries. Newton sought to expand the scope further and explained that "It's meant to be Shaw and his contemporaries. Let's play Shaw amongst his contemporaries and see what happens."[24] Potential selections now included any play written during Shaw's lifetime. This effort to enhance the festival's artistic reputation rested fiscally on annual programming that balanced commercial, experimental, and Shavian offerings.

The commercial portion of each season appealed to the broadest possible audience and included a vintage musical (Romberg, Berlin, Porter), a mystery (especially Agatha Christie), and a farce (especially the Aldwych farces of Ben Travers). These popular offerings sought to generate the revenue needed to allow the inclusion of more provocative pieces, especially those written by Continental playwrights such as Gombrowicz, Andreyev, Wedekind, Strindberg, and Jarry. This approach also permitted Newton to assume box-office risks elsewhere by mounting politically sensitive works such as the 1995 revival of Harley Granville Barker's *Waste*, a drama whose plot involves an illegal abortion and the only play that season without a corporate sponsor.

The festival's international reputation rested on its Shaw productions, and here also Newton charted new theatrical territories. While traditional stagings of Shaw's most popular plays continued, the festival produced his neglected works and shorter plays and engaged in staging experimentation. Newton's own preoccupation was to view Shaw's plays through a surrealistic lens, and these explorations exposed new, often disturbing, aspects of plays like *Misalliance* and *Heartbreak House*.[25] Other directors stretched beyond the predictable. In 1982 Denise Coffey staged a dark *Pygmalion* that focused on a naked power struggle and added Shaw as a narrator and occasional actor (including Mrs. Pearce). Neil Munro directed a 1993 modern-dress production of *Saint Joan* in which the trial scene assumed the atmosphere of a nationally-televised Congressional hearing in which Joan sat facing the investigating panel with her back to the audience, which followed her responses on two banks of four monitors that transmitted a closeup of her face. In 1996 Shaw again appeared on stage, this time as the silent creative force in Glynis Leyshon's staging of *The Simpleton of the Unexpected Isles*.

Newton also made significant changes in the festival's organization. He hired resident designers and put an increased emphasis on the visual

Fig. 1. Mary Haney (Joan) laments the unwillingness of the high court to believe in her powers in the Shaw Festival's 1993 production of *Saint Joan*, directed by Neil Munro. Photograph by David Cooper. Reproduced by permission of The Shaw Festival and Mary Haney.

aspects of production. He replaced the star approach to casting with a more permanent acting company; the immediate result was a 1980 ensemble in which forty-eight actors were new. The company remained unusually stable, enhanced in part by Newton's policy of listing artists as members even when they are not involved that season. The perennial presence of actors such as Michael Ball, Jack Medley, David Schurmann, Jennifer Phipps, and Robert Benson allowed Newton not only to build a cohesive acting ensemble but also to foster actor recognition and audience loyalty.

The funding of a festival of the scope and size of The Shaw is challenging. Newton began his administration with an inherited deficit of more than $700,000 and a funding situation where "We have only a ten per cent subsidy from government at all levels, and we raise another ten from sponsors, so 80 per cent must be raised from box office. If the RSC and

Fig. 2. Al Kozlik appears as Bernard Shaw in the Shaw Festival's 1996 production of *The Simpleton of the Unexpected Isles*. The play was staged by Glynis Leyshon. Photograph by David Cooper. Reproduced by permission of The Shaw Festival and Al Kozlik.

the National had to do that they'd close down." Newton added that "if you don't break even you're in real trouble."[26] In recent years, however, Newton needed to be more tolerant of deficits. Following the 1989 season, the theater faced a 1.1 million dollar shortage. The accumulated deficit was $910,000 after the 1990 season; $1.4 million, 1991; $840,000, 1993; $838,000, 1994; $780,000, 1995. During this same period, the annual budget grew from ten to twelve million dollars. It should be noted, however, that while deficits are always undesirable, they are in the arts community a part of a fiscal way of life that allows an organization to maintain artistic quality while providing a rationale for increased governmental, corporate, and individual giving. It is perhaps for this reason that Newton recently stated that despite the deficit, "The Shaw is not in a crisis at the moment."[27]

Having completed its thirty-sixth season, The Shaw is the recognized center for professional Shavian production; its scale and stature are presently without rival among existing Shaw festivals. Between April and October it offers more than seven hundred performances of some ten plays in its three theaters as well as an impressive array of auxiliary activities including music, Tuesday question sessions, Friday chats, Saturday conversations, Shaw seminars, teachers' days, and student enrichment programs. In 1995 the festival enjoyed its most lucrative season, selling more than 290,000 tickets and generating receipts of nine million dollars. The success of The Shaw also inspired the creation of the Shaw festivals in Texas, Pennsylvania, Wisconsin, and Colorado.

In 1979 I began The Houston Shaw Festival on the campus of the University of Houston—Clear Lake where I was a professor. This suburban campus was located midway between Houston and Galveston and offered a pleasant wooded environment. The campus had two theaters, and the festival initially used the black-box facility because it provided both an intimacy and a flexible staging and seating arrangement. The university also offered a financial basis from which to launch the venture by supporting the artistic director's planning and management activities, providing teacher-artists' salaries, and supplying student actors and technicians.

Having visited The Shaw, I was convinced that Houston would support a similar festival. I saw in Shaw's plays an irresistible combination of entertaining wit and contemporary significance, and confidently labeled my venture "the first annual Bernard Shaw Festival." I also proclaimed my intention to do the entire canon before a play was repeated. Snubbing superstition, the festival opened on Friday, 13 July, with a production of *Getting Married*, followed the next evening by *Arms and the Man*. The plays ran in repertory for twelve performances, with special celebration activities held on Shaw's birthday. The total attendance that summer was only

Fig. 3. Susan Meyers (Candida) explains "Prossy's Complaint" to a bewildered Jody B. Sanders (Morell) in Robert G. Everding's staging of *Candida* for the 1980 Houston Shaw Festival. From the personal collection of Robert G. Everding.

1,040, but in the discussion sessions following each performance patrons expressed their enthusiasm for the concept and their conviction that my "Shavian congregation" would grow. Fortunately the festival did not run a deficit that season although it was totally funded through ticket revenues. The following season solidified funding by securing patron and business sponsorships and by adding matinee performances of a children's play.

My programming built each season around a Shavian theme: Shaw's views on happiness (*Heartbreak House* and *Too True to Be Good*), marriage (*Candida* and *The Philanderer*), parents and children (*Misalliance* and *Fanny's First Play*), religion (*Major Barbara* and *Androcles and the Lion*), and human will (*Village Wooing*, *The Man of Destiny*, and *You Never Can Tell*). Shaw's viewpoints were quoted and explained in the program and provided the focal point for the audience talkback sessions that were held after every performance. To attend these often-heated discussions was to experience how stimulating and controversial Shaw's ideas remain today. Indeed, some patrons did not wait for the post-performance period to express their reactions, for twice during the run of *Major Barbara*, patrons exited in protest during the Salvation Army scene and wrote later to express their outrage over the play's religious ideas.

Fig. 4. The 1987 Houston Shaw Festival staging of *The Devil's Disciple* with Tom Baird (Dick Dudgeon) and Katherine Hallowell (Judith). The production was directed by Brandon Smith. Reproduced by permission of the University Archives at the University of Houston—Clear Lake.

The festival's first acting ensemble consisted of unpaid community actors and graduate students. Most had never performed in a Shaw play, a fact not missed by the Houston *Post* reviewer who accurately bemoaned the lack of style. However, the company's enthusiasm over the challenge of acting Shaw led many of them to return for future seasons and thus allowed the gradual development of an experienced troupe of Shavian actors. Fortunately, Houston's professional resident company and its several semi-professional theaters provided a pool of talented actors who were available for summer employment. In 1985 actors received salaries, and five years later the festival gained an Equity II small professional status.

My departure brought new artistic directors and many changes, both of which furthered the festival's growth. Konrad Winters (1985–86) introduced an apprentice training program and formed the Houston Shaw Society. Alan Kreizenbeck (1987–89) hired the first Equity actor and secured the festival's first grants from Exxon and the Houston Cultural Arts Council. Mac Groves converted the festival to an Equity house, expanded

programming to include "works in the Shavian tradition of socially relevant comedy," and initiated an ambitious five-year plan. Nevertheless,
while the festival was fiscally solvent during its thirteen seasons, it failed
to establish its economic independence from the university and therefore
did not survive the institution's termination of its theater program.[28]

The American Shaw Festival began in 1982, the creation of Bruce Wall,
a British-born and RADA-trained actor with London and Off-Broadway
credits. The festival occurred in the historic 800–seat Mount Gretna Playhouse on the grounds of the Pennsylvania Chautauqua, a rural setting
nestled in the Stone Mountain hills. The playhouse had a tradition of
professional summer theater and served as the home for an annual summer music festival that was initiated in 1976 and that one national publication listed as one of the six best small music festivals in the United
States.

Wall's project prospectus compared Shaw's festal potential with existing Shakespearean festivals and argued that "out of Shaw's canon of fifty-
seven plays (Shakespeare only has thirty-eight to his credit) are many
which remain theatrical hallmarks . . . [and which] live on in many languages and traditions because of their universality." He added that "patrons of the American Shaw Festival will leave the theatre having heard
actors speak something more than bitter complaints followed by bemused
smiles."[29] Wall outlined his plans for a four-play season, a professional
company, a student acting academy, and a symposium featuring Clive
Barnes and Jean Stapleton. In December 1981 the company previewed
its initial season by presenting to the Bernard Shaw Society a reading of
Candida in the style of a live radio broadcast. The production featured
Jan Granger, Michael Allinson, Bruce Wall, Louis Zorich, James Walker,
and Paddy Croft.

The festival's first season ran for five weeks, presenting *Candida* and
Mrs Warren's Profession in repertory for fifteen performances, followed by
twelve performances of *The Importance of Being Earnest* and six of *The Day
After the Fair;* there was also a symposium on "The Woman Question in
Shaw" and a Wildean tea party. The American Shaw Festival continued
for four more summer seasons. Shavian offerings included *Misalliance,
How He Lied to Her Husband, Major Barbara, Pygmalion, Arms and the Man,
The Millionairess,* and *Press Cuttings* as well as original compilations by Wall
such as *A Shavian Sextet: A Pastiche for Six Voices* (1983) and *In, On,
Around & About Love* (1984). These Shaw offerings were combined with
other works such as *Hay Fever* and *The Browning Version* (1983), *The Chalk
Garden* and *The Glass Menagerie* (1984), and *Painting Churches* and *A Doll's
House* (1985). One performance of each play was followed by an audience
talkback session and each season included a Shaw Symposium. In 1984,
for example, the topic was "Theatre Critics and Shaw: Love or Hate and

Why?" In November 1984 the festival held a fund-raiser off-Broadway at the Parson School of Design where its concert reading of *A Little Bit More of Pygmalion* featured Carole Shelley, Remak Ramsay, Brenda Forbes, and Bruce Wall. It was reportedly irreconcilable differences between Wall and the Mount Gretna Playhouse's board that led to the festival's demise.

In 1983 Montgomery Davis began the Milwaukee Shaw Festival. Davis studied at Princeton University and the Webber-Douglas School of Dramatic Art in London before commencing on an acting career in the United States and Canada. In 1979 he founded the Milwaukee Chamber Theatre, a small mobile professional company that toured five states presenting small-scale theater performances in informal, intimate settings. In 1982 the enterprise became a resident theater company and offered its first subscription season; in 1993 MCT established residence in the 360–seat Broadway Theater Center. Today Davis still serves as the Artistic Director of this salaried company. The company's initial Shaw festival in 1983 ran five days in April and offered *Don Juan in Hell* and Jerome Kilty's *Dear Liar;* its 1996 festival presented four Shaw plays in twenty-four performances over a twenty-three-day period in late February and early March. Its 1997 season included a production of *The Apple Cart* and *Smash!,* a new stage adaptation of *An Unsocial Socialist.* In these sixteen seasons the festival staged twenty-six different Shaw plays.

The festival's mission statement emphasizes its commitment to present Shaw's plays not as museum pieces but as still-potent political forces relevant to the issues of our times. Since the 1989 festival, Davis structured each season around a specific socio-political theme and included non-Shavian scripts to offer modern perspectives on that issue. That season focused on the political troubles in Ireland by combining three Shaw plays (*John Bull's Other Island, O'Flaherty, V.C.,* and *The Admirable Bashville*) with Ron Hutchinson's *Rat in the Skull,* a powerful 1984 drama depicting an act of police brutality motivated by the national attitudes and antagonisms discussed in Shaw's plays; the festival also featured a public lecture by Tom Hadden, an Irish criminologist and founder of a political periodical, who discussed the English colonialism, religious prejudice, and terrorism at the center of the four plays. The 1992 season presented *Misalliance, Farfetched Fables,* and *The Lady's Not for Burning* in an examination of family life; in 1995, *Candida,* and *Oleanna,* offered varying views on the New Woman. Recently the festival enlarged its offerings with the addition of annual "Shaw Shorts" by Screaming Penguin Productions, a company of festival alumni that in 1996 produced *Press Cuttings* and *The Land of Heart's Desire.* Davis indicates that he has reserved the five-play epic *Back to Methuselah* for his millennial contribution.

The festival is also committed to providing its community with "a complete immersion in Shaw's view of the world"[30] and offers an array of

Fig. 5. Durward McDonald (Sir Pearce), Ruth Schudson (Mrs. O'Flaherty), and Norman Moses (O'Flaherty) in *O'Flaherty, V. C.,* directed by Montgomery Davis for the 1989 Milwaukee Shaw Festival. Photograph by Mark Haertlein. Reproduced by permission of The Milwaukee Chamber Theatre.

ancillary educational activities, including "Viewpoint" lectures, panel discussions, and "Meet the Artists" post-performance talkback sessions. Scenes are performed at a local bookstore, and an outreach program entitled "He Said, She Said, Shaw Said" visits local schools to present a chalktalk on G.B.S. The festival maintains connections with the Canadian festival and has an advisory panel that includes Christopher Fry, Denise Coffey, Dan Laurence, Margot Peters, Bernard Dukore, and Fred Crawford.

The Milwaukee Shaw Festival is part of the company's subscription season and receives external funding for the festival and its auxiliary programs. The festival costs approximately $100,000 annually and generates some $85,000 in ticket revenue. The company reported that its 1995–96 season generated the highest attendance, sales, and contributed income in its history and that its fiscal year ended with a $50,000 surplus.

Tucked up some nine thousand feet in the Colorado Rockies, the old

Fig. 6. The 1989 Milwaukee Shaw Festival production of *The Admirable Bashville*, directed by Jewel Walker. Pictured (left to right) are J. D. Nelson (Paradise), William Finn (Trainer), Lynn Allen (Lydia), Norman Moses (Master of the Revels), Jim Beasley (Lord Worthington), and James DeVita (Cashel Byron), Photograph by Mark Haertlein. Reproduced by permission of The Milwaukee Chamber Theatre.

mining town of Silverton is a summer tourist destination and also the site for another attempt to establish an annual summer Shaw festival. In 1989 A Theatre Group fittingly staged *The Shewing-up of Blanco Posnet* in Zhivago's, a restaurant that boasts a western-movie-set exterior. The festival was the inspiration of Marianne Fearn, who holds a doctorate in theater and is a member of the Society of Stage Directors. The following summer the community group officially made the Shaw festival part of its summer stock season and staged both *Overruled* and *Don Juan in Hell*. In 1991 the festival moved to the 1901 Miners Union Theatre on the top floor of the American Legion Building and produced *Too True to Be Good* and *Village Wooing* on its thrust stage. In recent years, however, the Shavian portion dwindled to a single play—*Major Barbara* (1994), *Arms and the Man* (1995), and *Mrs Warren's Profession* (1996).

Conspicuous by its absence from this discussion of recent Shaw festivals is a British contribution. The most promising ventures occurred at Malvern, where summer productions resumed in 1965. Its initial season ran 8 July–2 October and presented four plays, including one Shavian offering, *You Never Can Tell*. In 1996 Bernard Hepton became artistic director of a resident company that featured Constance Cummings, Helen Christie, John Gregson, and Betty Marsden; the three-week summer season offered five plays, including *Androcles and the Lion* and *The Man of Destiny*. In subsequent years, however, the theater shifted to mixed programs that found Shaw a very infrequent visitor; the theater ceased operations again in the mid-1970s. When the Malvern Festival Theatre reopened in 1977, it sought to revive the festival idea by creating an intriguing dual focus on Shaw and Elgar. That season the Royal Shakespeare Company performed *Man and Superman* from 24 May through 11 June, followed by a brief three-city tour, all as prelude to a fall run in the West End; the production featured Susan Hampshire and Richard Pasco and was accompanied by mealtime readings of *Don Juan in Hell* by actors attired in Edwardian evening dress. In 1978 three companies visited Malvern to present Shaw plays: Yvonne Arnaud Theatre produced *Pygmalion;* Abbey Theatre (Dublin) performed *You Never Can Tell*, starring Cyril Cusack; and the Old Vic presented Eileen Atkins in *Saint Joan*. The following summer the Birmingham Repertory Theatre visited Malvern to celebrate the fiftieth anniversary of the festival's founding and to recognize Sir Barry Jackson's centenary with productions of *Misalliance* and *The Elder Statesman* by T. S. Eliot, productions enhanced by a film retrospective of the original Malvern Festival and a photography exhibition entitled "GBS as Seen by Himself and Friends." In 1980 a touring production of *Heartbreak House* with Anthony Quayle and Honor Blackman appeared from 19 May through 1 June. While this scheme of visiting professional companies offered the potential for a revived festival, it was never fully developed and soon evaporated, leaving Malvern summers without a Shavian presence.

It is perhaps unfair to hold Malvern alone responsible for the absence of an English festival when the concept itself, even as a one-time basis, has been so generally ignored.[31] Michael Coveney perhaps touches upon one explanation when he suggests that "Far from being in the happy position of Shakespeare, whose reputation no production can enhance or undermine, Shaw's place in the heart of the British playgoer is distinctly insecure because of a suspicion that his credibility will fade in direct proportion to the amount of public scrutiny attended his works."[32] Unlike North America, where Shaw is generally appreciated, England appears unsure about the playwright's stature. On the one hand there are impressive professional revivals at the national theaters and prestigious summer festivals; on the other hand, the general revival pattern is sporadic, and critical commentary too often focuses its discussion on a given production's ability to overcome its loquacious, boring, and irrelevant playwright.[33] While there is encouragement in a recent announcement concerning London's Stockpot Productions' intention to stage Shaw's complete works, the fact remains that there is yet no British move afoot to honor Shaw with a festival in the image of Stratford.

Resistance to the concept of a Shaw festival is not restricted to the United Kingdom, for there are also skeptics on the other side of the Atlantic. These pundits raise questions about viability and integrity, concerns perhaps best answered by the record of the very festivals that they criticize.

One objection is that "the Irish playwright's work, unlike Shakespeare's, cannot be the staple of a five-month summer repertory season."[34] Certainly this comment cannot refer to the Shavian canon, for as both Brian Doherty and Bruce Wall correctly noted, Shaw wrote more plays than Shakespeare (albeit some of these are not full-length works) and an equal number of recognized masterpieces. At the core of this objection is the belief that only a limited number of Shaw's plays are producible and even fewer relevant, but the festival record suggests the contrary. Recent festival productions demonstrated that the major plays are not time-bound, one-experience vehicles but rather possess complex dramatic textures that invite multiple examinations; as Christopher Newton suggested, each of Shaw's masterpieces contains "a number of stories buried in it, and each period of history will find the story that is important to it."[35] The Shaw staged *Pygmalion* four times, once in each of the past four decades, all with different directors and all markedly varied in tone and theme. Productions of the so-called minor plays generally revealed them to be effective stage pieces that entertain and enlighten audiences. Moreover, as the history of Shakespearean productions suggests, scripts have their time. Shakespeare's "lesser" work *Troilus and Cressida* spoke powerfully to audiences during the Vietnam war period, and recently *Measure for Measure* received multiple revivals because it contains ideas and attitudes that resonate with contemporary audiences. Similarly, Shaw's neglected works such as *The Philanderer* and *The Simpleton of the Unexpected Isles* are now finding new appreciation.

The festival record also indicates that the concept of a Shaw festival is economically viable. While festivals employed varied levels of and approaches to funding, there is a common pattern of institutional longevity that suggests a high degree of fiscal stability. In 1997 The Shaw completed its thirty-sixth and the Milwaukee Chamber Theatre its sixteenth year, and both festivals experienced record attendance in their most recent seasons. The Houston and Hedgerow ventures existed for thirteen and nine seasons, respectively, and neither ceased operations because of fiscal difficulties. This longevity is due in large part to that automatic Shaw audience identified by Edmund Wilson, a claim echoed in Christopher Newton's report that "we sell about 270,000 seats every year and the Shaw plays are always among the best sellers so he must be finding an audience."[36]

Another criticism centers on the inclusion of non-Shavian works and the effect those selections have on a festival's integrity. For instance, Christopher Newton's programming evoked considerable concern that this dilution of the Shavian presence reduced the Shaw festival to a drama festival with Shaw plays. A festival's integrity, however, should not be measured solely by the exclusivity or number of Shaw plays but by the overall emphasis on its dramatist. Barry Jackson provided insight on this issue when he explained that Malvern "started off predominantly a Shaw Festival . . . but the poor wretched audiences found a week of G.B.S. far too much—their brains were completely fagged after 2 or 3 nights and so they asked if they couldn't have some other plays."[37] Jackson's remedy was to offer a range of dramatic literature stretching from the medieval to the modern, most of which offered scant perspective on Shaw's work, yet Shaw remained Malvern's centerpiece and the touchstone by which the world knew and measured that festival. Basil Langton and Bruce Wall balanced their Shavian seasons with Broadway revivals, but the context of lectures and apprenticeships left little doubt about the festivals' purpose; the Milwaukee Chamber Theatre produced a single Shaw script in a two-play festival, but Mamet's *Oleanna* shed light on *Candida* and its contemporary relevance. Any evaluation of a festival's integrity must look not only at its programming but also at its overall activities.

Concern is also often expressed about textual integrity whenever a production deviates from traditional staging or interpretation. Such revisionism has its critics because (as we have seen particularly with Shakespeare) experimentation can move beyond the script with bewildering absurdity; however, it also can work within a play's integrity to reach audiences in profound ways by discovering new textual territory or addressing contemporary socio-political concerns. For example, the experimentation at The Shaw expanded, even altered, perceptions about certain scripts, and future explorations could make significant contributions to our deeper understanding of Shaw's dramaturgy. As the Milwaukee Chamber Theatre's mission statement reminds us, Shaw was a political playwright who sought to change the daily lives of his audience. Rather than relegating productions to period pieces, festivals have the opportunity to explore when and how a given script responds to the historical moment and thereby engages its contemporary audience with a force and effect not unlike that created by the play in Shaw's own lifetime.

Critics also point to the paucity of existing Shaw festivals, particularly in comparison with the number of annual festivals that honor Shakespeare. It is true that today the summer Shakespearean festival is a cultural staple, seemingly appearing everywhere and attracting everyone. In July 1995 the San Francisco Bay area offered seven different outdoor Shakespearean festivals—on a glen and in an amphitheater, at a winery and on the beach, in a park and touring the parks. One is tempted to complain that the world is perhaps overly littered with the Bard and that interpretive excesses have reached such a degree that the theater-going public is ripe for a new patron saint for its summer cultural pilgrimages. However, it is more prudent simply to point out that this Shakespearean phenomenon is a relatively recent occurrence. At Shaw's death, four Shakespearean festivals existed in the English-speaking world, only one of which was fully professional. A decade later the number increased to twelve, but two of the original four were no longer in operation, and the majority were still amateur. This is not to say that within the next few decades the number of Shaw festivals will rival those of Shakespeare. Shaw attracts a different, more limited audience. However, the Shavian evolution is still young in festival terms, and there is ample justification to expect the creation of new festivals.

Despite Shaw's initial resistance to theaters dedicated to his plays, he announced in 1939 that "I am a booster of festivals." He added that he had planted a mulberry tree in Malvern and that "as the Festival habit grows from the seed sown in Malvern I hope to plant many mulberry trees."[38] The past half decade is a record of those further plantings. Not all these festivals exist today, but each contributed to an expanded recognition of Shaw's genius and the development of the festival concept. Also, these ventures collectively undertook a wide array of programming schemes, fiscal arrangements, and auxiliary activities that today provide valuable insights for those individuals who seek to plant their own mulberry trees in the days ahead.

Notes

My appreciation to the following individuals who aided in my research on Shaw festivals: Fred D. Crawford, Montgomery Davis, T. F. Evans, Al Franklin, Denis Johnston, Douglas Laurie, Neil Havens, Christopher Newton, Patricia Pate, and Konrad Winters.

1. Bernard Shaw, *Collected Letters 1911–1925*, ed. Dan H. Laurence (New York: Viking, 1985), p. 901.

2. Gerald Willem Van Loom, "Of Pilgrims and Players," *Theatre Arts Monthly* 34 (July 1950): 50.

3. Frank Marcus, "Green Room," *Plays and Players* (November 1968), p. 56.

4. Dan H. Laurence and Nicholas Grene, eds., *Shaw, Lady Gregory and the Abbey: A Correspondence and a Record* (Gerrards Cross: Colin Smythe, 1993), p. 119.

5. Norman MacDermott, *Everymania: The History of the Everyman Theatre Hampstead 1920–26* (London: Society of Theatre Research, 1975), p. 32.

6. T. C. Kemp, *Birmingham Repertory Theatre: The Playhouse and the Man* (Birmingham: Cornish Brothers Limited, 1948), p. 36.

7. Vivian Elliot, " 'Genius Loci': The Malvern Festival Tradition," *SHAW* 3 (1983): 192.

8. See "G. B. S. at Hedgerow," *New York Times* (23 July 1939), sec. 9, p. 1. Deeter said that "I am tired of festivals" and that the current season might be the last because the commitment upset planning and limited the mounting of new additions to the repertory.

9. "Draft Board Fights Ruling of Roosevelt," *New York Times* (20 October 1942), p. 5.

10. Harold Rubinstein, *Bernard Shaw in Heaven* (London: William Heinemann, 1954), p. 18.

11. Basil Langton, "A Shaw Repertory Theatre," *Shaw Bulletin* 3 (May 1952): 6.

12. Ibid., p. 5.

13. Burns Mantle, ed., *The Best Plays of 1959–60* (New York: Dodd, Mead, 1960), p. 43.

14. Quoted from Simon Callow, *Charles Laughton: A Different Actor* (New York: Grove Press, 1987), p. 212.

15. Warren S. Smith, "G. B. Shaw at 119—Indications of Immortality," *New York Times* (2 November 1975), sec. 2, p. 5.

16. Edmund Wilson, *The Sixties: Last Journal, 1960–72*, ed. Lewis M. Dabney (New York: Farrar Straus Giroux, 1993), p. 205.

17. Byron Pumphrey, "Why Not Shaw?" *Frontier* (June 1959), p. 18.

18. Byron Pumphrey, "Shaw with Shakespeare," *Frontier* (June 1962), p. 19. See also Charles Meredith, "Towards a Shaw Theatre," *California Shavian* 3:6 (November-December 1962): 2–6.

19. Quoted in *California Shavian* 3:6 (November-December 1962): 8–9.

20. Brian Doherty, *Not Bloody Likely: The Shaw Festival—1962–1973* (Toronto: J. M. Dent & Sons (Canada) Limited, 1974), p. 7.

21. Arthur R. Day, "The Shaw Festival at Niagara-on-the-Lake in Ontario, Canada, 1962–1981: A History" (unpublished Ph.D. dissertation, Bowling Green University, 1982), p. 101.

22. Ibid., p. 103.

23. Lisbie Rae, "Making Sense of Shaw: Newton at the Shaw Festival, 1980–1993," *SHAW* 15 (1995): 134. For further insights see Lisbie Rae, "The Christopher Newton Years at the Shaw Festival: 1980–1993" (unpublished Ph.D. dissertation, University of Toronto, 1993).

24. Day, "The Shaw Festival at Niagara-on-the-Lake," p. 205.

25. See particularly Keith Garebian, *George Bernard Shaw and Christopher Newton: Explorations of Shavian Theatre* (Oakville: Mosaic Press, 1992).

26. Michael Leech, "Shaw Thing," *Plays and Players* 388 (January 1986): 30.

27. John Bemrose, "Diabolically Good Diversions," *Maclean's* (10 June 1996), p. 62.

28. For a detailed overview of the Houston Shaw Festival, see Monique A. Haverkorn, "A Theatrical History of the Houston Shaw Festival 1979–1992" (unpublished M.A. thesis, University of Houston—Clear Lake, 1993). The archives of the Houston Shaw Festival reside in the library at the University of Houston—Clear Lake.

29. Bruce Wall, "American Shaw Festival: Summer '82 and Beyond," p. 5.

30. Milwaukee Chamber Theatre, "The Shaw Festival: A Mission Statement" (1994), p. 1. This undated document was supplied by Montgomery Davis.

31. One notable exception is the annual productions and programs offered one weekend each July in the garden area at Shaw's Corner, Ayot St. Lawrence, in celebration of Shaw's birthday.

32. Michael Coveney, "John Bull's Other Island," *Plays and Players* 18:7 (July 1971): 47.

33. See particularly Alan Seymour "Misalliance," *Plays and Players* 237 (June 1973): 50, and "Subtext," *Plays and Players* 451 (July 1991): 4.

34. Mark Czarnecki "A Festival Does Not Live by Shaw Alone," *Maclean's* 93:24 (16 June 1980): 38.

35. John Bemrose, "Energizing the Stage," *Maclean's* (15 June 1992), p. 53.

36. Letter to me, 18 January 1995.

37. Elliot, " 'Genius Loci': The Malvern Festival Tradition," pp. 206–7.

38. Bernard Shaw, "On the Festival Habit," *Independent Shavian* 16:2–3 (Spring 1978): 24–25.

Michel W. Pharand

"ALMOST WHOLLY CEREBRAL": RICHARD ALDINGTON ON BERNARD SHAW

In a manner of speaking, it was the mother of Richard Aldington (1892–1962)—soldier, poet, novelist, essayist, linguist, and translator—who "introduced" her son to Bernard Shaw. In 1908, shortly after young Richard's first poem was published in a London periodical, he wrote his first short story, and his mother sent a copy to Shaw. "What she wrote to him I don't know," wrote Aldington in his 1941 autobiography, *Life for Life's Sake,* "nor what her motive was, unless she thought that Mr. Shaw might turn his satire on me and drastically cure me of the itch for writing. If so, she was disappointed." This is how he recalled Shaw's letter:

> "Madam,
>   Your son has obviously too much literary talent to earn his living in an honest way.
>   I enclose a guinea which he is to spend in some thoroughly selfish manner.
>   Yours faithfully,
>   *George Bernard Shaw.*"

Aldington concluded, "I believe I was so revolted by Shaw's cynicism that I insisted on giving [the guinea] to my mother. As to Shaw's opinion, who am I to dispute it? If earning money by writing is dishonest, I can only say that I have done my best to follow in his footsteps."[1] Shaw's "review" of Aldington's first prose fiction did not make a favorable impression on Aldington.

Frequently cantankerous but more often than not astute in both judgment and taste, Aldington may nonetheless have been a little off the mark in some of his views on *Frank Harris on Bernard Shaw* (1931).[2] The 408-page book by Frank Harris (1856–1931), one-time editor of the *Saturday Review*—for which Shaw was dramatic critic from 1895 to 1898—received from Aldington an eloquent but on the whole negative review, mostly because of its subject. Indeed, he seems to have had nothing against Harris, whom he may have known personally, judging from a passing reference in his autobiography: "I got Reggie [Turner] to talk about Oscar [Wilde]'s death, and I am happy to inform the world that Reggie gave me his word of honour that there is no truth to Frank Harris's sensational account—though I don't suppose anyone who knew Harris ever believed it" (*Life*, p. 377).

Harris's first biographical essay on Shaw appeared in *Contemporary Portraits: Second Series* (1919), with a coda by Shaw entitled "Shaw's Portrait by Shaw, or How Frank Ought to Have Done It."[3] Little did he suspect that this was only a prelude to the rewriting of a much longer Harris biography fourteen years later. And as he did for Archibald Henderson, Hesketh Pearson, and Thomas Demetrius O'Bolger, Shaw provided Harris with letters that found their way—often verbatim but at times self-bowdlerized by Shaw—into the book. In fact, according to Stanley Weintraub, "Harris completed only sixty-five faltering pages before his health cracked altogether and ghostwriter Frank Scully took over, completing the job by the use of paid researchers and Shaw's letters. . . . As far as Shaw was concerned, it was mostly his book."[4]

Thus, when Harris died debt-ridden, Shaw undertook to rewrite the book and see it through the press not only to emend his imaginative biographer's facts, but also to assist financially Harris's widow, Nellie. Upon learning of Harris's death, Shaw sent her a check, mitigating the implications of "charity" by saying that she could repay him out of the book's royalties. Furthermore, to increase sales, he included under his own name a postscript in which he went so far as to claim that Harris had completed the book except for correcting the proofs. To cover his tracks, Shaw destroyed the corrected galley proofs, with the exception of the postscript (which he gave to Nellie). The posthumous, largely rewritten "Unauthorised Biography" sold 27,000 copies on publication day in London alone.[5]

Aldington encountered Shaw again more than two decades later when he debunked the T. E. Lawrence ("of Arabia") legend. In his research for *Lawrence of Arabia: A Biographical Enquiry* (1955), Aldington consulted the correspondence between Lawrence and the Shaws (in the British Museum), especially the letter to Charlotte of 26 March 1924 that recounted (albeit allusively) Lawrence's rape by the Turkish Bey at Deraa. Aldington

wrote to Eric Warman on 23 February 1955, "Yet the interpretation of
L's tortured psychology and the motives—stated by himself—for entering
the RAF are contained in those letters and only in those letters!"[6] Aldington indicated in the same letter that he was also familiar with Blanche
Patch's *Thirty Years with G.B.S.* (1951). Although Lawrence's *Seven Pillars
of Wisdom* (1926) had been revised by Shaw and proofread by Charlotte,
Aldington believed, as he wrote to Alison Palmer on 8 February 1962,
that "G.B.S. re-wrote the book."[7]

From the following review, it is clear that Aldington was disenchanted
with Shaw both as an individual and as an ideologue. Never one to disguise his feelings or attenuate his opinions, Aldington writes with outspoken vigor about a man whom he paradoxically respected as a journalist
and essayist, yet disparaged as a playwright and political analyst. The
irony was that the cutting remarks about Shaw that Aldington quoted
from Harris and approved enthusiastically were very likely written by
G.B.S. himself as Harris's unacknowledged ghostly ventriloquist. Aldington never knew.

[*Aldington's review, which appeared in the* Sunday Review *(London) on 6 December 1931, is from an undated, unsigned single-spaced typescript, leaves numbered [1]–3, from The Richard Aldington Papers, Collection 68, Box 23/2,
Special Collections, Morris Library, Southern Illinois University, Carbondale. I
would like to thank Ms. Shelley Cox, Rare Books Librarian, for her generous and
invaluable assistance and Mme. Catherine Aldington for her permission to publish
her father's review. Aldington's text © 1998 by the Estate of Richard Aldington.*]

Bernard Shaw. By Frank Harris. (Gollancz. 8/6.)

By Richard Aldington

The first thing to be said of Frank Harris's book on Bernard Shaw is that
it is entirely and pleasurably readable. This is meant as high praise, since
too many of the books a reviewer has to read are unluckily chiefly distinguished by various shades of dullness. I may have been tempted to gallop
through the book by the very facility of reading, but that only means
that I found myself interested from beginning to end—an all too rare
experience with new books. Whatever Harris's faults as a writer, he had
personality and vitality (especially remarkable in a man of his age)* and

*Harris turned seventy-five on 14 February 1931.

managed to get them into these pages. His rather bludgeoning style may
not be exactly a model, but it enabled Harris to flail his way through a
subject with real gusto. I do not know whether Mr Shaw touched up the
writing in addition to correcting the proofs and making sundry revisions,
but it strikes me as one of Harris's brightest efforts. The fact that Mr Shaw
helped Harris with this book and then passed it through the press softens
my heart towards him. True, it is excellent publicity; true, Mr Shaw utterly refuses to authorise it and gives himself the last word in a postscript;
but in the course of the book he is required to take some shattering
blows.* A smaller man would not have seen the book through the press;
he would have tried to get it suppressed. One up to Bernard Shaw.

   The character of Frank Harris as it appears in his books is that of a
rather conceited braggart and adventurer with more than a tendency to
arrange facts for the purpose of flattering himself. But he also appears as
a warm-hearted, full-blooded, intelligent man with a scrupulous regard
for what he considered essential truths, a passion for defending the
under-dog, and any amount of courage in violently asserting and defending his views. Upon the whole, rather a lovable sort of man—so long as
you managed to avoid knowing him personally.† He adopted a brave but
dangerously unpopular attitude during the War, for which I admire him;
he made and lost a great deal of money; with the possible exception of
F. M. Hueffer,‡ he was the most intelligent literary editor London has
seen for fifty years; in Ercles-Casanova vein§ he wrote a long book about
himself§§ which shows an ardent but healthy imagination and restores

*In a letter to Hesketh Pearson on 8 October 1938, Shaw referred to "My autobiography
by Frank Harris" and stated, "I need inbunking, not debunking, having debunked myself
like a born clown" (Bernard Shaw, *Collected Letters 1926–1950*, ed. Dan H. Laurence [New
York: Viking, 1988], p. 512).

   †In his postscript, Shaw quotes Oscar Wilde: "Frank Harris has been received in all the
great houses—*once*" (Harris, p. 392).

   ‡Hueffer, later Ford Madox Ford (1873–1939), was founding editor of the *English Review*.
During 1914, Aldington served as Ford's secretary and helped write *When Blood Is Their
Argument* (1915), "one of Ford's attempts to answer George Bernard Shaw's anti-war propaganda" (*Literary Lifelines: The Richard Aldington—Lawrence Durrell Correspondence*, ed. Ian S.
MacNiven and Harry T. Moore [London and Boston: Faber & Faber, 1981], p. x). As a
result, Aldington was almost certainly familiar with Shaw's controversial *Common Sense about
the War*, which had appeared as a supplement to the *New Statesman* on 14 November 1914.

   §"Ercles" is a variant of Hercules. Shakespeare, in *A Midsummer Night's Dream*, Act I, scene
2, has Bottom say that he "can play Ercles rarely" and then recite a passage that he describes
(incorrectly) as "This is Ercles' vein, a tyrant's vein." Aldington sees the "Ercles-Casanova
vein" differently. Hercules had many love affairs, and on one night he fathered fifty-one
sons by forty-nine of the fifty daughters of Thespius. The association of this with the numerous conquests of Giacomo Casanova (1725–98) would make the "Ercles-Casanova vein" an
appropriate description of Harris's memoirs.

   §§The notorious *My Life and Loves* (three volumes, 1923–29, with a fourth added after
Harris's death) is analogous to Casanova's posthumous autobiography, *Mémoires de J. Casa-*

one's faith in the 19th century; he also went to prison. He was a bit of a Pietro Aretino* in his way, and as such immensely sympathetic when contrasted with the colourlessly virtuous (on paper) London literati. He was almost the only genuine adventurer in the literature of his day. I can only hope that he enjoyed his life as much as he said he had; he deserved it.

This (as I see him) is the man whose posthumous work is the estimate of a very different sort of man and writer. Timid, prudent, somewhat bloodless and gutless, ready to follow up any idea to the verge of action, possessed of astonishing verbal virtuosity, the literary inspirer of the most ignominious failure among modern governments, Mr Shaw was cast by the Life-Force to play the part of lord of the London literati, the ancestral inventor of the Bloomsbury snigger. His exaggerated and brilliantly self-fostered reputation rests on far flimsier foundations than that of Anatole France, and will crumble with even more astonishing swiftness.† This, not because he lacked abilities, but flesh and blood; not because he was a revolutionary, but a supporter of political prize-fighters and petty bureaucratic tyranny; not that he was a selfish disregarder of other people's happiness, but that his ignorance of human nature is such that he could only maim not foster life, could only produce a complicated politico-social-economic machine, instead of a new spirit. I would rather be back in the trenches than live in Bernard Shaw's utopian paradise of statistical eunuchs. I would rather pig along with the warm (if smelly and beery) humanity of London slums than dwell in Shaw's vegetable-garden suburbia. He would make the world one sickening Switzerland‡ if he could find a Lenin to do it for him.

---

nova de Seingalt (twelve volumes, 1826–38), which made his name synonymous with "libertine." Charlotte insisted that the first volume of Harris's autobiography be burned, page by page, in the fireplace (*Playwright*, p. 205). Aldington's later fictional treatment, *The Romance of Casanova: A Novel*, appeared in 1946.

*Pietro Aretino (1492–1556), an Italian satirist who dubbed himself the "scourge of princes," was forced to leave Rome because of his 1524 collection of *Sonetti lussuriosi* (Lewd Sonnets).

†Although faulted for the thinness of his plots and for a lack of creative imagination, the skeptical, ironic Nobel-winner Anatole France (1844–1924) was considered in his day the ideal French man of letters. John Steinbeck had made a similar analogy in an unpublished letter of 14 April 1928: "He [Shaw] and Anatole France will be buried together and will be forgotten together" (quoted from Jay Parini, *John Steinbeck: A Biography* [New York: Henry Holt, 1995], in John R. Pfeiffer, "A Continuing Checklist of Shaviana," *SHAW* 16 [1996]: 239).

‡Cf. Aldington, writing from Switzerland to Eric Warman on 20 May 1938: "Switzerland. Ha, ha! Palace of the League of Nations, roads like billiard tables, no hooting of cars, trams as smooth as prams, lake, mountains, snowcrests, protestants, neatness, . . . the most respectable suburbia in the world. . . . It is a bourgeois utopia, and I should go crackers if I had to live here. The only thing lacking to the place is Bernard Shaw, who ought to be the

Bernard Shaw is a great literary journalist, which is just as rare as any other kind of great writer. He is a most fluent and effective pamphleteer, expounding his convictions with splendid clarity and vigour, buffeting his opponents, and animating his words with verve and wit. Moreover he has an innate gift of theatre which he has disciplined to a high state of efficiency. So much so that he has not always been able to resist the temptation to play a part himself—that of a new sort of stage Irishman in London. At the same time this excellent stage-craft has enabled him to give vigour, interest and even a semblance of life to ideas on the stage which, in the hands of a less splendid virtuoso, would have been flaccid and dull. But I cannot see him as a great creative artist, because he is almost wholly cerebral. There is no deep physical life in his writings, and his feelings are abstract and without passion—I don't mean sexual passion, though that is true as well. His writing is not of things, people, situations and relations, feelings, passions, but of ideas about them. I do not complain because the people of his plays exist at one or two removes from life, because that is a condition of all art. In spite of the real inventiveness which produced them and the more than admirable skill with which they are manoeuvered, I find they do not move or interest me as people. In fact, they are not people; they are skilfully disguised microphones. Is it unjust to say that this is because he sees human life as a series of problems to be solved or despaired of, and not as an adventure to be shared and lived? He talks much of the Life-Force, but does he ever make us feel it? He admires Jesus, but believes that with equal incomes the Kingdom of Heaven will be added unto us. He believes that the quality of life can be improved by material organization, as if the collective happiness of robots were worth a hang. His plays move or collapse according to whether assent is given to or withheld from the ideas which are their structure. You must be a Shavian to admire and love Shaw as an artist. Who cares, who knows that Balzac was a Catholic and a royalist when reading Le Curé de Tours and La Duchesse de Langeais?*

I find a good deal of support for my view of Mr Shaw's writings in Frank Harris's book, which is not mere denigration, but the reduction of an inflated reputation to something nearer its true proportions. So long as praise is confined to him as a kind of philosophe-playwright-wit-propagandist I am all for him; what I will not have is the assertion that he is either an artist, a thinker or anywhere near a complete human being.

Swiss mascot, and swim in the lake, eat lettuce in Jaeger underclothes and guide intelligent women to socialism for a modest retaining fee of 30,000 a year. It is the epitome of enlightened unimaginative virtue, the peak quotation of sober righteousness and making money 'honestly.' . . . It's quite unbearable." (*Richard Aldington: An Autobiography in Letters*, p. 156)

*The monumental *La Comédie humaine* (1829–47) by Honoré de Balzac (1799–1850) has 2,000 characters appearing in nearly one hundred completed novels that span five decades.

Harris lets him off rather lightly as "inconsistent," but I should say it is a frenzy of incoherence for a man to be "a scoffer and religious at the same time; an atheist and pew renter, a Socialistic supporter of war, a peace-loving Fabian favouring a strong Army, a libertarian eulogising Musso-lini, a zealous champion of State control fighting the Government censor, a believer in freedom advocating compulsory equalisation of incomes, a zealot of 'the true joy of life' scoffing at love and sex" . . . That is typical enough of these reformers en pantoufles*—realists for themselves and idealists for other people. And he can salve his conscience with a quibble in a crisis, as in the matter of the Boer War. He quoted Ibsen as silencing a pro-Boer audience by saying: "Are we really for Oom Paul and the Old Testament?"† But that wasn't the point. The point was: "Do we really believe in a big nation stealing a little nation's property by force of arms?"

As to his standing as an artist, I cannot do better than quote Harris again:

"But I cannot find it in me to praise him above all men.‡ He will not live. His rhetoric is racy, intuitively good, but it lacks inspiration; and though often fine, never reaches genius. . . . Though he remains a writer of importance, his plays on re-reading are dull. Only a few seem likely to me to live.§ . . . He is the wittiest author of our time; he may even be the wittiest in English literature. But his plays, almost all of them, lack vitality."

This is higher praise than I should give, because I think Shaw's wit is far too often mere Oscarian verbalism, while I find all his plays dull. But let that pass. Shaw's letters about the European War§§ disgust me. They are simply upper-class London, and utterly remote from the reality. They might have been signed by Lloyd George. I should not have thought that an Irishman could be so smug.§§§ But all things, apparently, are possible with the Life-Force.

"What, then, did he accomplish or give to the world that will secure him immortality? Nothing that I can see. How could he? All that he had§§§§ was a clear eye for seeing what the trouble was. He didn't kill, nor was he killed by it. All he did was to spit putty balls at it from his ivory tower, and laugh."

*The French expression "en pantoufles" means "in slippers." Aldington is implying that Shaw was a mere theorist uninvolved in active struggle.
†"Are we really on the side of Mr. Kruger and his Old Testament?" (Harris, p. 303).
‡"beyond all men" (Harris, p. 382).
§"seem to me likely to live" (Harris, p. 382).
§§See Chapter XXI, "In War and Peace," in Harris, pp. 300–325.
§§§Aldington would have particularly resented Shaw's remark to a soldier who stated that "If I had known all that in 1914, they would never have got khaki on *my* back." Shaw replied, "That is precisely why I did not tell you in 1914" (Harris, p. 318).
§§§§"All he had" (Harris, p. 384).

Notes

1. Richard Aldington, *Life for Life's Sake: A Book of Reminiscences* (New York: Viking, 1941), pp. 59–60. Subsequent references to *Life* appear parenthetically in the text.

2. *Frank Harris on Bernard Shaw: An Unauthorised Biography Based on Firsthand Information, with a Postscript by Mr Shaw* (London: Victor Gollancz Ltd.; Garden City, N.Y.: Garden City Publishing Co.; New York: Book League of America; New York: Simon and Schuster, 1931). The publication date in England and America was 27 November 1931. Subsequent references to Harris are to the British edition.

3. Frank Harris, *Contemporary Portraits: Second Series* (New York: Frank Harris, 1919), pp. 313–45.

4. Stanley Weintraub, *The Unexpected Shaw: Biographical Approaches to G.B.S. and His Work* (New York: Frederick Ungar, 1982), p. 20.

5. *The Playwright and the Pirate, Bernard Shaw and Frank Harris: A Correspondence*, ed. Stanley Weintraub (University Park: Penn State University Press, 1982), p. 254. For the background to Harris's biography, see pp. 216–60. *Playwright* reprints the text of Shaw's postscript on pp. 260–67.

6. *Richard Aldington: An Autobiography in Letters*, ed. Norman T. Gates (University Park: Penn State University Press, 1992), p. 275.

7. Ibid., p. 320.

Leon Hugo

THE QUEST FOR SHAW:
AN INTERVIEW WITH
MICHAEL HOLROYD

This interview will focus on Shaw and the work you have done on him. By way of
introduction and to place Shaw in the context of your career as a writer, let's spend
some time on your earlier years. Would you tell us first about your education;
possible influences (any Shavian ones via Hesketh Pearson?); your decision to be-
come a writer, specifically a biographer?

I feel considerable sympathy for Osbert Sitwell, who described his education in *Who's Who* as having taken place "during the holidays from Eton."
I also went to Eton, my family having raised a double mortgage on the
house to send me there. The plan was that I should rescue the family
fortunes by studying chemistry, physics, and advanced mathematics,
thereby qualifying myself for a splendidly paid job in the new scientific
age. Unfortunately I had no natural scientific or mathematical abilities. I
argued so obstinately with my father over this that he decided I must put
my gift of obstinacy to some economic use. He therefore persuaded me
to take up the law where, he pointed out, I could argue for profit to my
heart's content. So I became an articled clerk in a firm of solicitors—a
Dickensian post in which, instead of receiving a salary, you paid your
employer. This was a further blow to the family's plummeting finances.
After a couple of years I came to the conclusion that I was only interested
in criminal law (which is really an interest in human nature rather than
law). So I abandoned law and did my two years' national service in the

army, an unnerving episode that proved to all who saw me that I was not a man of action. I emerged, a maverick and largely unemployable figure, good for nothing but writing. The peculiar advantages that this unconventional education gave me as a future biographer of Bernard Shaw will be immediately obvious to all readers of *The Annual of Bernard Shaw Studies*.

Your first biography was on Hugh Kingsmill in 1964, then on Lytton Strachey in 1968–69, and then on Augustus John in 1975–76. There were also various "occasional" pieces, including a novel, A Dog's Life, *in 1969. What would you like to tell us about these works?*

I read literature, not at any university, but at my local public library. It was there, in my late teens, that I came across the biographies, essays, and novels of Hugh Kingsmill. What F. R. Leavis was to many members of my generation, Kingsmill was to me. My first book, a very bad one, was a Life of Kingsmill—a labor of love that was turned down by some fourteen publishers who insisted on returning it to me as if it were some tennis ball sent over to them for that purpose. Eventually it was accepted by that doyen of British publishing, Martin Secker, who allowed me an advance on royalties of £25 (what Kingsmill would have called more of a retreat than an advance). Kingsmill, however, remained as stubbornly unknown after the appearance of my book as he had been before it.

One of Kingsmill's closest friends had been Hesketh Pearson, whom I got to know during the writing of my biography. He became something of a father figure to me, generous, encouraging, fun. I learnt a good deal from Pearson about the organization of biographical narrative. He had been an actor—very good, it was said, when a part suited him and remarkably bad when it didn't. The same was true of his biographical performances, though he had more freedom to choose his subjects as a biographer. His style had been influenced by Bernard Shaw. It was assertive and had about it an air of epigrams. His pen portraits were done in primary colors, and it is only when you look closely that you can see the solidity of the underlying draftsmanship. It was Pearson who took me to my first productions of Shaw plays in London. But it is probably Kingsmill's attitude to G.B.S. that has been more influential.

I had hoped to intersperse novels with biographies, but my first attempt at a novel, *A Dog's Life*, was met by the threat of a libel action, and eventually the book was published only in the United States. This setback put an end to my career as a novelist, though I suspect I may have transferred some of the story-telling I wanted to try in novels to the narrative of what we call non-fiction.

No one would suggest that any of your earlier publications, Lytton Strachey *and* Augustus John *in particular, are "apprentice" works, yet if we bear in mind that we are looking ahead to your biography of Shaw, we can perhaps see them as preparing you for that task. Comment?*

Kingsmill had been labeled, in so far as he wrote biographies, as being a disciple of Lytton Strachey. I examined this categorization in my book on Kingsmill and grew interested in Strachey's writings. This set a pattern for the future, a minor character in one biography developing into the subject of my next biography—a process that sometimes gives the sensation that they are choosing me rather than the other way around. Augustus John played a small but significant part in *Lytton Strachey*; Bernard Shaw sat to Augustus John and even superintended John's painting of General Montgomery. All my subjects lived in approximately the same hundred-year span, and most of them met each other. But they each represented a different cultural and political philosophy: Kingsmill pure individualism; Strachey the beliefs of the Bloomsbury Group that were satirized by Shaw in *Heartbreak House*; Augustus John the anarchy of Bohemianism; and Shaw for the most part the radicalism of the Fabians. What I have been attempting to do in my biographies is to chart these cultural and political cross-currents in Britain from the middle of the last century to the middle of the twentieth century.

On to Shaw. You were commissioned by the Shaw Estate to write his biography. How did this come about? Had you any idea what you were letting yourself in for when you accepted the commission?

The invitation I received to write the authorized biography of Bernard Shaw came out of the blue. I did not know how I had been selected. In fact the decision to invite me was made by a committee chaired by Lord Wolfenden representing the three residuary legatees of the Shaw Estate (the British Museum, the National Gallery of Ireland, and the Royal Academy of Dramatic Art). I did not know the members of this committee, nor did I discover until recently that they had taken the advice of a distinguished biographer who had fortunately liked my *Lytton Strachey*.

I was terrified by the immensity of the task, though I knew I would never forgive myself if I were too cowardly to take it on. Up till then I had dealt with the families of my subjects (some of whom would beg me to think of another subject) rather than with committees. In my mid-thirties I felt I was growing respectable and even mature. Fortunately this proved not to be so—or not wholly so.

You were probably guided by personal interest in your choice of subject in the three biographies that preceded Shaw. *Did the fact that this was a commission and not perhaps your choice color your approach to the task, at least initially? In what ways, if at all, did you see the Shaw biography as complementing your Strachey and John biographies?*

One factor that attracted me to Shaw was that he appeared to fit into the pattern of my biographical subjects I have already described. I didn't find that he contradicted Strachey, but that he complemented him. Both wanted to change Victorian values, but they had different priorities of change. I also welcomed Shaw because I wanted to do something rather different from what I had already done.

Initially he mystified me. He appeared a mass of paradoxes that, while attracting great attention to himself, acted as a form of self-concealment. He was, for his time, startlingly informal, yet not often intimate with people: a shy trumpeter and drum-beater. He wrote of course with extraordinary brilliance, but did that brilliance not blind as well as illuminate? And how to interpret his jokes? His poetry lay within those jokes, but was he not taking jokes a little far by surrounding himself with so many humorless disciples, including some of his translators and biographers? Like other Irish writers, Beckett and Swift for example, he seemed a natural pessimist, dark and unrelenting, yet with a moral commitment to optimism and cheerfulness. He was lonely and gregarious, had highly sophisticated ideas, and went through a series of emotionally immature relationships. He was not, I believed, politically naïve—yet he had championed Stalin. He was surely not insensitive—yet he wrote benignly of Hitler and Mussolini. He presented himself as unappealingly asexual, yet a number of his beliefs were based, not on reason, but on a sexual instinct. He was man of unbribable integrity who compromised for reasons of assumed political pragmatism; a skillful and far-seeing campaigner for noble causes who regularly undermined his own campaigns. He was a natural individualist and an ideological collectivist, an embarrassment to England as well as to Ireland, a bloodless revolutionary, physically timid and sometimes curiously unenterprising, who advanced some of the most radical and heterodox ideas of the twentieth century. How was I to accommodate such a phenomenon, to find the man behind the superman? Could I discover a genuine working relationship with this strange and formidable "man of genius" with whom I was to spend some fifteen years? What I wanted was a partnership of integrity; some rhythm and style natural to myself that might match the pace and assertion of this spring-heeled marcher. The difficulty was that he appeared so dissimilar to myself (though appearances can of course be misleading). But I have never written about people who obviously resemble me (after lives of Strachey, John, and Shaw I remain clean-shaven, which I take as a symbol of my independence). Not having gone to a university, I look on my biographical subjects as my teachers. I knew that, however difficult I might find it, Shaw had a good deal to teach me. And he had.

You would have been well advanced in your research for the biography when you and Paul Levy produced The Genius of Shaw *in 1979. Your reasons for apparently interrupting yourself in this way?*

This is an awkward question to answer. Dan H. Laurence, as the greatest Shaw scholar in the world, had hoped to crown his career in Shaw studies by writing the authorized Life of G.B.S. He was extremely disappointed not to have been asked to write it. He had previously experienced difficulties with Max Reinhardt, the publisher of Shaw's Letters in Britain, and after my appointment as authorized biographer of Shaw, he quarreled with the Society of Authors, which acted as literary agent to the Shaw Estate. I had been chairman of the Society of Authors between 1973 and 1974, and it may have seemed from a distance that I occupied an inside track and had been granted the appointment as a favor. In fact I was invited to write the biography by the Shaw Estate in 1969 but was obliged to delay my start until 1975, when my *Augustus John* came out. The Society of Authors believed that when Dan and I met and talked together, everything would sort itself out. But regrettably this didn't happen. It may have been my fault—I had had no experience of academic scholars (even roving academic scholars unfettered by tenure) as colleagues before. I did not, I dare say, comprehend their concerns as well as I do now. I was told that the Shaw Estate did not want to load Dan Laurence with the biography on top of his Shaw bibliography, his four-volume edition of the Shaw letters, his work as adviser to the Estate, and his various other Shavian commitments. That smacked of a monopoly to them, and they preferred to risk inviting a new and younger writer to take on the job of the Shaw biography. It certainly was a risk, and it may have appeared as something of an insult to some fine Shaw scholars on the other side of the Atlantic. In any event, Dan Laurence resigned as editor of the Shaw Letters, and I was asked to hold my biography in abeyance until things were sorted out by the Shaw Estate. It was during that interval that I produced *The Genius of Shaw* (not co-edited with Paul Levy incidentally). Fortunately in due course Dan Laurence was persuaded to continue editing Shaw's letters.

Let's consider your basic research on the biography first. Would you tell us how you set about tackling—and containing—the life you were contending with?

The first thing I did was to go and live in the Rathmines district of Dublin. For the best part of two years I was within a mile or so of Synge Street, and I would also go walking near Torca Cottage at Dalkey. I sometimes worked at the National Library of Ireland, looked at pictures purchased by Shaw's money in the National Gallery of Ireland, and generally tried

to acclimatize myself to Shaw's early years. During this period I read
pretty well all Shaw's books and quite a number about him. All this
helped to prepare me for stage two—which was traveling to the great
manuscript collections in the United States and Britain. I wanted to ab-
sorb myself in Shaw's world so that I instinctively knew, when reading his
correspondence for example, what was of genuine significance. I constructed what must now seem a flint-age information retrieval system:
files of letters and excerpts from letters arranged alphabetically; a subject
index; a chronology (including an itinerary that is now lodged in the
British Library); files dedicated to individual plays and books; and something, over which I often lost my temper, called cross-referencing. These
were the poor accoutrements with which, like Don Quixote, I set out on
my quest.

In your "Double Preface" to the 1995 Noonday Books edition of Lytton Strachey
*(Farrar, Straus and Giroux) you speak appreciatively of the help you received from
most of Strachey's relatives and friends. Did you find the same co-operation when
gathering material on Shaw?*

The chief difference between writing *Bernard Shaw* and writing my earlier
biographies was that with G.B.S. I did not deal with families, but with
libraries. Almost all the manuscript material I needed to see was held in
public collections round the world, not in the attics and cellars of private
houses. The atmosphere in which I worked was therefore very different—less one of privilege, but more impersonal. I was unused to being
searched for guns and knives, to having my pens confiscated, to being
required to sign legal documents before I could examine manuscripts.
On the other hand the manuscripts I saw had been sorted and prepared
and were often beautifully presented, having been rescued from the ram-
shackle conditions with which I was familiar. I stepped from the amateur
world into the professional world. The experience was new to me. I
needed expert rather than personal help: and almost always I received
it.

*On to the writing and formulation of your ideas. Did you find the mountain of
secondary material on Shaw—the biographies, the half-biographies, the anecdot-
age, the unending stream of critical and interpretative works—a distraction? How
did you cope with it?*

The good books on Shaw were enormously valuable to me; the bad books
(of which there were many) a depressing distraction. But after a while I
became pretty quick at sorting out the good from the bad, and finding
what I needed. Later on I was amused to see that some critics, working
by precedent, described my use of works by Shaw scholars as being "derivative," while my departures from these works struck them as "unor-

thodox"; whereas other critics described the former passages as "well-researched" and the latter as "original."

Did you find Shaw's autobiographical writings a help or a hindrance? Was he a congenial "companion" during those solitary years of research and writing?

I found Shaw's autobiographical writings both a help *and* a hindrance. For a start they were composed with such a shimmer of confidence, such power of assertion and imaginative comedy, that it was extremely difficult not to copy down whole paragraphs and pages under the illusion that one had oneself grown brilliantly prolific. Testing to find where pain had been transmuted into entertainment, and retrospective adaptation shone more happily than actual experience, became a more complicated business and developed into part of the texture of my narrative.

It is sometimes alleged that Hesketh Pearson's *Bernard Shaw* is peculiarly valuable because G.B.S. grabbed Pearson's pen and wrote large sections of the book himself. The same might be said of Archibald Henderson's *Playboy and Prophet* and Frank Harris's *Bernard Shaw: An Unauthorised Biography*. I yield to no one in my liking for Pearson's biographies, but despite the oblique interest of Shaw's contributions done in Pearson's style, this Life is not among his best books. The fact is that Shaw was an awkward collaborator. He distrusted biography and interfered with his biographers' texts so as to turn the record of his lonely pilgrimage into a sociological history lesson, with his emotional deprivation converted into a financial balance sheet. He wanted his biographies to provide endorsement of his political beliefs, and he feared that if his background was seen as singularly wayward, and his birth as possibly illegitimate, then this might tend to invalidate his politics, and divert his political thinking eccentrically from the mainstream of the twentieth century. But by presenting himself as the immaculate child of his writings and becoming, as it were, the very author of himself, G.B.S. made himself appear curiously inhuman to modern readers. I saw part of my job as deconstructing the mythical G.B.S. and restoring to Shaw his humanity. As a young man in late Victorian England, he had called for the revolution in biographical writing that Lytton Strachey was later to begin with *Eminent Victorians*. But when in middle age Shaw became the subject of biographies himself, his attitude changed. "Reality" and the "inner life," he affected to believe, had "no place in individual portraits," and he overrode inner reality with dramatic stage effects, which nevertheless carry a subtext of reality. In 1911 he wrote that "when an autobiography does not agree with a biography, the biography is probably right and the autobiography wrong." I interpreted this as an appeal for a truthful posthumous biography, in so far as the truth can be captured, and did my best to write one. I did not want G.B.S. to reach back and do to me what he had done to many of my predecessors. But then I did not believe that the posthumous Shaw would want this either. We were collaborators of a different sort.

As a companion he was exhilarating, unsettling, inspiring, irritating, a mixture of wonderful directness and deviousness. Living with him, writing about him, probably changed my life—but perhaps I too changed his a little. I did not surrender to him, did not feel that I had opposed him. But I was often anxious over not being able to do it well enough. For my ambition was to find a good place for his Life in what I believe has been a golden age of biography.

Giving a public reading in the United States recently, I found I could not continue with my account of Shaw's death, but stood there silent for almost a minute clutching something sharp in my hand to bring myself under control. I thought afterwards how disgusted G.B.S. would have been with me; but then I reflected that he might perhaps have congratulated me on having raised the dramatic tension of the performance (which I certainly had). There were few things Shaw despised so much as sentimentality and persistent efforts to please. I think that even hostile critics would agree that I had avoided these.

The research and writing of my biography took far longer than I had calculated—or allowed myself to calculate. For many years I went into hibernation and lost contact with my readers. I remember feeling like a marathon runner who runs alone and does not know whether he is doing rather well or has left the course. I showed no one anything, but kept going until I was approximately three-quarters of the way through when my literary agent, his patience finally crumbling after ten years or so, demanded to see *something*.

At what stage did you decide on a tripartite division of the life and the themes of the three volumes—"The Search for Love," "The Pursuit of Power," and the "Lure of Fantasy"?

The three-part division gradually became clear as I worked but did not stare me in the face until I had reached about two-thirds of the way through the narrative. The subtitles of the three volumes were chosen by me, at my publisher's request, in 1988. They were intended to suggest, in a simple way, the dominant theme or subject matter of each volume. I did not, however, begin with, or work to, any thesis. I came with an open (some might say empty) mind and followed what I found to be the greatest current of energy and interest. Other biographers would very likely find other currents. That, it seems to me, is the nature of literary biography, which I think of as an invitation by the biographer to his or her subject to write one more book posthumously and in collaboration. If the collaboration works, then the reader may have something that transcends reductive criticism. I was surprised that critics did not pick up many points of reference, the "intertexuality"—my use of Fielding's *Tom Jones*, for example, and my reasons for using it.

Did you begin at the beginning and continue, volume by volume, methodically to the end, or work on each "division" of Shaw's life more or less simultaneously?

I began at the beginning (which happened to be Shaw's death) and went on, not always very methodically, to the end—and then beyond the end. I did attempt to report his death in 1934, but this was unavailing. Most of my experiments to get ahead of myself on some theme or subject were the results of anxiety and not very successful. I was sometimes obliged to destroy up to fifty pages and try another sequence of connections, like a chess player who finds a middle or endgame does not work after what seemed a promising beginning. I wanted to build a narrative structure rather like a brick wall, carrying along each line of chronology or theme until it came to a natural end, then working in parallel on another line of narrative until that also finished aesthetically. I then went over the completed narrative, amending, reducing, correcting, and I hope generally improving it. I did this several times. The published work is substantially different from the first draft.

Would you comment on the critical and public reaction to each volume in the U.K. and the U.S.A.?

Many reviewers were very generous about the book. In Britain there were, as I recall, two main objections: that Shaw was no longer regarded as a world-serious writer and did not therefore "deserve" such a long biography; that my advance on royalties had been "obscene" and I needed to be taken down a peg or two.

I had not realized how deeply disliked Shaw had become in Britain, how unfashionable his work now is. Some people assumed that I intended to write a work of propaganda that would raise Shaw's status and justify my investment of time on his biography. This was nicely balanced by devotees of G.B.S. elsewhere who thought I had been too hostile to him, especially early on. To be fired at from both extremes at the same time is somewhat bewildering and not wholly comfortable, but it may in the long run not be such a dishonorable position to occupy in connection with a writer who is still extremely controversial.

My advance on royalties for *Lytton Strachey* had been twice that I received for *Hugh Kingsmill*: in short, £50. No one remarked on it at the time. But the £625,000 I was offered by Chatto & Windus in 1987 took people's breath away. They reacted as if I were a lottery winner receiving an immense check. In fact I was being offered a middle-age pension which gave me security and reflected the fact that I had worked for ten years without any payment from Chatto. This money was to be spread over more than ten years (at the time of writing this I have not yet received it all). There can be no doubt that this bought me some unpopularity in Britain.

But none of this, so far as I am aware, troubled reviewers and readers in the United States or Canada, or anywhere else in the world. What did trouble some of them was my irony (the tone of someone writing in an old country that does not always translate well into younger cultures) and my lack of academic status. In the United States most leading biographers are academics; in Britain they are a maverick crew of self-employed writers. I comforted myself with the fact that Shaw himself had not been to a university, and hoped that the advantages would outweigh any shortcomings.

Then there was the unexpected and very short fourth volume, The Last Laugh. *Your justification for this?*

I had not planned *The Last Laugh,* but remembering Shaw's criticism to the effect that many plays ended just when they were getting really interesting, I was emboldened to add this financial postscript, bringing Shaw's affairs into contemporary times. This pendant to the main biography is mainly a satiric commentary on the late twentieth century, showing how the love of money, rather than its actual use, has become "the most important thing in the world." I liked to think that in investigating how his estate has been handled I was, as G.B.S. might have put it, "carrying on Shaw's business."

You came in for a lot of criticism, principally from Shaw scholars, for dispensing with the usual apparatus of research—footnotes and the citation of sources and so on. Do you think you have adequately silenced those critics with the publication of the Source Book?

I doubt it, though the irritation has probably become less inflamed by now. I have given my reasons for separating the critical apparatus from the narrative (I did not dispense with it). I can see that my initial withholding of the notes disconcerted some critics who wanted to know what items of information were "new," who felt that they would be expected to know this, and yet who could not quite be certain without a crib at the end. My reasons for introducing this system were essentially Shavian reasons, and the exasperation it produced on some reviewers very adequately recaptured the sort of irritation G.B.S. himself so often provoked. But Shaw scholars, it seemed to me, should be open to innovation, on the side of change, amenable to experiment, prejudiced in favor of what is new. Otherwise they have no business to be in Shavian territory at all.

"The line [the biographer] tries to follow points towards empathy without veering off into sentimentality and maintains a detachment that stops short of incompatibility." This (I need scarcely tell you) is part of your "credo" as biographer of Shaw, stated in the opening passage of the biography. Do you think in retrospect that you were in tune with Shaw's life and works throughout, in terms of this "credo"?

It seemed to some Shaw scholars that I was too detached from Shaw during his early life and only "won over" to him when he was quite old. I understand what they are saying, but this is not what actually happened. I did not change my attitude halfway through, and I do not now regard Shaw differently. I knew when I was writing that first volume what the tone of the last volume would be—that was part of the general strategy of the book. Some reviewers of the first two volumes predicted what the last volume would turn out to be. Not being quite right about this, they concluded that I had changed course. But I hadn't. There is, I hope, a feeling of evolution in the book; but there is no Road to Damascus.

Should you be asked to prepare a shortened revised edition of the biography, what, if anything, would you excise, revise, or alter? Is such an edition likely in the near future?

My contract requires me to write a one-volume condensation of the multivolume biography, and I am doing this now. I am working as I always work, which is to say I am working instinctively rather than to any preset formula or prescription. Of course I correct errors where I spot them; and I try to keep up with Shaw scholarship. I began this exercise quite tentatively, crossing out with regret some passages that had taken me so much trouble to construct. But now I have warmed to this work, and developed what is almost a lust for attacking the old text. I plan to go through it all four or five times before I get the final synthesis.

It's not conceivable that you have finished with Shaw or he with you. Would you tell us about your Shavian activities since publication of the last volume? Your campaign to get more of Shaw's money diverted to the British Library comes to mind; also your role as lecturer, speaker, and promoter (I avoid the word "apostle") of Shavianism round the world. And a final word on the state of Shaw studies in the U.K., on Shaw on stage in the U.K. in the mid-nineties?

What interests me most these days is the unpopular or neglected Shaw. I have lectured at the London School of Economics in London, and at Brown University, Rhode Island, on Shaw's communism. I have written a program essay on *Too True to Be Good* for the Shaw Festival Theatre at Niagara-on-the-Lake (of which I am an International Governor); and led a seminar at the Orange Tree Theatre at Richmond on Shaw's late plays during the run of Sam Walters's production of *The Simpleton of the Unex-*

pected Isles. I have also been involved in seminars on *Heartbreak House* and *Misalliance* at the American Repertory Theatre at Cambridge, Massachusetts, during the productions of those plays. In London, I organized a Shaw exhibition at the National Portrait Gallery (and lectured on Shaw's films there), and have spoken on G.B.S. on British Council tours abroad (I am just off to Barcelona University to represent Shaw at a celebration of Ireland's winners of the Nobel Prize for Literature). I also joined a band of desperadoes in Dublin campaigning for Shaw's birthplace to be made into a museum and (with less complete success) campaigned to have that part of Shaw's money which is taken by the British Museum diverted onto its proper course to the British Library (for which Shaw himself obviously intended it). Part of that campaign involved playing the part of Michael Holroyd opposite Sir Ian McKellen's Shaw in *Mister Shaw's Missing Millions* on National television. The latter was excellent, but the former I thought miscast—it needed Albert Finney to bring out the subtlety of the biographer's character. In addition to this, I have been instrumental in getting the first professional production of *The Philanderer* performed with its original last act. It was done at the Hampstead Theatre in London (and later at Niagara-on-the-Lake). I was involved too in beginning a Shaw summer school in Dublin and a Shaw Festival in Carlow.

Making an inventory of all this has rather appalled me. I have enjoyed doing such things because each one was something new, or something that needed to be done. But I do not intend to hang around repeating myself on G.B.S. until, a gnarled and fossilized creature, I become a figure of pity and ridicule. Knowing when to shut up is a considerable accomplishment, and one not always mastered by G.B.S. himself. For fear of becoming a monster bore I have refused invitations to Shaw events, explaining truthfully that I have little new to say and must move on elsewhere.

There is one thing I would like to achieve on behalf of Shaw, and that is to help raise the level of Shaw productions in the United Kingdom to that I have seen at the Shaw Festival Theatre at Niagara-on-the-Lake and at the American Repertory Theatre at Cambridge, Massachusetts. We do not need in London more performances of *Pygmalion* and *Saint Joan*. At the very least we should see *Jitta's Atonement*. But what we really need is a genuinely dramatic (and dramatically cut) *Back to Methuselah* directed by that most "operatic" man of the stage, Richard Jones, at the Royal National Theatre. I hope the new Artistic Director of the National, Trevor Nunn, will someday do this. But: How long, O Lord, how long?

Jeffrey M. Wallmann

SEE NO EVIL, HEAR NO EVIL, SPEAK NO EVIL: THE ALIENATION FACTORS IN SHAW'S DRAMAS

In the concluding speech of *Too True to Be Good,* Shaw's protagonist Aubrey confesses to the strong disillusionment felt by the author: "I am ignorant: I have lost my nerve and am intimidated: all I know is that I must find the way of life, for myself and all of us, or we shall surely perish."[1] Indeed, throughout *Too True to Be Good* the autobiographical note is unmistakable as Shaw expresses his own bitterness and anguish over the brutal insanities of World War I and the subsequent follies of the Geneva negotiations. When Aubrey says, "I am by nature and destiny a preacher," it is Shaw speaking of his own ministry from the pulpit of the stage. "But I have no Bible, no creed: the war has shot both out of my hands" (4: 719).

Millions are said to be like Shaw, suffering from an alienation born of despair and acting it out by their indifference or hostility toward others or toward society's institutions, workings, and goals. Understandably, the term has grown quite popular. Important in the writings of many whose ideas have had great influence—Marx, Hegel, Fromm, Camus, Sartre, to name a few—"alienation" has been employed in connection with a broad spectrum of major problems and issues. Reference has constantly been made to it in respect to the compartmentalization of our lives, the stunting of our personalities, the "death of God," the loss of meaningfulness in life, and the growth of neurotic behavior and superficiality in our relationships. There is scarcely an aspect of human existence that has not been linked, openly or by implication, to "alienation."

Yet although there is no single general meaning of "alienation," most writers have tended to define it in one specific way or another in their work. Not so Shaw. Woven suggestively throughout his dramas, "alienation" is used by Shaw in several different senses, ranging from our loss of independence to our involvement in labor that is devoid of any originality, spontaneity, or creativity. The phenomenon that concerns Shaw most, however, is the dehumanization of mankind, most frequently in the contexts of our relation to society, to others, and to our essence, our own true nature. That mankind has an essence or true nature is, of course, the assumption underlying Shaw's argument for the existence and purpose of a Life Force.

Perhaps what comes to mind most often when we hear of alienation is the estrangement of certain groups and individuals from the society in which they live. Shaw, however, characteristically dramatizes alienation as estrangement *in* society rather than *from* it, portraying society—that is, the social, economic, political, and cultural order—as so structured that it tends to make individuals alienated in various ways. In this, Shaw was clearly influenced by Marx, who stated that "The alienation of the worker in his product means not only that his labor becomes an object, an external existence. . . . [It] means that the life which he has conferred on the object confronts him as something hostile and alien."[2] And like a brilliant prosecuting attorney, Shaw puts Victorian capitalism into the witness box, making it confess to the avarice, cruelty, deception, hypocrisy, thievery, and waste of talent and lives that lie behind its accumulation of wealth.

Thus in *Widowers' Houses,* Shaw presents a classic portrayal of the abuses of private ownership of property. He attacks the rationales of exploiters and collectors of rent in the excuses given by the miserly-minded, money-obsessed agent Lickcheese: "Look at that bag of money on the table. Hardly a penny of that but there was a hungry child crying for the bread it would have bought. But I got it from him—screwed and worried and bullied it out of them. I—look here, gentlemen: I'm pretty seasoned to the work; but theres money there that I couldnt have taken if it hadnt been for the thought of my own children depending on me for giving him satisfaction" (4: 522). Lickcheese fits Marx's comment that since money appears to command everything, it is the master of everybody.

Granted, at times Shaw allows individuals to win out over intimidation by the social order. For example, self-confidence overcomes intimidation in such plays as *Captain Brassbound's Conversion, Caesar and Cleopatra,* and in particular *Pygmalion.* First Alfred Doolittle announces he can no longer assert his will and be happily and "undeservingly" poor because he is "intimidated," fearful of a life he has not chosen. Then Liza is intimidated by Higgins who, representing society, pressures her into becoming a socially acceptable lady. She comes fully alive, however, only when she at last asserts her individuality and engages Higgins in a contest of wills.

More often, Shaw portrays his characters as in *Back to Methuselah*, where they are helpless amid cultural complexities, emmeshed in an unfathomable economic system, and exploited by the few who control the levers of finance and politics. In Don Juan's opinion, for example, in *Man and Superman*, although man was devising war machines by which to murder his fellows, man had already devised machines of greed by which those on top had been grinding those below into poverty and suffering. In *The Man of Destiny*, Napoleon rules by ruling his subjects' imaginations. Julius Caesar in *Caesar and Cleopatra* and King Magnus of *The Apple Cart* inspire disorganization and awe in those opposing them by the sheer dint of their personalities. In "The Revolutionist's Handbook," Shaw asserts that the "ministers" of "democratic republics" are "experts in the art of dodging popular enthusiasms and duping popular ignorance" (3: 704). In *Major Barbara*, the elite keep power through violence: "the ballot paper that really governs is the paper that has a bullet wrapped up in it (1: 436). No matter the method, however, as Shaw makes clear in his preface to *Misalliance*, "What corrupts civilization, religion, law, and convention (and they are at present pretty nearly as corrupt as they dare) is the constant attempts made by the wills of individuals and classes to thwart the wills and enslave the powers of other individuals and classes" (4: 64).

Whether in works by Shaw or by anyone else dating all the way back to Wolfram von Eschenbach's *Parzival* in the twelfth century, intimidating someone to accept social proscriptions at the expense of individual will produces in the person an alienation known traditionally as the Waste Land. More specifically, the Waste Land is where force and not love, indoctrination and not education, authority and not experience prevail in the ordering of lives and where the laws and duties and rituals are consequently unrelated to the actual inward realizations, needs, and potentialities of those upon whom they are imposed.

When intimidation is combined with the exploitation or opposition of individuals or groups, the resultant alienation appears as a synonym for a feeling of bitterness or apathy. Shaw in this regard is right on target when he portrays the poor, especially the working poor, as allowing themselves to be robbed blind and kept from power out of detached indifference. "[T]he pious citizen who would like to be a better man goes on behaving just as he did before," Shaw declares in "The Revolutionist's Handbook," "And the tramp who would like the million does not take the trouble to earn ten shillings . . ." (3:709). "[I]t is for the poor to repudiate poverty when they have had enough of it," Shaw remarks caustically in the preface to *Major Barbara* (1:310). In *Heartbreak House*, Hector Hushabye is an apathetic lover and husband, drifting vacuous and discontented "like a damned soul in hell" (1:563). Early on he breaks the heart of Ellie Dunn, who grows increasingly disenchanted as other illusions are stripped away—Boss Mangan's money is as ephemeral as Hector's romantic lies; Captain Shotover's supposed wisdom is mainly fumes out of a rum bottle—until she is left naked and vunerable to reality, eluding utter despair only by envisioning an Armageddon of bombs.

Moreover, the tyranny that money holds over the agents and victims of capitalism is also a tyranny over those who out of decency and compassion attempt to better society. The essence of *Major Barbara* is the argument that civilized idealism cannot influence the world of violent free enterprise: at play's end, both Cusins and Barbara agree to compromise with power beyond their control, finding it easier to preach to the comfortably converted and sell armaments to national governments than to sell either product to the poor. Trevor Whittock finds that "One implication is that Barbara's faith rested on shaky foundations because it assumed that spiritual welfare could be separated from the material consequences of life. . . . No faith can be sustained which ignores the basic conditions of survival."[3]

Nor are the well-intentioned and the poor, working or not, alone in suffering alienation. Shaw takes the position expressed by Marx that the rich capitalist "knows the realization of the essential powers of man only as the realization of his own excesses, his whims and capricious, bizarre notions" (156). Capitalists, then, especially those in the upper brackets of ownership or management, are estranged from rivals as well as from their labor force. Thus, in *Heartbreak House*, Shaw portrays Boss Mangan as a vindictive exploiter and warmonger who skirts insanity when he discovers that he is impoverished. And Andrew Undershaft, despite mitigating nuances in his character, worships wealth and believes that honor, justice, and truth are "the graces and luxuries of a rich, strong, and safe life" (1:385). To Shaw, a life based on the good of money alienates a human being from being human; whatever crimes Mangan, Undershaft, and other capitalist rogues may have committed, the far greater crime is that which robbed them of their humanity. Shaw could never accept the existentialist answer that the "criminal" was only a response to the "absurdity" or inherent "cruelty" of life. The problem was a socio-economic one, and he sought a socio-economic answer, although for Shaw—as for Marx—the overcoming of alienation does not involve the achievement of unity with society.

Although as a socialist Shaw saw a need to subordinate personal behavior to public order, he nonetheless feared suppression of valuable impulses by the "artificial system of morality" infinitely more than license and chaos. He also implies in his plays a distinction between decisions that disregard human considerations and decisions whose "spill-over" outcomes carry in themselves a de facto disregard for human considerations. Cruelty caused by the latter, he believes, is the consequence of ignorance. For example, in "The Revolutionist's Handbook" Shaw repeatedly claims that a democratic majority is simply a majority of ignorance and passion: "Now we have yet to see the man who, having any practical experience of Proletarian Democracy, has any belief in its capacity for solving great political problems, or even for doing ordinary parochial work intelligently and economically" (3:704). "[T]o hand the country over to riff-raff is national suicide, since riff-raff can neither govern nor will let anyone else govern except the highest bidder of bread and circuses. There is no public enthusiast alive of twenty years' practical democratic experience who believes in the political adequacy of the electorate or of the bodies it elects" (3:728). Of course, the result is politicians like the one described in Part 3 of *Back to Methuselah* as elected to the House of Commons: "He was released from the County Lunatic Asylum a fortnight ago. Not mad enough for the lethal chamber: not sane enough for any place but the division lobby. A very popular speaker" (2:95).

However, Shaw suggests that the political institution of the state makes harmful decisions on purpose, imposing laws and duties that result not in our betterment as claimed, but in keeping the powerful in power and corrupting the free development of our selves. To illustrate, laws in *The Sanity of Art* are portrayed as moral crutches, to which we cling long after they have become archaic hindrances and that prevent us from thinking or acting on our own. Duty is a similar deception, a similar refuge. In *The Devil's Disciple,* Major Swindon wants to do his duty although his duty involves a lethal travesty of justice. Judith tries to do her perceived duty of clearing up Dudgeon's mistaken identity, but in the process acts according to her romantic illusions rather than her personal convictions. As Don Juan says in *Man and Superman,* "Hell is the home of honor, duty, justice, and the rest of the seven deadly virtues" (3:604).

Additionally, Shaw condemns as malevolent institutions such socially ensconsed big businesses as education, medicine, and science. Indeed, insofar as an established educational system is concerned, Shaw would likely agree with Ralf Dahrendorf that the production and distribution of knowledge may not be indispensable.[4] In the preface to *Misalliance,* for instance, Shaw charges that schools are prisons meant to keep children from annoying their parents and that instructors are sadists who teach out of the desire to beat their pupils. As well, the play itself satirizes class education under capitalism. Gunner, attempting to assassinate the capitalist Tarleton, admits that his melodramatic ways derive from reading lurid novels in the public library and learns from Tarleton that his mother's affair with Tarleton was not her ruination but her salvation.

To digress from his dramas, Shaw probably put his opinion of state

education best in an early novel, *The Irrational Knot,* wherein the protagonist Conolly indicts British schooling: "But what you call her education,
as far as I can make out, appears to have consisted of stuffing her with
lies, and making it a point of honour with her to believe them in spite of
sense and reason. The sense of duty that rises on that sort of foundation
is more mischievous than downright want of principle. I don't dispute
your right, you who constitute polite society, to skin over all the ugly facts
of life. But to make your daughters believe that the skin covers healthy
flesh is a crime."[5]

As for medicine, virtually the entirety of *The Doctor's Dilemma,* including
the preface, castigates the medical profession as having a vested interest
in ill health, with doctors grubbing for profit by operating unnecessarily,
diagnosing fashionable diseases, prescribing expensive cures that do not
cure, and forming associations solely to conceal medical malpractice. Science fares even worse although Shaw seems to distinguish somewhat between accidental problems created by developing technology and
predictable disasters caused by calculated actions. For example, new energy sources can ease human toil, yet in some areas have impact on
human health. Shaw rages against such problems, real or fancied, and
scolds the scientific and technological community for presuming objectivity and authority and for experimenting brutally on hapless animals. The
alienating effect arises, inevitably if unintentionally, from scientific ad-
vances dislocating what had once been a stable universe: "All is caprice;
the calculable world has become incalculable" (*Too True* 4:695). No doubt
Shaw would have joined Robert Nisbet in counseling scientists not to "ad-
vise governments, save mankind, make public policy or build empires,"
but instead to restrict themselves to the "search for truth."[6]

Shaw lobs his most vitriolic volleys at the conscious misuse of science
and technology, particularly for purposes of warfare. *The Man of Destiny*
and *Arms and the Man* ridicule the illusionary romance of war and the
irrationality of duty and honor amid the grisly horror of battle. In *Man
and Superman* and the preface to *John Bull's Other Island,* Shaw describes
the depths of terror and violence into which England and Europe were
sinking, and in *Major Barbara* he exposes the dangers of international
arms manufacturing—along with the message that just as munitions slay
thousands, so capitalist industry as a whole starves, cripples, and kills millions. Just as *Major Barbara's* weapons-merchant Andrew Undershaft influences the government for his own gain, so all plutocrats manipulate
the body politic in order to keep the profitable secrets of modern science
carefully guarded from all but the sufferers themselves. In *Heartbreak
House,* war is shown as maintained by lying to the civilian population,
thereby making journalism highly profitable. Yet equally infuriating to
Shaw is the inability of the home front to grasp war's awful reality—a

clear alienation. The last act closes with bombs falling on an oblivious England, bombs from so high above that the enemy is estranged from the consequences, alienated from the havoc and death that the bombs wreak.

Similarly, Shaw denounces the social institution of marriage, gleefully charting the ills and weaknesses of wedded bliss. "Shaw's criticism of our marriage laws is so radical and so well known, that it obscures the meaning of the many delightful marriages glimpsed in his plays," notes feminist critic Barbara Bellow Watson, adding, "When Shaw does treat marriage as a happy ending, that is not with a view to personal happiness, but as a reminder of the supra-personal meaning with which he endows even the most fragile flirtation."[7] Arnold Silver concurs: "A cosmic Life Force has to be invoked to explain marriage and to obscure thereby the individual's own responsibility for his marital fate."[8] Still, Shaw is not beyond excoriating marriage and, as Watson points out, linking marriage to Marxist philosophy. "Under capitalism, marriage means economic slavery for the dependent woman. . . . In *Getting Married* Shaw's indictment of marriage is consolidated, and the various ways in which marriage can become slavery are both dramatized and described" (208).

Sometimes Shaw exposes the moral hypocrisy of marriage and similar social institutions by comparing them with more odious alternatives. In *Major Barbara* and *Widowers' Houses*, he uses reproachful occupations to dramatize his points, and in *Mrs Warren's Profession* he uses prostitution for more than simply to assail marriage although, according to Watson, "the parallel between marriage and prostitution has a historical foundation in the venerable custom of buying wives and shows itself in our own times in the demand for virginity in brides and absolute fidelity in wives" (208). Shaw goes on to use prostitution in a three-pronged attack. First, that although Victorians regard prostitutes as social abominations, their moral virtue by itself is a feeble consolation lacking any real influence in the world. Second, by pointing sarcastically to prostitution and the sheer physical sex act as the "facts" of love, Shaw suggests that capitalist society erodes the mutual growth, aid, and affectionate understanding that should accompany sex—obviously implying estrangement within even the closest relationships. Third, that so far as the ruling classes are concerned, there is no difference between a brothel and a sweatshop as long as the profits are sufficient and the owners are absent from the scene of the degradation. As Shaw states in his preface to *The Three Unpleasant Plays*, "At present we not only condemn women as a sex to attach themselves to breadwinners, licitly or illicitly, on pain of heavy privation and disadvantage; but we have great prostitute classes of men: for instance, the playwrights and journalists, to whom I myself belong, not to mention the legions of lawyers, doctors, clergymen, and platform politicians who

are daily using their highest faculties to belie their real sentiments . . ."
(3:xxviii).

In Shaw's world, others besides prostitutes experience social alienation
because they belong to a particular group. For instance, since he views
religion as functioning to smooth over conditions that should be acknowledged and resisted—"the opiate of the people," in Marx's words—devout
believers are often characterized as alienated from other groups or from
society in general, until and unless they have a "conversion" to reality.
"Beware of the man whose god is in the skies," Shaw cautions in "The
Revolutionist's Handbook" (3:737). So, as martyrdom grows nearer for
Lavinia in *Androcles and the Lion,* her Christian faith dissipates until she
no longer believes, and she realizes like Dick Dudgeon that she must die
for no reason at all. Barbara in *Major Barbara* may think that she can cure
people's souls, but she knows that she cannot cure their poverty, which
Christianity serves to perpetuate. In the final crisis, reality as usual wins
over idealism, economics over theology, capitalism over Christianity.
Saint Joan is a "costly but noble tension," according to critic Richard Gilman, "between Church and State and between their institutional necessi-
ties and those of the individual."[9] In mounting this struggle between
individualism and the state, as portrayed by a petrified theocracy that
controls Joan's society, Shaw is able to expose the core of the Waste Land
of the modern soul, the epitome of alienation. Believers estranged from
their faith, from their God or gods, experience a sense of desolation, first
in the loss of identification with any spiritually compelling group and,
second, in a loss of a dimension of experience or a sense of being that is
any more awesome than provided by society at large. But Joan does not
buckle to the Church, her will resolute to the end: "If you command me
to declare that all that I have done and said, and all the visions and revelations I have had, were not from God, then that is impossible: I will not
declare it for anything in the world. . . . And in case The Church should
bid me do anything contrary to the command I have from God, I will not
consent to it, no matter what it may be" (2:399).

Although appalled, theologians and believers have been hard pressed
to deny the alienation suggested by such dramatizations. Originally, Ju-
daism and Christianity challenged the faithful to estrange themselves
from nature, society, and themselves. According to the Old Testament,
Hebrews were not supposed to be "like all the nations" but a people
apart, without even a sense of community to compensate them for their
alienation from other nations; rather, instead of an idealized community,
the Hebrew Bible provides a succession of imposing leaders—Moses, Eli-
jah, Amos, Hosea, Jeremiah—who are themselves strangers among their
own, even while reminding the people that they should be separate and
distinct. In primitive Christianity, the feeling was widespread that nature

was the enemy, sex was evil, the body was a prison, and this world belonged to the devil. Indeed, Paul offered the classical formulation of religious alienation: "I do not understand my own actions. For I do not do
what I want, but I do the very thing I hate" (Romans 7:15).

Very few persons are caused anguish when recognizing that they are
entities separate from all others. Indeed, most philosophers and psychol-
ogists believe that such awareness is a healthy process that supposedly
occurs "automatically" in the course of human development. Shaw, however, agrees more with Erich Fromm's contention that relations between
men, particularily modern men, have the "character of alienation" in that
"instead of relations between human beings, they assume the character
of relations between things."[10] This parallels the Marxist concept that
alienation in our "human" or social life causes us to risk losing the potential to grow through and discover ourselves in it. Instead, we tend to
experience ourselves as abstractions, according to Fromm, the self
"merely the subjective disguise for the objective social function of man in
society" (118, 117). Indeed, the seeds of estrangement are inherent in
every relationship because "The phenomenon of alienation" is an "effect
of Capitalism on personality."[11]

Not surprisingly, considering Shaw's abhorrence of capitalism, the general drift of his dramas is that the more personal the relationship, the
more delusional and destructive the resultant alienation. In *Candida*, Reverend Morell is convinced that his wife cannot love him because she does
not love him for the right reasons—his right reasons—and spends the
play tormented and degraded by suspicion until, at the climax, he demands that she choose between his supposed rival Marchbanks and himself. The dopey Ferrovius in *Androcles and the Lion* and the much deeper
Captain Shotover in *Heartbreak House*, albeit very dissimilar characters,
are each in his own way self-righteous, self-deluding men of precarious
self-control, with the treacherous habit of perceiving what they choose in
exterior reality. The theme of deception dominates *Man and Superman*.
Don Juan terms Hell the "Palace of Lies," the "home of the unreal,"
where "you call your appearance beauty, your emotions love, your sentiments heroism, your aspirations virtue, just as you did on earth; but here
there are no hard facts to contradict you, no ironic contrast of your needs
with your pretensions, no human comedy, nothing but a perpetual romance, a universal melodrama" (3:616–17).

As well, Shaw sees the impatience of children to be on their own as a
vast rift between them and their parents. He has a point. According to
one historian of student movements, "alienation was the chief slogan-
word of the protesting students in America, Japan, and Russia."[12] Shaw
in the preface to *Misalliance* blames such alienation on the capitalist system in which a child "cannot realize its parent's humanity," cannot con-

ceive of its parents' "having had youth, passions, and weaknesses, or as
still growing, yearning, suffering, and learning" (4:81). As evidence,
Shaw presents a number of children, such as Vivie Warren, Gloria Clandon, and Ann Whitefield, blithely ignoring their mothers, who are usually shocked and discouraged by the behavior of their offspring. In *The
Irrational Knot,* they have nobody to blame except themselves: "If she had
been taught the truth in her own childhood, she would know how to face
it, and would be a strong woman as well as an amiable one. But it is too
late now. The truth seems natural to a child; but to a grown woman or
man, it is a bitter lesson in the learning . . ." (253).

The absence of active concern does not entail the adoption of an exploitive orientation toward others. The latter constitutes yet another distinct relation, that of one regarding others as things or instruments to be
used for one's own selfish gains. In Shaw's dramas, some of the women
characters are nice, at least some of the time, but when they are bad,
heroines in particular are the personification of predators using others
as a means to personal ends. Such women are at times in a battle but
always on the hunt, for while men seek freedom, they seek the mate most
suitable for providing for their future children. As Silver puts it, "Shaw
has now to insist—in plot, characterization, and preachment—on the
woman as ruthless aggressor and the man as helpless victim" (142). Desmond MacCarthy quotes Shaw when arguing that Ann "is a bully and a
liar and by 'unscrupulously using her personal fascinations to make men
give her what she wants,' she is also 'something for which there is no
polite name.' [Tanner] knows that she will think his aspirations and efforts to reform society absurd and thwart him in so far as she dares in the
interests of the family."[13]

Shaw's battle of the sexes ranges from duels of witticisms between, say,
Magnus and Orinthia or Leonard Charteris and his women, to active
pursuits, such as when Hypatia Tarleton chases Joey Percival up a hill
and he chases her back down. When gloves come off, however, Shaw's
ladies tend to catch their men by using cunning and deceit, baited with
beauty. In *Widowers' Houses,* Blanche Sartorius craftily acts innocent until,
pretending wounded pride, she maneuvers her victim, Harry Trench, a
doctor no less, into an embrace that is discovered by his friend Cokane
and her outwardly respectable father. The dentist Valentine in *You Never
Can Tell* is a philanderer avoiding marriage until he meets Gloria Clandon, who refuses conventional seduction. She is a "twentieth-century"
girl who lives by reason and eschews emotion—or so she makes it appear,
as she weaves Valentine into capturing himself in as devious a net as a
black widow spider's web. Frequently love is the lure: "On the subject of
that late-flowering luxury called love," Watson observes, "Shaw maintains

his respect for the mysteries, subtleties and inconsistencies which remain even after the last reasonable word has been said" (209).

Clearly, what respect Shaw has for love is not extended to the sweet sentiments, pious professions, and dainty coy charms that were eagerly sought and cherished by infatuated males, as was the wont of late Victorian romances. Shaw respects in the sense that one respects rattlesnakes. His women charm, certainly, but by the same means that carnivores attract their quarry, with a ruse of witless innocence for protective coloring. According to Watson, "Above all, he grants sexual freedom to women on absolutely equal terms, his feminine 'varietists' being, if anything, more at ease with themselves and more delightful to others than the philandering men" (209). And no wonder; as Watson points out, more often than not the snare is sex. "The Shavian woman outrages the 'womanly' idea further by being the aggressor in sex. . . . [Shaw] endows his huntress with tact, wit, personal charm, and a strong sense of her own individuality, instead of making her the ferocious woman more timid authors imagine" (205).

The running of quarry to earth is less a conscious act than an instinctual drive. For Watson, "In the woman who interests Shaw, the woman who is a vital genius, even unscrupulous or promiscuous behavior is interpreted as the working of the evolutionary appetite through the promptings of her unconscious self" (205). This leads, of course, to plot-entangling confusions and misunderstandings, and to despairing laments like the outcry by *Heartbreak House*'s Hesione Hushabye: "Why are they not satisfied? Why do they envy us the pain with which we bring them into the world, and make strange dangers and torments for themselves to be even with us?" (1:529).

More importantly, whether the combatants are aware of it or not, their relationship demands a surrender of individuality to the Life Force, which "subdues man to its purpose, and thereby moves the race to its next higher level."[14] In *Man and Superman*, for instance, John Tanner is warned of his fate in time to bolt across Europe, but Ann Whitefield tracks him remorselessly to Granada, where he goes down "fighting for my freedom, for my honor, for my self, one and indivisible" (3:683). Intuitively Tanner realizes that in marriage he cannot remain himself, "one and indivisible." But neither of them can, as MacCarthy notes: "Both Ann and Tanner, in submitting to their attraction for each other, become servants of the will of the world. They are the instruments towards creating the superior race of the future—ultimately the Superman" (33).

Although Shaw does write of struggles continuing after the marriage, Watson notes that generally he has the husband "compelled to sacrifice his inclinations and even his principles when they are in conflict with his obligations to his wife and children" (208). For Silver, "If the woman decides on motherhood . . . the man must accommodate her. If she chooses not to be a mother, the choice also is hers, imposed on her by the Life Force" (129). For the most part, successful marriages are dramatized as having sexual fires banked, no longer driving the couple berserk with uncontrollable urges—an image derived, Silver contends, from Shaw's own celibate marriage. Surely that would help explain the Hushabyes' speaking nostalgically if not desirously of long-gone passions:

> HECTOR. That was a confounded madness. I cant believe that such an amazing experience is common. It has left its mark on me. I believe that is why I have never been able to repeat it.
> HESIONE [*laughing and caressing his arm*] We were frightfully in love with one another, Hector. It was such an enchanting dream that I have never been able to grudge it to you or anyone else since. I have invited all sorts of pretty women to the house on the chance of giving you another turn. But it has never come off. (1:524)

The surrender of individuality and subsequent cessation of sexual passion might well be termed a Waste Land alienation in its most intimate form. At the end of *Captain Brassbound's Conversion,* Brassbound gazes yearningly at Lady Cicely Wayneflete and asks whether she is in love with another man:

> LADY CICELY [*shaking her head*] I have never been in love with any real person; and I never shall. How could I manage people if I had that mad little bit of myself left in me? Thats my secret.
> BRASSBOUND. Then throw away the last bit of self. Marry me.
> LADY CICELY [*vainly struggling to recall her wandering will*] Must I? (1:686–87).

For those like Shaw who believe that we have an essence, a true self, it follows that we are engendered by the distortions of life in an exploitive society. The self-alienation that results differs from class consciousness, however, or the knowing by the exploited of how and by whom they are exploited. It is instead a psychological conflict, an internal incapacity to determine whether we create our own acts or are driven by forces separate from ourselves. And to the extent that we cannot distinguish between actions that we think are our own and those we think are due to outside pressure, we impoverish ourselves. Self-delusion, then, is one form of self-alienation.

For Shaw, such alienation is best opposed through knowledge and self-awareness. In the preface of *Major Barbara,* he concludes, "If a man cannot look evil in the face without illusion, he will never know what it really is, or combat it effectually" (1:338). His dramatic remedy consists mainly of stripping away the illusions—Trench's illusions in *Widowers' Houses* about the innocence of interest, the Petkoffs' in *Arms and the Man* about war, Morell's in *Candida* about women and marriage, and so on—by taking, Ronald Peacock notes, "an unconventional character, a person with the gift of insight and freedom," and impinging it "upon a group of conventional social animals, and the impact reveals at every turn stock notions and reactions, prejudices and dishonesties, in short the illusionary, the unreal, the irrational."[15] Shaw finds, alas, that what is wrong with mankind is stupidity: "Stupidity made sordid and cruel by the realities learnt from toil and poverty: Imagination resolved to starve sooner than face these realities," Don Juan argues in *Man and Superman* (3:618). Indeed, Shaw himself decries in the preface to *Too True to Be Good* that the ignorance of audiences and critics is so deep and so lulling that they adamantly resist enlightenment "as if I had hit them in some new and unbearably sore spot" (4:609), and despairs even more in "The Revolutionist's Handbook" that ". . . Man will return to his idols and his cupidities, in spite of all 'movements' and all revolutions," so "We must therefore frankly give up the notion that Man as he exists is capable of net progress" (3:712–13).

Undeterred, however, Shaw campaigns against deception, especially of oneself. He does so, according to John F. Matthews, "by revealing through action the contrast between appearance and reality."[16] One of the triumphal achievements of his plays is his penetration into internal or subjective life, exploring the psychologies shaped by the transformations of social life and the problems and dilemmas that they have brought forth. Characteristic of his writing is his stubborn fidelity to reality—or rather, his view of reality—and part of this discovered reality is the delusions that alienate humanity. It is one of the themes of a host of dramatic works. *The Devil's Disciple,* for instance, presents a classic portrayal of delusion. Although invading British troops arrest Dick Dudgeon by mistake, Major Swindon considers hanging him anyway. Dudgeon, in a fit of honor, refuses to imperil the real rebel's life by talking. The rebel minister's wife, Judith, naïvely believes that Dudgeon is motivated by love for her. Eventually Dudgeon sees that he is deceiving himself as the commander is deceiving himself and Judith is deceiving herself, and he confesses to her that his sacrifice is not for love, but for nothing at all—a rather existential view.

Yet Shaw is not existentialist. The plots of his plays usually revolve around the sort of extreme situations preferred by existentialists, and his protagonists often do compromise their private values as existentialist heroes do. However, existentialists find that the fact of death makes the reality of life "absurd," leaving individuals lonely and impotent in the face of an implacably hostile or indifferent universe. Unable to accept the concept of a mindless and meaningless universe, Shaw assumes that it has order, reason, coherency, and a mysterious primal urge he calls the Life Force that guides evolution ever upward. To move from our present stage of ignorance to an ultimate condition of knowledge involves discarding dead, unreal conventions, in particular repudiating romantic love and renouncing the idea of duties—as one of the maxims in "The Revolutionist's Handbook" states, "The golden rule is that there are no golden rules" (3:731). Thus, the ideological struggle for progress is not an existentialist struggle of one form of alienation against another, but a struggle of humanization against alienation.

A step in humanization is a discovery of truth. Hence, the disillusionment that many of Shaw's characters undergo leads occasionally to death or to surrender of the future, but most often to shedding of obsolete attitudes and the subsequent ascent to a clearer vision of reality. As such, the heroic model is Dick Dudgeon, who knows what he wants and wills his way to it. He reappears in a more villainous form as Andrew Undershaft, the incarnation of self-expression rather than self-suppression, the image of the Life Force in action.

Perhaps the more important self-alienation, at least to Shaw, is the disparity between one's actual condition and one's essential or true nature. This ideal essence is embodied in Shaw's Superman, which John Simon asserts is attained through "the power of creative evolution . . . and willed longevity, gradually leading toward immortality, a mankind that has learned how to harness the Life Force."[17] Creative evolution is unavoidable, inexorable, lifting us like it or not, but it also is Lamarckian in that through our own learning and striving, our acquired characteristics can be inherited. So alienation from oneself may be construed in terms of a disparity between the way we are and the way we should be along our evolutionary climb.

This is the sense of the Life Force implicit in Shaw's dramas and his "fundamental issue," according to Whittock, "that men must move forward with the movement of life itself, serving with their creative energy that ultimate Creative Energy which makes what will be" (14). This struggle toward a spiritualized and immortal being is not original with Shaw, however. Friedrich Schiller held that every individual carries within himself an ideal man and that it is his life's task to be in harmony with this ideal.[18] More than two millennia earlier, Heraclitus of Ephesus said, "I sought myself," which Walter Kaufmann interprets as marking alienation: "The prime source of any feeling of futility, frustration, and anxiety lies in the self."[19] Nevertheless, to the extent that we can consciously strive, can willfully counter the suppressions and inhibitions imposed by society, we are accountable for failures to be the self we should be and, thus, for our unhealed separation from our true self. Indeed, having to seek oneself or to become oneself obviously implies the possibility of not finding or not becoming oneself, of remaining a stranger to oneself—self-alienation. Shaw's ultimate expression of alienation from oneself is in the third act of *Man and Superman,* insofar as it can be interpreted symbolically: Hell is the condition of the soul resulting from living out one's lies; such alienation from one's true self is the only true death.

If rebellion against the establishment were a sign of alienation, Shaw would have to be considered a paradigm of alienation. Shaw's dramas embrace not only the awareness of alienation in society, but increasingly the expression of his own alienation. Behind his expression of alienation lay a deepening subjectivism, Shaw becoming more absorbed in his internal or subjective life, especially after the outbreak of World War I. His "unpleasant" plays in particular often poignantly reveal his own longings, fears, and frustrations, while his outer-world outlook reveals what he is estranged from, finding in it few if any ties or common ground with his own being. As he declares in the preface to *Major Barbara,* ". . . I am, and have always been, and shall now always be, a revolutionary writer, because our laws make law impossible; our liberties destroy all freedom; our property is organized robbery; our morality is an impudent hypocrisy; our wisdom is administered by inexperienced or malexperienced dupes, our power wielded by cowards and weaklings, and our honor false in all its points" (1:336).

It is tempting, then, to categorize Shaw as an "organized professional" who is the "prime victim and exemplar of self-loss in contemporary society."[20] Certainly characteristic of recent times is the vast amount of scientific and artistic talent involved in the network of industrial monopoly production, with talented people too alienated from their own creative skills, no longer having free play of their imaginations and growths of their minds, but following patterns set by sales departments. Since our true selves rebel against social function, according to Georg Lukács, among others, the only way to cease being alienated is to cease being social creatures.[21]

This is brave talk, this shooting for perfection on one's own terms. In reality, to withdraw from the troubles of our fellows, to see ourselves in perpetual struggle against a hostile and absurd world, produces an alienating art. Shaw was too much the social creature and commercial beast for that; it would be a mistake to confuse the disillusion that Shaw felt with the nihilistic direction taken by Hemingway, Fitzgerald, and other between-the-wars existentialists, or by the postwar novelists like Bellow and Pynchon who were moved by the impulse to dissidence. Rather, Shaw transmitted eloquently what he learned from others and their own engagements with society, perceiving if only intuitively that collective integrity makes individual integrity more possible, even in what seems to be so purely personal and individual an art as writing. More akin to Balzac, Tolstoi, Dreiser, and O'Neill, Shaw reveals his alienated self as an understandable human being through whom playgoers can learn something about themselves and shows how the forces at work in society are reflected in conflicts in the individual. In the humorous and satirical process, Shaw helps break down the isolation of people by giving them a consciousness of the world they were collectively shaping, creating in effect a kinship between playwright and audience through an illumination of the forces affecting them all.

Consequently, the artistically complex and socially disruptive dramas concocted by Shaw have contemporary value. In one fashion or another, his characters are either playing social roles and thus abdicating their true selves or are outsiders trying to keep and develop their individuality, thus alienating themselves from society. The tragic alternative between alienation or self-alienation that Shaw faces in his dramas is the same dilemma that we confront today. One legacy of Bernard Shaw lies in the dramatic acknowledgment that life seems a difficult or impossible course between individualism and society, between reality and illusion, between the Scylla of alienation and the Charybdis of self-alienation.

Notes

1. Bernard Shaw, *Complete Plays with Prefaces*, 6 vols. (New York: Dodd, Mead, 1962), 4:720. Subsequent citations of Shaw's plays and prefaces appear parenthetically in the text.

2. Karl Marx, *The Economic and Philosophic Manuscripts of 1844* (New York: International Publishers, 1964), p. 108. Subsequent citations appear parenthetically in the text.

3. Trevor Whittock, " 'Major Barbara': Comic Masterpiece," *Theoria* 51 (October 1978): 7.

4. Ralf Dahrendorf, "The Denunciation of the Outsider," *Zeit* (4 April 1975), p. 3.

5. Bernard Shaw, *The Collected Works of Bernard Shaw*, Ayot St. Lawrence Edition (New York: Wm. H. Wise, 1930), 2:253. Subsequent citations appear parenthetically in the text.

6. Robert Nisbet, "Knowledge Dethroned," *New York Times Magazine* (28 September 1975), p. 46.

7. Barbara Bellow Watson, *A Shavian Guide to the Intelligent Woman* (London: Chatto & Windus, 1964), p. 208. Subsequent citations appear parenthetically in the text.

8. Arnold Silver, *Bernard Shaw: The Darker Side* (Stanford: Stanford University Press, 1982), p. 142. Subsequent citations appear parenthetically in the text.

9. Richard Gilman, "The Special Quality of Joan," *Common and Uncommon Masks: Writings on Theatre 1961–1970* (New York: Random House, 1971), p. 66.

10. Erich Fromm, *Escape from Freedom* (New York: Rinehart, 1941), pp. 126–27. Subsequent citations appear parenthetically in the text.

11. Erich Fromm, *The Sane Society* (New York: Fawcett Premier Books, 1955), p. 111.

12. Alfred Kurella, *Ourselves and Our Strangers* (Berlin: Franz Schneekluth Verlag, 1970), p. 18.

13. Desmond MacCarthy, *Shaw* (New York: MacGibbon & Kee, 1951), p. 33. Subsequent citations appear parenthetically in the text.

14. Warren Sylvester Smith, *Bishop of Everywhere: Bernard Shaw and the Life Force* (University Park: Penn State University Press, 1982), p. 27.

15. Ronald Peacock, "Shaw," in *The Poet in the Theatre* (New York: Harcourt Brace Jovanovich, 1960), p. 89.

16. John F. Matthews, *George Bernard Shaw*, Columbia Essays on Modern Writers, No. 45 (New York: Columbia University Press, 1969), p. 29.

17. John Simon, "The Definitive Bernard Shaw," *New York Times Book Review* (2 November 1975), p. 2.

18. Friedrich Schiller, *On the Aesthetic Education of Man*, ed. and trans. E. M. Wilkinson and L. A. Willoughby (Oxford: Clarendon Press, 1967), p. 17.

19. Walter Kaufmann, *From Shakespeare to Existentialism* (Boston: Beacon, 1959), p. 26.

20. Harold Rosenberg, *The Tradition of the New* (New York: Horizon Press, 1959), p. 281.

21. Georg Lukács, *History and Class Consciousness*, trans. Rodney Livingston (Cambridge, Mass.: MIT Press, 1971), pp. 72, 157.

Bernard F. Dukore

EVIDENCE AND INFERENCE:
THE PHILANDERER

On 14 November 1991, the Hampstead Theatre Club in London presented, in its first preview performance, the world première of Bernard Shaw's original version of *The Philanderer*: that is, the production employed the text of his original final act. Press night of Shaw's dramatic Opus 2 was on 19 November, and the last performance was on 2 January 1992. This final act appeared in 1981 in a holograph facsimile edition[1] but has not yet been published in typeset form.

According to his diary, Shaw began the play on 29 March 1893.[2] On 11 May, he told William Archer that he had "all but finished" it, and on 5 June, he wrote to Elizabeth Robins that he had finished it.[3] Although his diary reveals that he read "the entire play" to Charles Charrington and Janet Achurch on 28 June, he apparently had completed only the dialogue. The diary entry of 11 July records that he "bought some chessmen to work out the stage positions," which he characteristically did before pronouncing his plays completed. Also characteristically, he continued to revise his plays before and even after they were performed and published.

"Surprisingly," Julius Novick notes in his introduction to the facsimile edition, Shaw dated the final leaf of the holograph text 23 August 1894, more than a year later (p. 447). Novick logically concludes that Shaw completed the play "in the summer of 1893; presumably the 1894 date represents some recopying or reworking" (p. xxiv). In addition to Shaw's reading the full dialogue on 28 June and his blocking the play with chessmen on and after 11 July, the reason for considering summer 1893 the time he completed *The Philanderer* is that his diary records nothing for *The Philanderer* between 11 July and 20 August 1893. The 20 August entry indicates that he "at last succeeded in beginning a new play," which is clearly a reference to his dramatic Opus 3, *Mrs Warren's Profession.*

Between 29 March, when he started to write *The Philanderer,* and 28 June, when he read its dialogue to the Charringtons, Shaw experienced a great deal of difficulty in composing this work—or, perhaps more accurately, in providing a conclusion for it. What he did is published in the holograph facsimile edition. Why he did it is a matter on which there has been considerable conjecture. The two can be hard to distinguish.

The program of the Hampstead Theatre Club's 1991 production contains a five-page essay by Michael Holroyd on Shaw's composition of the play, which is a reworking of Holroyd's analysis of the subject in the first volume of his biography of Shaw.[4] Holroyd records Shaw's progress in writing *The Philanderer* whenever he had an odd hour or apparently even fifteen consecutive minutes. On 12 June, says Holroyd in both note and book, referring to Shaw's diary entry, Shaw was "horrified" at its excessive length, for "it took me over three hours to read it" (p. 285). He spent the next several days, including the morning of 17 June, cutting and otherwise revising the work. At 3:30 P.M. on that date, according to his diary entry, he "read it all to Lady Colin [Campbell], who pointed out to me that the third act at which I have been working ought to be put into the fire. This opened my eyes for the first time to the fact that I have started on a quite new trail and must reserve this act for the beginning of a new play." On 22 June, Shaw's diary records, he "wrote a new scene for the beginning of the new third act of the play, as suggested by Lady Colin." In both book (p. 286) and program note, Holroyd partly quotes and partly paraphrases these passages, which appear to constitute his sole evidence of why Shaw changed the concluding act of *The Philanderer.*

According to the program note,

> His years of impoverished rejection and neglect had taught Shaw that he must rely on no one's opinion but his own. Yet now he *meekly* accepted Lady Campbell's dismissive judgement. There were pragmatic reasons for this. . . . She was better qualified than anyone Shaw knew to judge what was then acceptable to public opinion on those matters of marriage and divorce that were explored in the last act of *The Philanderer. What she told him in effect was that his last act was ahead of its time and that, if he wanted to get his play performed, he must write a more conventional ending and Shaw, hungering to have his play performed, did put aside his original act.* [Italics are mine.]

This note is substantially the same as the passage in Holroyd's book:

> She was . . . a sensitive judge of public opinion. *What she told Shaw was that no audience in the early 1890s would easily accept the last act as he had written it.* He was in his thirty-seventh year. After that tiny taste of success with *Widowers' Houses,* he hungered to have his play produced. *But by substituting her suggestion for his original inspiration he was going against much that he claimed for himself as a dramatist.* . . . *[H]e had become an artisan, manufacturing an ending according to plans and specifications laid down by Lady Colin Campbell.* [p. 286; italics are mine]

Although Shaw "had compromised," Holroyd adds that "his compromise had led nowhere" since the Independent Theatre rejected *The Philanderer* (p. 289). Is there any evidence to support the italicized passages, a source that documents the paraphrases of Lady Campbell's statements about what audiences would accept, the "plans and specifications" she provided, Shaw's going against his own grain, and his meek willingness to "compromise" his vision for commercial success? Holroyd gives no sources for any of these italicized passages or for the view that Shaw "had compromised" his play.

At the end of 1894, says Holroyd, Shaw wrote to Janet Achurch, paraphrasing Lady Campbell's admonition: "I am struggling with an almost overpowering temptation to burn The Philanderer" (p. 286). According to Holroyd's Source Notes, Shaw made this statement in a letter dated 10 December 1894.[5] The citation indicates the British Library, Add. MS 50561, fols. 51–52, but these folio leaves contain a letter *to* Shaw, dated 22 December 1894. When Holroyd graciously searched his notes for the correct attribution, he found a 3″ × 5″ index card with the quotation and date that appear in his Volume I, but with the provenance of the letter inadvertently omitted. A copy of this letter undoubtedly exists somewhere in his massive records of data for the three-volume biography, but unfortunately it has been misfiled. Does this letter contain another statement that might support the biographer's view? I do not know, and neither does Holroyd. Although he has searched for it, it has not turned up.

There seems to be no other evidence, beyond Shaw's statement in his diary, of why he changed the ending of the play. The portion of Holroyd's Source Notes (p. 188) that would provide the necessary documentation, published or still unpublished, cites none. Holroyd's other explanations of why Shaw did what he did are purely inferential (that is, not substantiated by data). All we know for certain is that Lady Campbell disliked Shaw's original third act so intensely that she suggested he burn it; that Shaw concurred with her view that this Act III moved the play in an entirely new direction; and that he "wrote a new scene for the beginning" of this act as she suggested. Shaw's statement is ambiguous as to whether her suggestion was for the entire third act or for only the first scene of that act.

Having examined what part of Holroyd's views rests on evidence, we are now in a position to summarize what part consists of inference. He infers what Lady Campbell suggested in addition to burning Act III, he infers why she suggested it, and he also infers why Shaw adopted what he claims she suggested.

When Shaw brought out *The Philanderer* in 1898 as one of the *Plays Unpleasant,* he published the revised third act. In Holroyd's program note, but not in his book, he makes another inference. "Shaw had done a very clever thing when drafting the substitute last act," he says, referring to the published Act III. "He had written it so that it could be played either as an alternative to his own ending or, penultimately, as an addition to it." The Hampstead Theatre Club chose the latter. When the Shaw Festival of Niagara-on-the-Lake, Canada, presented the North American première of Shaw's original *Philanderer* in repertory from 18 June through 24 September 1995, it adopted a shrewd stratagem. As in the London production, Shaw's original Act III followed his printed Act III as a fourth act, but of the Shaw Festival's fifty performances of *The Philanderer,* only eight were the four-act version. The Shaw Festival gave its audiences the option of which version to see, or whether to see both. Its decision of how many performances to give of each version may derive partly from its own misgivings about the original last act. It may also derive partly from its perception that only sixteen percent of its public would want to see the longer rather than the shorter work—a practice that conforms to its scheduling of *Man and Superman* in both three and four acts, the latter (with the Hell scene) having fewer performances than the former.[6] Furthermore, its program note by Brian Tyson appraised the discarded act as a "new trail" and explained its dramatic relationship to the play that precedes it, but it made no inferences about Shaw's motives in discarding it.[7]

Because of the accessibility of Holroyd's biography, other theatrical producing organizations may follow the Hampstead Theatre Club's lead and print his explanation, using the words in his book, or paraphrases of them, in their programs. Yet, intriguing as his inferences may be, he offers no evidence to substantiate them, and there seems to be none. Since readers of such program notes, and indeed some readers of Volume I of his biography, may accept his inferences as valid, it is important to examine them carefully and to suggest another way to interpret the evidence.

Let me now offer an alternative to Holroyd's view—buttressed both by evidence and by some inferences of my own that I will distinguish from the evidence. First, Shaw's stated reason for canceling his original Act III and writing a new one, that Lady Campbell made him aware of "the fact that I have started on a quite new trail" in the original third act, conforms to the evidence of that act, which appears in the holograph facsimile edition. The play that Shaw printed in 1898 is about courtship, involving two men and two women. It ends, less than twenty-four hours after it begins, with one woman accepting a marriage proposal by one man and the other woman rejecting a marriage proposal by the other man. The canceled final act, which occurs four years later, is chiefly about divorce. As Brian Tyson argues, "although Shaw never did use his abandoned act for the beginning of a new play, parts of it appear in his disquisitory treatise on the subject of matrimonial problems, *Getting Married,* fifteen years later."[8] Indeed, the first, and the major, piece of evidence that Tyson presents—parallel passages from the two plays—is a discussion of the conditions of divorce (pp. 94–95).

Second, when Shaw republished *The Philanderer* again and again over the half century that followed its initial publication, he had ample opportunity to give the world what, by the mid-twentieth century, it had become ready to accept. He did not do so. Instead, he reprinted the revised third act. Not only did he withhold publication of the third act that he had read to Lady Campbell, he appears not to have referred to it. If Shaw had cleverly written a substitute last act, as Holroyd claims, so that it could be performed either as an alternative to his original ending or plugged in as a preceding scene to it, why did he not publish it as such? After all, he published two alternative prologues to *Caesar and Cleopatra,* a third act that might be detached from *Man and Superman,* an induction and an alternative to it for *Fanny's First Play,* and two alternative endings to *The Millionairess.* I infer that Shaw was not suppressing a dramatic effort that would have prevented acceptance by a large audience, because no evidence exists to support the contention that he did so for this reason, and that he was not cleverly providing alternative texts, simply because he did not make one of these alternative texts public. Both what he did and what he failed to do validate the conclusion that he remained convinced that the original final act was dramatically deficient for the reason he gave: it moved the play in a new and different direction.

Another argument supports this viewpoint. During the summer that Shaw completed *The Philanderer,* either the same month or the month after, he began to write a new play. Is it likely that a dramatist who, in Holroyd's words, so "hungered to have his play produced" that he "compromised" by revising it according to commercial specifications, including "a more conventional ending," in order that audiences of his time would more easily accept the work, would write, as his next play, *Mrs*

Warren's Profession? *Mrs Warren's Profession* is hardly the type of play an author would compose if he were lusting for commercial approbation at any price. Like Holroyd's argument, this one is inferential. However, it conforms more closely to Shaw's habitual dramatic practice. As he declared in his 1898 preface to *Plays Pleasant,* published at the same time as *Plays Unpleasant,* between "public-spirited" theater producers who pursue their business "with the minimum of profit and the maximum of . . . quality" and those who "aim simply at the maximum of profit with the minimum of risk," there exists "a career, no harder of access than any cognate career, for all qualified playwrights who bring the manager what his customers want and understand, or even enough of it to induce them to swallow at the same time a great deal that they neither want nor understand. . . ."[9] With his printed version of Opus 2, Shaw pursued that career without, to use a word associated with Opus 3, prostituting *The Philanderer.*

Notes

1. Bernard Shaw, *The Philanderer: A Facsimile of the Holograph Manuscript,* intro. by Julius Novick (New York: Garland Publishing, 1981).

2. Bernard Shaw, *The Diaries 1885–1895,* ed. Stanley Weintraub (University Park: Penn State University Press, 1986).

3. Bernard Shaw, *Collected Letters 1874–1897,* ed. Dan H. Laurence (London: Max Reinhardt, 1965), pp. 395, 397.

4. I saw the production on Press Night and again on a matinée performance in December. Although Holroyd's program note is unpaginated, its brevity (five pages) should present no difficulty to anyone having access to it in tracking down quotations. References to what he says in Volume I of his biography are from Michael Holroyd, *Bernard Shaw: The Search for Love* (New York: Random House, 1988). Erroneously, Holroyd's program note records the start of composition as 14 March 1893 (when, according to his diary, he bought a one-shilling notebook "to begin new play"). Holroyd's book correctly cites 29 March (pp. 284–85).

5. Michael Holroyd, *Bernard Shaw: The Shaw Companion* (London: Chatto & Windus, 1992), p. 188.

6. According to a friend, the Shaw Festival may have miscalculated since some people were unable to obtain tickets for the performance of the four-act version on the night he attended.

7. I was unable to attend the Shaw Festival in 1995, but three colleagues who were aware of my interest in *The Philanderer* sent me copies of the program. I thank all of them: Fred D. Crawford, T. F. Evans, and Dan H. Laurence.

8. Brian Tyson, "Shaw's First Discussion Play: An Abandoned Act of *The Philanderer,*" *Shaw Review* 12 (September 1969): 94.

9. Bernard Shaw, *Plays Pleasant* (London: Penguin Books, n.d.), p. 11.

Rodelle Weintraub

EXTRACTING THE ROOTS OF SORROW: *YOU NEVER CAN TELL* AS DREAM PLAY

In July 1895, Bernard Shaw made an abortive attempt to write the play that we now know as *You Never Can Tell*. As a London theater critic, he had found the 1895 season dismal and depressing. Plays based on the predictable old formulae failed. New plays had little that was new or challenging about them, and after they, too, failed, the managers were too timid to encourage radical new plays. In his end-of-season review, he bemoaned that the theater manager "responds to the demand for honest, wholesome, English murder, suicide, and adultery, . . . and lo; bottomless disaster, worse than the worst Ibsen ever threatened. . . . The press proclaims a masterpiece; where is that masterpiece now? . . . That safe old hand Sardou, playing the safe old game according to the safe old rules, fails ignominiously. Those safe old hands . . . cautiously playing the new game according to the safe old rules, fail. . . ."[1]

By 1900, little had changed. Max Beerbohm protested that "Several farces and melodramas have been withdrawn lately after the shortest of runs, for the simple reason that they were not good enough for the public. To provide something beneath the public is quite as disastrous as to provide something above it." But Beerbohm added, "In the latter case disaster is no ignominy. Might it not sometimes be courted?"[2]

Too many *fin de siècle* plays were what we might now describe as "soap-operas." Actors and actresses were miscast. Shakespeare was still bowdlerized, and the audience had to suspend more disbelief than should be required to accept the goings-on on the stage. The 1895 season had ended for Shaw with a poorly conceived, badly staged production of *Two Gentlemen of Verona*, followed by an even worse *A Midsummer Night's Dream* and a not especially well-acted *Twelfth Night*.

By the time Shaw returned to the writing of *You Never Can Tell*, the apprentice playwright had written all but the last of his *Plays Pleasant and Unpleasant*, exploring various ways of developing a new art form for the theater. But these, too often, while challenging actors, directors, critics, and audiences with new ways of seeing things, were still presented in familiar forms. Despite the polemics of *Widowers' Houses* and the send-up of Ibsenite new women in *The Philanderer*, they remained boy-meets-girl romantic comedies. *Arms and the Man*, his first success,[3] was received as boy-meets-girl, boy-gets-girl romantic farce although it was the first of Shaw's plays to have a dream sub-text. *Candida*, his *Doll's House*, was his "would-the-wife-be-adulterous?" play. But his play's wife, rather than being a fallen woman, is a Madonna. Although Shaw in *Mrs Warren's Profession* attacked the causes for prostitution and sensitively examined parent-child relationships, the play could not get past the censors because it did not censure prostitution. Shaw felt that drama should do more than merely entertain, and in his plays Shaw the polemicist tried to educate the audience. Still, there is little of serious content in *Man of Destiny*. Will the mysterious stranger let Napoleon find out that his wife is unfaithful? Is the mysterious stranger a man or a woman? Will the mysterious stranger have an affair with Napoleon? There is no hint of homosexuality here, as there may be in *Mrs Warren*. The stranger, who in the guise of a man had stolen the Lieutenant's horse, pistols, and dispatches, proves to be a woman.

In December 1895 Shaw returned to *You Never Can Tell*, the last of the *Plays Pleasant*, and, breaking free of the restraints of 1890s theater, introduced theatrical techniques that foreshadowed the drama of the mid-twentieth century. The second-act luncheon scene in which the waiters bring plates of food to the table, snatch them away, and repeat the pattern until the meal is finished but never eaten was seen as a radical innovation six decades later when the preparation of food was treated in a similar manner in Arnold Wesker's 1959 play *The Kitchen*.

The play was so far advanced for the stage of the 1890s that the actors, who could not understand it, could not perform it.[4] In 1900, Max Beerbohm, an astute drama critic who did not always appreciate Shaw, having attended a matinee of *You Never Can Tell*, wrote

> I attended one of the six *matinees*. . . . Such innocent laughter is seldom heard in London, . . . the house was quite full and everyone in it was roaring with laughter throughout . . . the play. *Six*

matinees! Why are the commercial speculators who control theatres so obtuse as not to run Mr. Bernard Shaw for all he is worth?
. . . In the course of the next decade or two, they will begin to get
some glimmering of this fact. Meanwhile, they shake their heads
and purse their lips and proclaim, "Very clever, no doubt, . . .
much too clever; over the heads of the public." . . . Reality and
sheer fantasy are inextricably entangled. . . . Serious characters
behave ridiculously, ridiculous characters suddenly become serious. . . . It is all very confusing.[5]

The play remains quite delightful, a witty farce with echoes of *The Importance of Being Earnest*. Children discover the identity of the father they do
not know, and the dialogue rings with references to earnestness. It is
indebted not only to Wilde but also to the Shakespeare that Shaw had
seen just before starting to write in 1895. What made the play difficult
for end-of-the-century actors and audiences was his understanding of
dreams and his incorporating that understanding into the subtext of the
play.

When the play opens, the children of a fatherless family—that is, one
in which the children do not know who their father is—have been
brought from their home in Madeira, a group of five Portuguese islands
off the Atlantic coast of Morocco, to a fashionable English seaside resort.
Because Dolly, one of the twins, has a toothache, she and her twin brother
Philip have gone to the dentist. Dolly, the dentist's first patient, is described as a young woman who *"clearly does not belong to the room, or even to
the country . . ."* (p. 669). Valentine,[6] who has no other name and will
be the love-smitten suitor, is an unsuccessful doctor turned unsuccessful
dentist. The twins invite him to join them for lunch, but he at first de-
clines because they do not know the identity of their father. As in *The
Importance of Being Earnest*, it is essential that one know who one's father
might be before one can be accepted in society. Valentine, who later
swears he is "in earnest" (p. 749), withdraws his refusal upon learning
that they do have an appropriate grandfather, the Canon of Lincoln.
When their elder sister, Gloria, and their mother, Mrs. Clandon, arrive,
Valentine (like Titania, the fairy Queen in *A Midsummer Night's Dream*
who, after having her eyes rubbed with love petals, falls in love with the
first creature she sees upon awakening) is smitten the instant he sees Gloria. *A Midsummer Night's Dream* is again recalled in the second act when
Valentine tells Gloria that she had "Thrown an enchantment on me" (p.
737). Mrs. Clandon exits, and Mr. Crampton, the dentist's landlord, who
has been waiting to have a broken tooth fixed and could possibly have
overheard bits of their conversation, enters. He remarks that Dolly looks
like his mother. The three young adults recall to mind his own family

that he has not seen in eighteen years. With another echo of Shakespeare, Dolly, learning that Crampton has a painful memory, advises him to "Pluck from the memory a rooted sorrow."[7] The children invite him for lunch, too. The act ends when the dentist has administered gas to the landlord and Crampton has fallen asleep.

What the audience expects, and what will occur, at least in the manifest play, is that the children will turn out to be his absent family, the father will be as rich as Dolly hopes he will be, and Gloria and Valentine will become engaged. Of course this hardly original farcical romance will have witty dialogue, comic misunderstandings, mixed identities, romance, and a courtship duel between Valentine and Gloria that could have been fought by Beatrice and Benedict in *Much Ado about Nothing*, which makes one wonder why it should have been so difficult for actors to perform. After all, all's well that ends well. But does it? As unpredictable as some of the bizarre action seems, all of it can be understood as the dreamings of the anaesthetized patient having a problem-solving dream stimulated by what had occurred and by what he may have overheard shortly before he lost consciousness.[8]

Nothing that occurs in Acts II, III, and IV need have any roots in reality. No character is introduced who could not in some way already have been known to Crampton. The family friend invited down from London to explain their parentage to the children is a former suitor of Mrs. Clandon. When the twins inform their mother that they have also invited someone to luncheon, Dolly calls him "Chalkstones" and "Crampstones" (pp. 707–8), the names she had given Crampton in the first act. Walter Boon, the waiter in the hotel, does not have to ask Crampton what he will have to drink. He already knows. The waiter, the staff, and the waiter's son are all known to the most influential businessman in the community. Mrs. Clandon is the wife who had deserted him; the children are the ones she had spirited from his household. No lines or quotations are uttered that Crampton would not have known and that could not have come from his memory. Significantly, the characters who say those lines could not have known them.

The twins are what Crampton might expect children brought up without his discipline to be. They are exuberant, undisciplined, self-possessed, and far more in control of others than would be expected of seventeen- or eighteen-year-olds. Yet much of their behavior seems more appropriate for prepubescents. Both M'Comas[9] and Crampton are distressed by their behavior. M'Comas in Act II exclaims, "My children know how to behave themselves" (p. 711). That Dolly can be quiet only by covering her mouth with her hands distresses Crampton, who thinks children should be seen and not heard. He also objects to her flamboyant way of dressing. Although he has not seen his family in more than eighteen years, the twins are not yet eighteen years old.

Mrs. Clandon still holds the radical ideas she had at the time when she—if she be Mrs. Crampton—had left him. M'Comas assures her that all her radical ideas are now well accepted except, in the playwright's subversive criticism of the *fin de siècle* drama, for one place—the stage.

Unbelievable coincidences abound. A woman who is required by the terms of her separation to remain distant from her husband and not allow him to be harassed by the children would hardly select for her return to England the seaside resort in which that man is prominent in business. Yet in Act II, not only has she done exactly that, but her children have invited this man to join the family for lunch. The Queen's Counsel brought in to help solve the problem proves to be the son of the waiter who would have been happier if his son had gone to the other bar and become a "potman." Instead of following the family tradition of service, the son has gone into the service of the Queen. In Victorian England, however, becoming a Queen's Counsel required proper breeding as well as education.

Incongruities and inconsistencies tumble over themselves. Dolly has renamed the waiter "William" because he reminds her of Shakespeare. Walter/William has also renamed himself, simplifying the spelling of his surname from *Bohun* to *Boon* because it seems inappropriate to him for a waiter to have a Norman name. The children are disappointed that the bohemian suitor of Mrs. Clandon's youth, Finch M'Comas, has cut his hair and no longer wears a sombrero, as he did when Crampton wooed her away from M'Comas. The once-radical revolutionary who drinks no spirits—nothing "heating"—has become a priggish solicitor, a conservative, teetotaling member of the bar. Dolly claims that the middle-aged M'Comas is wooing her, yet he already has a family, including, presumably, a wife. The Q. C.—the play's second member of the legal profession—is introduced to the family as an ominous-looking masquerader who enters wearing a false nose and hooded cape, unrecognized by his father.

Philip and Dolly, having been absent from England and educated in the most advanced late-nineteenth century methods, would never, under their mother's radicalized tutelage in Madeira, have known the lines that English public-school boys of the earlier nineteenth century would have had to memorize. Crampton most likely would have had to learn and recite school pieces such as the speeches from the by-1895 unfashionable and derided eighteenth-century tragedy *Douglas* by John Home. Yet when Philip is asked his name, the twins respond,

PHILIP. . . . My name is—
DOLLY [*completing his sentence for him declamatorily*] "Norval. On the Grampian hills"—
PHILIP [*declaiming gravely*] "My father feeds his flock, a frugal swain"—(p. 706)

In the poem Norval, who does not know the identity of his father, is slain by his stepfather. Valentine, in describing his wooing methods to Mrs. Clandon, uses naval imagery with which he would have had no experience (pp. 749–50). Crampton, whose study was filled with model ships, is a well-known yacht builder.

Three characters, Gloria, Valentine, and Dolly, repeat variants of the same refrain, "Never, never, never, while grass grows or water runs" (pp. 756, 782), lines from Henry Thoreau's "Concord" in *A Week on the Concord and Merrimack Rivers*.[10] Published in the United States in 1849, it became well known in England in the 1850s–60s. Thoreau's writings were very popular and influential in mid-century British intellectual circles. It is more likely that the bohemian that Mrs. Clandon married would have been well acquainted with Thoreau than would Gloria and Dolly.

Philip exclaims, "On with the dance: let joy be unconfined" (p. 786), from Lord Byron's "Childe Harold's Pilgrimage," another poem that Crampton would have had to memorize in school but with which Philip, with his unconventional upbringing, may never have been acquainted. Unquoted, but possibly anticipated by the audience, many of which would have had an education similar to Crampton's, would have been the next line, "No sleep till morn. . . ." In his dream plays, Shaw left language hints that what we are seeing might be a dream. On Crampton's entrance in Act II, he exclaims, "Those steps make me giddy. [*He passes his hand over his forehead*]. I have not got over that infernal gas yet" (p. 713). In Act IV, shocked that his son had appeared wearing a false nose, the waiter echoes Crampton's words: "[*He clings to a chair to support himself*]. I beg your pardon, maam. A little giddiness—" (p. 773).[11] In *You Never Can Tell*, Shaw is far more subtle in leaving his clues than he is in other dream plays.

Strindberg noted that characters split in a dream, doubling, multiplying. Here there are three fathers: M'Comas, Walter/William the waiter, and Crampton. It is difficult to imagine what there was about Crampton that could have attracted Mrs. Clandon to him and that altered so much that she later fled from him. M'Comas explains that the marriage was an unsuitable one, purely accidental incompatibility of taste. She claims in the dream segment that she fled because of the whip he bought to discipline the children and that early in the marriage she "never discovered his feelings. [Instead] I discovered his temper, and his—[*she shivers*] the rest of his common humanity" (p. 761). Could the whip, which represents the incompatibility of their class and attitudes, also represent his "common humanity"?[12] M'Comas, who is supposed to be her representative, defends Crampton as one who lacked the veneer of civilization, the art of being charming. Could the young M'Comas—a rebel with long hair and sombrero whose lack of veneer might have appealed to the rebellious daughter of a cathedral dean—be that aspect of Crampton that had originally attracted Margaret? But having married and joined the family firm and the family itself, Crampton might have had to cut his hair, shave his beard, and become as respectable in his own way as M'Comas has become in his. Mrs. Clandon, dancing with M'Comas, exclaims that she has not "danced since the soirée at South Place twenty years ago" (p. 791). She expects M'Comas to know exactly what soirée they had attended, but twenty years before she had still been living with her husband and was the mother of the infant Gloria. When Dolly needs someone to kiss and M'Comas refuses her, she kisses Crampton.

Walter/William is suave and calm in a way that neither M'Comas nor Crampton can manage. He is satisfied with his station in life and seems without the inner conflicts that have ravaged Crampton. Yet he is dissatisfied with the upwardly mobile career his son has chosen, rejecting his home and family. The waiter, who must always be correct in manner and attire, is dismayed that his son should appear in a "false nose" (p. 773). Valentine learns from Walter the waiter that his wife, as is Mrs. Clandon, was of a commanding and masterful disposition (p. 794) and that the marriage was happy from time to time. The waiter Walter would never have permitted himself to dance with a hotel guest as Walter/William does with Dolly (p. 791). But a father might amuse a daughter by dancing with her.

As the roles split and shift and multiply, we can see Valentine as young Crampton the suitor. In Act IV, we can almost hear the conversation of some twenty years earlier:

> **[He, the young bohemian]:** . . . [B]e sensible: it's no use. I havnt a penny in the world.
> **[She, the daughter of the Canon of Lincoln]:** Cant you earn one? Other people do.
> **[He]:** I never could: youd be unhappy. . . . I should be the merest fortune-hunting adventurer if— . . . youre throwing yourself away. . . . [*To the Q.C.*] Give her some advice.
> **[Q. C.]:** She wont take it. When youre married she wont take yours either. [*To Her*] oh no you wont: you think you will; but you wont. He'll set to work and earn his living— [*To Him*] oh yes you will: you think you wont; but you will. She'll make you. (pp. 790, 792–93).

The two sons, Philip Clandon and Walter Bohun, have not followed their fathers' example, nor have they been educated to follow their fathers' professions, nor use their fathers' surnames. Walter/William says of his son that he has inherited his mother's "commanding and masterful disposition" (p. 794), a description that fits Philip every bit as well as Bohun. In the final act, Philip dances in with his sister Dolly and Walter Bohun exits, dancing with the other sister, Gloria.

Dolly, Gloria, and Mrs. Clandon in the manifest play are daughters and mother. In the underlying dream, Dolly (whose dress is described by the waiter as "pretty and tasty no doubt, but very choice and classy, very genteel and high toned indeed") "Might be the . . . daughter of a [Cathedral] Dean . . ." (p. 780). Mrs. Clandon is a Dean's daughter. Bohun tells Crampton that he would want Dolly "to give up dressing like a stage columbine in the evening and like a fashionable columbine in the morning," but "she wont: never" (p. 782), any more than her mother was willing to give up her unconventional ways. The middle-aged Mrs. Clandon, in her present dress, has ruled out any attempt at sexual attractiveness, having cultivated ideas rather than passion. Gloria is all passion. Her dress at first appearance "*seems conventional when her back is turned,*" but when she turns to face the audience, that conventionality becomes, Shaw says, scattered—making her very sexually attractive: "*A dangerous girl, one would say, if the moral passions were not also marked, and even nobly marked, in a fine brow*" (p. 680). On board ship all three women have been proposed to by the same man.

The relationship between Gloria and her mother is more like that between companions than between mother and child. Mrs. Clandon never asks her children anything, yet she seems to know Gloria's every thought. Gloria, like her mother, does not think the conditions of marriage are such that a self-respecting woman can accept. She has no intention of marrying, and she and her mother expect Gloria to continue her mother's work. In the second act, there is a "duel of sex" between Valentine and Gloria. In the third act, the "duel" takes place between Valentine and Gloria and Mrs. Clandon. In the last act, Valentine tells Gloria he wishes he could marry Mrs. Clandon, who is "worth six of" Gloria. Rather than being offended, Gloria is pleased (p. 788).

In working out the play, whether on the manifest level or the dream level, the frustrated Crampton has located his missing family. The children have learned the identity of their father. Bohun assures Crampton that although Crampton thinks that he might like to have the younger children live with him, Bohun knows better: Crampton would not really like the arrangement. A reunion could not be consummated. Mrs. Clandon has succeeded in returning from exile without losing her children. The family, however reestablished, will continue apart.

As an audience, we can take our choice among alternatives—comedic dream, Wildean spoof, intellectual farce, family fable, harlequinade—or we can have them all. Dream or not, the morals and standards claimed by radical ideologues for the new century are found wanting at their extremes just as the standards of the waning century have been proved no longer relevant. New values need a humanity and a flexibility exemplified by the originality of the twins' behavior that rejects authority old and new. Since we have a choice between Crampton's reality or Crampton's dream, we have the modern world of unresolved endings rather than the tidy but unreal box-office conclusions of the nineteenth-century stage; of perceptions that are as good as, or better than, realities; and of what Shaw called "original moralities" rather than second-hand ethical inheritances at odds with experience. In size of cast and variety of acting roles, the play comfortably meets the needs of the future repertory theater. For a theater dominated by actor-managers who rewrote even Shakespeare to give themselves starring roles, Shaw presented a cast of ensemble characters, no one overwhelming any other and each a star turn. As we come to understand them, their charm resonates more attractively now than it did to their first puzzled players, audiences, and readers. In *You Never Can Tell*, Shaw ushered in the theater of the twentieth century.

Notes

1. Bernard Shaw, "The Season's Moral," 27 July 1895, in *Our Theatre in the Nineties* (London: Constable, 1932; reprinted 1948), 1: 191–92. Also later reprinted in B. F. Dukore, ed., *The Drama Observed* (University Park, Penn State University Press, 1993), 2: 401–2.

2. Max Beerbohm, "Quo Vadis and Nil Praedicendum," 12 May 1900, in *Around Theatres* (New York: Simon & Schuster, 1900), p. 78.

3. As well as being a critical success, *Arms* established Shaw as a playwright. Shaw's royalties (£341 15s. 2d.) from the first year's run enabled him to give up his job as a music critic. See Bernard Shaw, *The Diaries 1885–1897*, ed. Stanley Weintraub (University Park: Penn State University Press, 1986), pp. 1002–3; and Michael Holroyd, *Bernard Shaw, Volume I: 1856–1898, The Search for Love* (New York: Random House, 1988), p. 306. The play ran in London and the provinces as well as in the United States and paid Shaw royalties for at least three years beyond the opening run. For Shaw's accounting of his 1894–97 royalties from *Arms*, see *The Diaries*, pp. 1055–58, 1104–6, 1108–9, 1149–50, 1153, 1164–66.

4. See Bernard Shaw, "*You Never Can Tell* (Chapter XVI of Cyril Maude's *The Haymarket Theatre*, 1903, written by Shaw)" *Collected Plays with Their Prefaces* (London: Max Reinhardt, 1970–74), 1: 797–802. All quotations from and references to *You Never Can Tell* are from this edition.

5. Max Beerbohm, "Quo Vadis and Nil Praedicendum", pp. 78–79.

6. Having reviewed *Two Gentlemen of Verona* in "Poor Shakespear!" (6 July 1895), Shaw was well aware that Valentine was one of the suitors in that play.

7. *Macbeth* (V.iii.38–44), referring to Lady Macbeth's madness after her loss of her father. Other allusions to Shakespeare include a reference to *Romeo and Juliet*. The last lines of Act III have Valentine say "and Gloria is the sun" (p. 766), recalling to the audience Romeo's "It is the east, and Juliet is the sun!" (II.ii.3).

8. "Dreaming makes connections more broadly than waking in the nets of the mind. . . . The connections are not made in a random fashion; they are guided by the emotion of the dreamer. . . . The dream explains metaphorically the emotional state of the dreamer. . . . Clearly dreaming makes connections between recently experienced material (day residue) and old memories . . ." (Ernest Hartmann, "Outline for a Theory on the Nature and Functions of Dreaming," *Dreaming* 6:2 [1966], reprinted **http://www.outreach.org/gmcc/asd/outline.html**.) See also Rodelle Weintraub, "Johnny's Dream: *Misalliance*," *SHAW* 7 (1987): 171–86; "Bernard Shaw's Fantasy Island: *Simpleton of the Unexpected Isles*," presented at IASAIL (1994) and published in *SHAW* 17 (1997): 97–105; and " 'Oh, the dreaming, the dreaming': *Arms and the Man*," in *Shaw and Other Matters,* ed. Susan Rusinko (Selingsgrove, Pa.: Susquehanna University Press, 1997), pp. 31–40.

9. "M'Comas" may be a pun on "Comus," a dramatic entertainment by John Milton (presented 1634) known to Shaw and most likely a school text known to Crampton. The plot combines the archetypal concept of a quest with the theme of enchantment. The three Travelers in the masque are two teenage children, a boy and a girl (Philip and Dolly?) and an Attendant Spirit, a guardian angel (Walter/William?). Masques combined story with dance (Act IV) and song, and were allegorical in nature.

10. Reprinted in *The Portable Thoreau* (New York: Viking, 1947), p. 139.

11. Shaw says of Walter, "*He ambles off through the window, having sounded the whole gamut of human happiness, from despair to ecstasy, in fifty seconds*" (p. 775). Erik Craig (1992) says, "While dreaming we entertain a wider range of human possibilities than when awake; the 'open house' of dreaming is less guarded" (quoted in Ernest Hartmann, "Outline for a Theory on the Nature and Functions of Dreaming").

12. The whip, a symbolic phallus, was a frequently used source of sexual gratification among public school-educated males of the nineteenth and early-twentieth century. W. E. Gladstone, after encounters with pretty prostitutes, during which he gave them Bibles, returned to his bedroom to whip himself. T. E. Lawrence (of Arabia) had himself whipped. A notorious house in St. John's Wood, in mid-Victorian London, purveyed whippings by women to such clients as the poet Swinburne. Genet surrealistically depicts such a scene in *The Balcony*. In this context one can take "common humanity" to refer to sexual intercourse.

Mark H. Sterner

SHAW'S SUPERWOMAN AND THE BORDERS OF FEMINISM: ONE STEP OVER THE LINE?

The catalogue of distinguished male writers who have fallen into critical disesteem due to feminist re-evaluation of the canon continues to grow. Recently numbered among them is Bernard Shaw who, curiously enough, was once considered an extremist on the subjects of equality and opportunity for women. Times change, however, and much of the corpus of Shavian dramatic literature has been dismissed as the stageworthy but rather puerile fantasies of a typically masculine, patriarchal sensibility. A case in point is *Man and Superman,* whose Ann Whitefield, originally intended as a twentieth-century stage incarnation of Nietzsche's "eternal feminine," has been reduced to a narrowly focused character bent on marriage to the man of her dreams and the ensuing bliss of motherhood. Although Ann Whitefield is certainly no ideal feminist by contemporary standards, it remains incumbent upon the dramatic critic to dismiss neither Shaw nor his projected Everywoman as heedless promoters of the patriarchy without a judicious hearing.

In a landmark essay entitled "Dancing Through the Minefield," Annette Kolodny attempted to codify some of the basic assumptions of the relatively new feminist critical theory. Perhaps the most crucial of these is the idea that power relations, specifically the power that males traditionally wield over females, are inscribed in the literary text, and that these relations are profoundly influenced by unacknowledged and unquestioned precepts of the culture.[1] Power relations between men and women constitute the dramatic core of *Man and Superman*; the crucial interpretive issue is whether Shaw brings the basis for these relations into question or merely portrays them, thereby lending tacit acceptance to the traditional sexual roles of late Victorian culture. Undoubtedly Shaw intended, as do the feminists who succeed him, to reinterpret history in order to give voice to the oppressed women of the world. He spoke passionately on the subject of women's emancipation, insisting that "unless woman repudiates her womanliness, her duty to her husband, to her children, to society, to the law, and to everyone but herself, she cannot emancipate herself. . . ."[2] Uttered before a meeting of the Fabian Society in 1890, these were radical sentiments, advocating nothing less than a revolution in the social roles played by women.

The action of *Man and Superman* (published for the reading public in 1903) is predicated on the struggle for dominance between the female principle (the biological Life Force) and the male (the intellectual process of creative evolution). These interconnected cosmic forces constitute a Shavian religion of sorts in which nature evolves toward greater organization and increased intellect through the linked processes of biological and cultural evolution. Shaw's peculiar and original conceit consists of the embodiment of these abstractions in characters who inhabit a familiar Victorian stage drawing room, characters who for the most part remain unaware of the universal implications of their actions. In addition, Shaw very conveniently links the realms of conscious and unconscious mind for his audience through a protracted dream sequence, during which the spectral forebears of the dramatis personae expound articulately upon the eternal struggle between matter and form. Thus the Philosophy comments upon and even influences the action of the Comedy, but the play remains stageworthily intact without it—so much so that Shaw saw fit to omit it entirely when he directed the play's 1905 London premiere.

Ann Whitefield is in many ways a comfortable inhabitant of this conventionalized stage world. She is an aristocratic young woman who seeks a suitable husband and father for her prospective children and who will apparently stop at no subterfuge, feminine tactic, or verbal deception in pursuit of her goal: one John Tanner, patrician socialist, deep thinker, and pre-eminently eligible bachelor. This sort of undivided matrimonial zeal would be suspect in and of itself in some contemporary feminist circles. How do Ann's aspirations measure up to the definition of a feminist protagonist provided in Janet Brown's *Feminist Drama*: "[The] feminist impulse is expressed dramatically in woman's struggle for autonomy against an oppressive, sexist society"?[3] Romantic love and matrimonial urges fly in the face of what many would consider genuine autonomy for a woman in Ann's historical and social position.

Shaw's reversal of gender roles in the ritual of courtship represents a fashionably shocking twist on Victorian dramatic conventions, but it also illustrates his quite specific ideas concerning human sexual relationships, as well as the connection of these relationships to the evolution of humanity to the ethereal heights. Shaw borrowed his anti-romantic stance from Schopenhauer, whose essay on the metaphysics of sexual love emphasized the very serious subject embedded at the root of all love affairs: the composition of the next generation. According to Schopenhauer, "This high importance of the matter is not a question of individual weal and woe, as in all other matters, but of the existence of the special constitution of the human race in times to come. . . . It is this high importance on which the pathetic and sublime elements of love-affairs, the transcendent element of their ecstasies and pains, rest."[4] The will of the individual is translated into the will of the species through the tragicomedy of courtship, and sexual passion is interpreted as the expression of the will to live of subsequent generations, a teleological trick of the Life Force. It is this mysterious and unyielding force of creative energy that suffuses Ann Whitefield with an irresistible passion for her artist-philosopher.

Man and Superman is charged with a sexual energy that is barely contained by the conventions of the Victorian stage. Shaw once referred to it as "a play entirely about sex."[5] The reversal of gender roles, combined with the social conscription of their outward behavior, forces the leading players into rather oblique expressions of their innermost feelings. Nevertheless, Ann continuously explores and extends the limits of her initiative with Jack, all the while risking her status as a decorous young lady worthy of a gentleman's consideration. Jack simultaneously wrestles with the repression of his equally strong desire for Ann throughout the play, ostensibly due to his belief that a true artist-philosopher should not dilute his attention to the betterment of humanity by consigning himself to the responsibilities of marriage.

The sexual intensity of the play derives largely from the degree of suppression that these characters exhibit, all in their own particular manners, in order to prevent the forbidden desire from rising to the surface and engulfing them. The desperation of Jack's flight, materialized in a strikingly theatrical automobile chase across the Continent, indicates an acute awareness of susceptibility on some level of consciousness as well as a recognition of Ann's dogged determination to succeed at practically any cost. There is in fact no logical reason for the pair's betrothal at the conclusion of the play. Jack succumbs solely because he finds himself in the thrall of Shaw's slippery but pervasive Life Force—an irrational, dionysian energy that ultimately proves too powerful for a mere genius to resist.

J. Ellen Gainor, author of *Shaw's Daughters*, finds the sexual metaphysics of *Man and Superman* objectionable primarily due to its radical split in gender roles. According to Gainor, the male hero retains both progenitive and cultural functions while the female heroine possesses purely biological ones.[6] She also reads Shaw's emphasis on the father/daughter relationship between Jack and Ann as an additional gender rift, particularly in terms of the stress on Jack's role as guardian/teacher over that of suitor. The power vested in these typically masculine roles is thus interpreted as an extension of the authority of the patriarchy. Shavian authority Margot Peters has noted an ambivalence in Shaw's attitude toward sex and domesticity, often expressed through a metaphorical association of eligible female characters with traps and snares; presumably these are intended for the capture of the independent masculine consciousness at the hands of a stagnating feminine domesticity.[7]

When Tanner makes pronouncements such as "Tavy: thats the devilish side of a woman's fascination: she makes you wish your own destruction,"[8] and then Shaw proceeds to illustrate the sentiment in terms of the play's dramatic action, these critics' exceptions seem well taken. It is only by examining the larger picture, as well as the detailed Shavian nuances that constitute it, that we are able to arrive at a full understanding and genuine appreciation of the character of Ann Whitefield. In reference to the mutual affection felt between the two former childhood companions, Ann gently nudges Jack: "Nobody could possibly misunderstand it. You do not misunderstand it, I hope" (77). Unfortunately, critics have too often misunderstood and misinterpreted the rather complicated character of Ann Whitefield, principally by assigning one facet of her personality too much importance while at the same time minimizing more significant factors.

Barbara Bellow Watson, whose *Shavian Guide to the Intelligent Woman* remains an invaluable reference for Shaw's female characters, acknowledges the Shavian tendency to distinguish between the feminine task of reproducing and nurturing human life and the masculine task of discovering knowledge. Watson believes, however, that Shaw remained quite cognizant of "the obvious fact that civilized women have artistic and intellectual impulses just as men have, and that woman's ability to act upon these impulses is hampered far more by social than by biological handicaps."[9] Watson has perhaps anticipated one of the central problems of current feminist thought: the social vs. biological basis for male domination. Many "radical feminists" argue that oppression results from the very construction of gender, from an insidious and irresistible biological force, rather than from the cultural role that the male plays within patriarchal society. Such a trend is dangerous, suggests feminist historian Ann Ferguson, because this kind of biological essentialism implies that sexual warfare is inevitable, ruling out "all but the most unrealistic separatist vision of social change."[10] In any case, this separatist position will not be dealt with as a reasonable objection to Ann as a feminist character since it would render the traditional comedic love chase inert from its very inception.

Shaw's optimistic belief in evolutionary change prompted him to create an Everywoman destined by a progressive Life Force to become a mother, but this fact does not preclude her from fulfilling any number of professional, intellectual, or artistic pursuits. If Jack occasionally plays teacher-adviser to Ann's submissive pupil, might not this be interpreted as fairly innocent role-playing, especially since it aids each of them in fulfilling their respective motivating desires (i.e., augmenting/diminishing the respective emotional distance between them)? When Tanner's rival Octavius Robinson declares his sister Violet a "womanly woman" at heart, Ann is unable to contain her pique at such conventional Victorian nonsense on the subject of women: "Why do you say that? Is it unwomanly to be thoughtful and businesslike and sensible? Do you want Violet to be an idiot—or something worse, like me?" (195) During this unguarded moment, Shaw's driven heroine allows the audience to glimpse not only her impatience with feminine stereotypes, but also a keen awareness of her own singleness of mind and the extremity of circumstance to which it has led. Ann's self-consciousness, sensitivity, and complexity, exhibited even during her overwrought pursuit of a mate, help to mitigate the boldly drawn sexual dichotomy of *Man and Superman.*

There is a traditional refrain in much of Shavian criticism that holds that Shaw was limited by his lack of life experience and that his characters reflect merely the multiple sides of the playwright rather than the reality of human behavior. To some extent this is true of all playwrights, but the assertion tends to stick to Shaw largely due to his relative inexperience with women. Elsie Adams, stalwart feminist and Shavian scholar, concludes that his female characters are primarily based on such literary types as temptress, mother, and goddess. Adams defines Ann Whitefield as an archetypal mother with a firm instinct for managing, a woman who would brook no interference from outside the family circle. She also includes Ann in that characteristically Shavian group of characters who use their feminine wiles to threaten and to deceive men: "Thus we are presented with the paradox of a man who can argue against the romantic idealization of women, but who nevertheless personally worships the mother-goddess figure he artistically creates."[11] Writing in the same collection, the invaluable *Fabian Feminist,* Gladys Crane insists, on the other hand, that Shaw created female characters distinguished both by their reality and by their individuality. The cardinal traits that Shaw brought to these characters reflected the changing reality of his times, according to Crane, and included those of self-awareness, self-evaluation, and a sense of personal worth.[12]

Such divergent and apparently incompatible views of Shaw's female characters are illuminated to a degree by Shaw's full-page description of Ann, which includes such typical physical details as *"well-formed . . . lady-like, graceful, and comely, with ensnaring eyes and hair."* But Shaw also utilizes terms suggesting Ann's inner depth, such as *"brave unconventionality"* and *"vital genius."* He characterizes his heroine as respectable and self-controlled, even though *"her pose is"* as a *"fashionably frank and impulsive"* young woman (54). Ann is depicted from the beginning as a complex and less-than-consistent figure. Her initial stage action in Act I consists of manipulating Jack Tanner and the patrician Roebuck Ramsden into an agreement to serve as her co-guardians, with the clandestine purpose of gaining more intimate access to Jack. This mission accomplished, Ann proceeds to deflate both men by using her pet names for them in front of one another. Ramsden becomes her dear "Granny," Tanner is christened "Jack the Giant Killer," while the fatuous Octavius Robinson is reduced to "Ricky-ticky-tavy."

When Octavius's sister arrives in the horrifying, disgraceful state of unwed motherhood, Ann confides to the assembled company, "Violet has done something dreadful. We shall have to get her away somewhere" (63). Jack is subsequently made to play the fool, valiantly defending Violet's shameful condition, only to discover that she has been secretly married all along. At the end of the act Violet reveals Ann's duplicity, announcing that Ann knew about her marriage all along. This sort of manipulation is further evidenced in the play's most lengthy scene: a ruminative interlude in which Ann goads her new guardian into confessing his childhood fondness for her, only to chide him subsequently for his lack of heroism, his egotism, and his dreadful political solemnity.[13] When Jack unchivalrously likens her to a boa constrictor, Ann seizes the opportunity to toss her feather boa around his neck, an overt sexual tease that she redoubles by putting her arms around him. When Jack revels in her "magnificent audacity," assuming that she is in love with Octavius and merely playing with him, Ann manages to disengage her arms with perfect composure: "But you should not jest about our affection for one another. Nobody could possibly misunderstand it. You do not misunderstand it, I hope" (77). Although Ann surely exploits her "feminine wiles" here, she can hardly be faulted for deception in making her very real sexual attraction explicit, at least on some level, to Jack—even as she ingeniously manages to follow the rigid rules of social decorum in her pursuit.

It is possible that we are not as free from sex-role stereotyping in the final quarter of the twentieth century as we would like to imagine. A flurry of empirical studies concerning gender stereotypes in the 1970s found that sex-role stereotyping remained pervasive despite the apparent fluidity of sex-role definitions during the period. In her book *Gender*

Communication, Laurie P. Arliss has summarized the findings of these studies in a catalogue of the feminine and masculine traits that respondents considered either typical or ideal. The following is her composite of feminine traits listed by respondents of both sexes during the 1970s: submissive, emotional, dependent, fragile, gentle, quiet, tactful, sensitive, yielding, verbal/language oriented.[14] From this list, presumably more enlightened than one constructed at the turn of the century, Ann Whitefield positively matches only two stereotypically feminine traits and is diametrically opposed to six of them.

For example, we can state without equivocation that Ann is highly emotional and quite verbal/language-oriented (she *is* a Shavian character, after all). Ann is certainly not submissive—not to the wishes of Tanner, Ramsden, Octavius, or her own mother—although she *feigns* total dependence on them concerning such matters as the designation of her guardian. This is part and parcel of her pose of conventional femininity that, granting the social exigencies of an hypocritical era, she was virtually forced to maintain. Similarly, while feigning a high degree of dependency, Ann remains fiercely independent in the pursuit of her ultimate goals. She is obviously neither fragile nor gentle, and by no means quiet, except when it suits her purpose of the moment. As the initiator in the love chase, Ann can hardly be seen as yielding. It is difficult to imagine that such a fundamental element of her character will change substantially after she marries Jack.

We are left with the feminine descriptors "tactful" and "sensitive." These adjectives may or may not be attributed to Ann, depending on the situation chosen for emphasis. Certainly she is tactful in handling the delicate situation of her guardianship, particularly when its outcome is crucial for her entrée to Jack. On the other hand, she treats her mother abominably and gives offense to the sensitive Octavius by coldly staunching the efflorescence of his passion when she no longer needs it to goad Tanner's reluctant courtship. Ann appears insensitive to the feelings and needs of others on a number of occasions, but even in the uncomfortable confrontation with Octavius there remains a sense that although the medicine was painful, it was necessary to help dispel the blindness of Octavius's compulsive romanticism. Is Ann thereby a creature of mere feminine instinct, or does she share some of Jack's keen wit and intelligence in handling the difficult situations with which she is confronted? In either case, she does not appear to represent the sterotypic feminine ideal of *any* era. If Ann Whitefield does in fact descend from literary typology, it is from such an assorted amalgamation of sources, coupled with purely Shavian invention, that she must be considered a true original.

The fact remains, however, that Ann may be a poor role model for feminists because she is a manipulator and a poseur. Instead of discarding the trappings of Victorian behavior, as any self-respecting New Woman would have done, Ann seems to exploit the very deviousness with which the female reputation had for so long been besmirched. Eminent Shavian scholar Charles A. Berst neatly sums up the critical response to Ann's complicated, seemingly objectionable personality: "Ann is metaphysically a potential mother for the Superman, biologically a predatory female, socially a guileful hypocrite, and personally a grown-up, determined little girl with a crush."[15] Charles Carpenter sullies her reputation further by contending that Ann's moral inferiority (that is to say, her hypocrisy) is the true obstacle in the sex chase and that she ultimately wins Jack only by discarding her veil of pretense, thereby ceasing to repel him morally.[16] But this is a classic case of blaming the victim: Ann cannot be the play's protagonist and its major obstacle at the same time. Ann's obstacle may be Jack, society, or creative evolution, but it is certainly not her own moral turpitude which is (a) mostly feigned, (b) existing primarily in Jack's mind as wish fulfillment, and (c) certainly not a feature of the Everywoman figure that Shaw forecasts in his preface to the play.

It is Tanner who prepares the audience for Ann's first entrance, upon discovering that he is bound to serve as her guardian, with these damning sentiments: "she has plenty of money and no conscience. All she wants with me is to load up all her moral responsibilities on me, and do as she likes at the expense of my character. I cant control her; and she can compromise me as much as she likes. I might as well be her husband" (49). Tanner's pronouncements, although surely quite real for him in this situation, must be taken with several grains of salt. A good deal of confusion has resulted from the notion that Tanner functions not only as the play's single protagonist, but also as its Shavian *raisonneur*. While serving as Shaw's political and philosophical mouthpiece to a degree, Tanner also functions as the comic butt of many a joke, such as when he so chivalrously defends the honor of the already-married Violet. We must be careful not to accept everything Jack says at face value since he is often grandiloquent, sometimes pig-headed, and occasionally dead wrong. He is, after all, an intensely interested observer and evidently quite an amateur when it comes to judging feminine character. Tanner is, for example, the first to hurl the epithet "hypocrite" at Ann, a slander that has been echoed by a veritable chorus of critics over the years. The fact is that Ann Whitefield, while certainly scheming and deceptive, never seriously pretends to be anything other than what she truly is throughout the action of the play.

The charges against Ann's character, if justified, would render Shaw's attempt at depicting the Everywoman quite inept. Either he intended audiences to receive Ann Whitefield as a representative recreation of the "inferior sex," in which case he should be regarded as an incorrigible member of the ruling patriarchy, or he was bent on creating something entirely different. If Shaw indeed intended a truly positive character, two options become apparent. The first possibility is that Ann is a genuine Everywoman whose powerful instincts, keen intelligence, charismatic personality, and, yes, even willingness to deceive in the service of her cause render her an authentic vital genius. The second is that while Shaw intended to create this kind of positive feminine role model, he was unable to do so as a consequence of the requisite blinders worn by members of the masculine gender. There is, perhaps, a third possibility: Ann Whitefield, although larger than life and generally admirable, is complicated beyond such simplistic interpretations by interwoven layers of very human needs and desires, a combination rendered even more intricate by a singular aptitude for role-playing.

Ann's complexity derives largely from the social role that she is forced to play: the elegant and eligible, although rapidly fading, Victorian flower. As with many of her real-life contemporaries, this role remained in unfortunate contradistinction to her given nature. Ann is confident, brimming with life, extroverted, independent, and highly engaged. She is also inexplicably driven by the Life Force in a need to co-operate with the evolutionary development of human society and consciousness. This circumstance impels her to seek out the intellectually and morally advanced John Tanner, who possesses the most suitable set of genes for the purpose. Ann is thus continuously required to tread a tenuous line between the requisite maidenly propriety and a rather brazen sexual appeal in order to ensnare this most intractable of prospects.

Much of the comedy in *Man and Superman* derives from the continuing revelation of Ann's complexity as she confronts this sensitive dilemma. In the words of Gladys Crane, "The pure delight in Ann's character is her superb control of her pursuing impulses, her marvelous channeling of her desire for Tanner into impeccably proper Victorian behavior which leaves Tanner confused and guilty and Ann shamelessly triumphant."[17] If Ann is constantly role-playing, it is because this is the avenue that an inheritance of privilege and intelligence provides for her in an untoward predicament. The fact that Shaw employs a reversed sexual chase as the occasion for comic laughter, coupled with the fact that Ann is forced to fall back on traditional feminine devices in order to accomplish her mission, has understandably evoked the ire of sensitive critics. But the aesthetic delight of the play derives largely from the subtlety, wit, and consciously controlled decorum of a woman who must play the man's role of pursuer without losing a jot of her feminine status in a rigidly conventionalized society. If Ann is manipulative and deceitful, it is primarily due to the fact that Victorian society failed to sanction a more direct course of action for a woman without dire social consequences, not because she is a stereotypic instance of female characterization invented by an unenlightened male.

Ann Whitefield has been assigned quite an assortment of roles by some estimable literary typologists. She has been diversely categorized as chaste heroine, siren, huntress, cat, mother, daughter, martyr, and goddess. Such a list appears to justify somewhat Shaw's assignation of the term "Everywoman." But it is the relative prominence of the role of archetypal mother to which feminists have taken greatest exception, and rightly so. Ann's genius for mothering is equated with Tanner's genius for thought in what appears to be nothing less than a sort of Shavian "separate but equal" doctrine. Elsie Adams concludes that while Ann may be vital, aggressive, even manipulative, she nevertheless perpetuates the insidious tradition of a woman serving someone else, albeit a higher cause, rather than herself.[18] Women's individuality, equality, and autonomy are the crucial issues at stake here.

In a Jungian-based study entitled "Ann and Superman: Type and Archetype," critic Sally Peters speaks to some of these concerns. Peters reminds us that the several dramatic types that can be discerned as elements of Ann's character, and the complexities that these various guises engender, should be considered against the backdrop of the universal-mythic role that she portrays in Shaw's philosophical interlude. Thus, while the Comedy often appears frivolous, it is to be understood as a necessary result of cosmic forces at work, of life becoming ever more transcendent and self-aware, of a world will that demands the conjugation of Ann and Jack.[19] In this light, Ann can be seen as an histrionic reflection of the "Queen Goddess of the World" archetype, a woman who both nourishes and consumes and who encompasses the multiple roles of daughter, sister, virgin, temptress, bride, and mother. "Ascribing this role to Ann implies both the humour inherent in all myth, as it perpetually renews itself in strange and marvelous forms, and Shaw's very special sense of the absurd."[20] It also helps to elucidate the rather perplexing plethora of roles that Ann portrays in the Comedy and indicates that Shaw did not intend to circumscribe Ann within the mother role so much as to expand her personality toward the all-encompassing capacities of the Goddess.

But the notion of the Queen Goddess still leaves Doña Ana with the mission of finding a father for the Superman. The parallel mission of Ann Whitefield consists of becoming a respectable nourishing mother. Tanner's view of conventional motherhood is explicit in his startlingly negative description of fashionable society: "A horrible procession of wretched girls, each in the claws of a cynical, cunning, avaricious, disillusioned, ignorantly experienced, foul-mouthed old woman whom she calls mother, and whose duty it is to corrupt her mind and sell her to the highest bidder" (96). Such vituperation against one of society's most sacred institutions is exceptional even for Shaw. Is it possible that he anticipated feminist objections to his Everywoman's unflagging superobjective and inserted these objections into the mouth of his iconoclastic hero as a means of self-defense? Shaw makes it abundantly clear, both here and elsewhere, that he is in solid agreement with the radical feminist belief that the family, as traditionally constituted, is a repressive institution that exploits the woman's reproductive capacity and keeps her in economic dependence. He believed that the Victorian institutions of motherhood and family served only to hinder the progress of the human race: "The truth is that family life will never be decent, much less ennobling, until this central horror of the dependence of women on men is done away with."[21]

J. Ellen Gainor argues that Shaw has conflated the womanly woman and the New Woman in the character of Ann Whitefield and that the resulting synthesis is compelled to "follow the demands of the Life Force—through the expression of sexual desire."[22] In other words, the Shavian attitude toward women has not progressed beyond that of crude physical exploitation and economic oppression. It is true that Shaw chose to write his *Gesamtkunstwerk* on the somewhat buried (and absurdly undramatic) theme of the evolution of the Life Force becoming ever more conscious of itself. Given the state of human knowledge and development at the turn of the last century, this necessitated standard biological reproduction, which in turn implied a healthy young male and a healthy young female in order to convey genetic matter and spiritual form safely into the future. Once these basic parameters are accepted, it seems incumbent upon the critic to evaluate the play with a view toward the articulation of such parameters.

Ann Whitefield is the true protagonist of *Man and Superman*, the initiator and propeller of the dramatic action and, appearances notwithstanding, decidedly *not* the typical feminine stage persona of the period. Without ever relinquishing her femininity, she easily dominates every male whom she confronts, displaying the unmitigated and decidedly unfeminine gall to pursue her desires in an active, efficient, and highly intelligent manner. Ann Whitefield is a dramatic character who lives and breathes on the stage, who induces the hearts of both sexes to beat faster as a result of her nerve as well as her charm, and who causes female conventionalists and male chauvinists alike to grit their teeth as a result of her audacity. The multiplicity of roles that she plays, roles that metamorphose as suddenly as the shifting array of characters that populate the Shavian stage, render Ann all the more authentically human. She is human because she is an individualist with a convincing motivating force as well as fully contrasting, even contradictory, moods and ideas. And she

is the victorious protagonist of an intellectual comedy—how many stage
heroines could boast of such pre-eminence at the time?

There are undoubtedly many feminists who would question the assumption that the creation of Ann Whitefield constituted a patronizing,
even chauvinistic, act. Jill Dolan, a feminist performance critic, maintains
that the compulsion of radical feminists to portray women's struggles
against a ubiquitous backdrop of patriarchal victimization leads to a flat-
tening of women's experience. "No room for questioning, doubt, or debate appears in this forum," according to Dolan, "which is constructed as
perniciously monolithic."[23] Ergo, the need to reject the Shavian Everywoman who, after all, requires a male to complete her mission. The cultural separatists have not seen Ann as she really is—a complicated, very
human, highly civilized, and extremely intelligent young woman with the
capacity for success in any number of endeavors. Moreover, Ann instinctively realizes that of all the careers open to a woman of her character
and position, a marriage to artist-philosopher John Tanner just might be
the most rewarding.

While it is ironic that Shaw chooses to question the assumptions of sexual power relations in patriarchal Victorian society by using a dominant
female who primarily desires to breed, this is entirely in keeping with the
generous use of paradox that typically abounds in the Shavian world.
Other plays have their fiercely independent Vivie Warrens and Lina Szc-
zepanowskas, but Shaw's singular subject here is the ineffable mystery of
creation, the relentless drive of the forces of biological and cultural evolution. Thus he presents a woman who is a "vital genius" with a strong
maternal bent and a talent for domesticity, a woman who displays the raw
courage, strength of character, presence of mind, intellectual talent, and
sheer determination to demand the best man for the job: the man she
loves, the man who will help create a race in the evolutionary direction
of the Superman. We can only presume that her more strident critics
would deny Ann Whitefield the freedom to choose a life—even a life of
co-equal love and partnership—with the most sympathetic and understanding of men.

Both Ann and Jack share attitudes and emotions that are traditionally
designated either masculine or feminine. Like many of Shaw's more advanced creations, they are androgynous in this respect. In contradistinction to recent radical feminist theory, the Shavian world view assumes
that nongendered existence remains a reality, that men and women share
some common ground, that there is still a mutual journey worth taking.
It remains incumbent upon feminist critics to reconsider the cogent advice of one of their own: "Since the grounds upon which we assign aesthetic values to texts are never infallible, unchangeable, or universal, we
must re-examine not only our aesthetics but, as well, the inherent biases

and assumptions informing our critical methods which (in part) shape our aesthetic responses."[24]

While it may be true that Ann Whitefield does not possess as much intellectual acumen as her paramour John Tanner, she does have the elements of character needed to make highly significant accomplishments. Shaw draws the members of his cosmic pair as significantly different, but nevertheless equal, a fact that in itself was a revolutionary change in the status of sexual power relationships. A salient characteristic is an underlying freedom from any genuine concern for what others may think of her, an emblem of Shaw's admiration for a woman who is able to swim free of the strangulating currents of conventional streams, even in the most conventional of societies. Ann's emotional independence from approval, in addition to her many other remarkable qualities, renders her a perfectly suitable mate for the world-betterer. Besides, they can make each other laugh.

Notes

1. Annette Kolodny, "Dancing Through the Minefield," in *Feminist Criticism*, ed. Elaine Showalter (New York: Pantheon, 1985), pp. 146–47.

2. Bernard Shaw, "The Quintessence of Ibsenism," *Major Critical Essays* (Middlesex, England: Penguin, 1986), p. 61.

3. Janet Brown, *Feminist Drama* (Metuchen, N.J.: Scarecrow Press, 1979), p. 1.

4. Arthur Schopenhauer, *The World as Will and Representation*, trans. E. F. J. Payne (New York: Dover, 1958), 2:534–35.

5. Quoted in "G.B.S. and a Suffragist," in *Fabian Feminist*, ed. Rodelle Weintraub (University Park: Penn State University Press, 1977), p. 241.

6. J. Ellen Gainor, *Shaw's Daughters: Dramatic and Narrative Constructions of Gender* (Ann Arbor: University of Michigan Press, 1991), p. 209.

7. Margot Peters, "The Sexual Politics of *Man and Superman*" (talk delivered at the Shaw Festival Seminar, Niagara-on-the-Lake, Ontario, 1992).

8. Bernard Shaw, *Man and Superman* (London: Penguin Books, n.d.), p. 60. Subsequent references are to this volume and appear in parentheses in the text.

9. Barbara Bellow Watson, *A Shavian Guide to the Intelligent Woman* (London: Chatto & Windus, 1964), p. 206.

10. Ann Ferguson, *Blood at the Root: Motherhood, Sexuality, and Male Dominance* (London: Pandora Press, 1989), p. 14.

11. Elsie Adams, "Feminism and Female Stereotypes in Shaw," in *Fabian Feminist*, ed. Rodelle Weintraub (University Park: Penn State University Press, 1977), pp. 158–59.

12. Gladys Crane, "Shaw and Women's Lib," in *Fabian Feminist*, ed. Rodelle Weintraub (University Park: Penn State University Press, 1977), p. 174.

13. In "Shaw's Scenario for *Man and Superman*," introduced by Charles A. Berst, *SHAW 16: Unpublished Shaw*, ed. Dan H. Laurence and Margot Peters (University Park: Penn State

University Press, 1996), p. 200. Berst notes that while this characterizing scene is one of the sketchiest in Shaw's original scenario, it ultimately became "the longest in the play."

14. Laurie P. Arliss, *Gender Communication* (Englewood Cliffs, N.J.: Prentice Hall, 1991), pp. 15–16.

15. Charles A. Berst, *Bernard Shaw and the Art of Drama* (Urbana: University of Illinois Press, 1973), p. 125.

16. Charles A. Carpenter, "Sex Play Shaw's Way: *Man and Superman*," *Shaw Review* 18 (May 1975): 71.

17. Gladys Crane, "Shaw's Comic Techniques in *Man and Superman*," *Educational Theatre Journal* 23 (1971): 13.

18. Adams, p. 159.

19. Sally Peters Vogt, "Ann and Superman: Type and Archetype," in *Fabian Feminist,* ed. Rodelle Weintraub (University Park: Penn State University Press, 1977), p. 52.

20. Ibid., p. 55.

21. Preface to *Getting Married,* in Bernard Shaw, *The Complete Prefaces, Vol. I: 1889–1913,* ed. Dan H. Laurence and Daniel J. Leary (London: Penguin Press, 1993), p. 441.

22. J. Ellen Gainor, "G.B.S. and the New Woman," *New England Theatre Journal* 1:1 (1990): 10.

23. Jill Dolan, *The Feminist Spectator as Critic* (Ann Arbor: UMI Research Press, 1988), p. 88.

24. Kolodny, p. 151.

Julie A. Sparks

AN OVERLOOKED SOURCE FOR ELIZA? W. E. HENLEY'S *LONDON TYPES*

Ever since 1914, when the glamorous Mrs. Patrick Campbell shocked London theater-goers by appearing as Eliza, the Covent Garden gutter-snipe with the appalling Cockney accent, critics and scholars have made an intellectual parlor game out of their search for Shaw's inspiration for the role. Shaw provided the first clue himself in a letter to Ellen Terry on 8 September 1897, soon after he saw Mrs. Campbell play Ophelia to Forbes-Robertson's Hamlet: " 'Caesar & Cleopatra' has been driven clean out of my head by a play I want to write for them in which he shall be a west end gentleman and she an east end dona in an apron and three orange and red ostrich feathers."[1] We cannot know how Shaw conceived his idea of a Galatea–flower girl from Mrs. Patrick Campbell's Ophelia (although it seems reasonable to assume that it had something to do with the "mad scene" when Ophelia passes out flowers to the assembled members of the court, who stand by shocked at her disheveled appearance and wild manner). Nevertheless, there has been much speculation about the literary and artistic precedents that may have influenced Shaw once his initial concept was formed, influences as various as Ovid and Plautus, Smollett and Burne-Jones. However, one late Victorian source that may have shaped the characterization of the "east end dona" has been over-looked, the sonnet " 'Liza" by the versatile Victorian man of letters William Ernest Henley (1849–1903).

Early in 1898 (only months after Shaw's letter to Ellen Terry) Henley published a collection of thirteen sonnets called *London Types* that includes this portrait of a flower girl (or, more probably, a vegetable seller) who sounds startlingly familiar to Shavians:

> *'Liza's old man*'s perhaps a little *shady*,
> *'Liza's old woman*'s prone to *booze* and cringe;
> But *'Liza* deems herself a *perfect lady*,
> And proves it in her feathers and her fringe.
> . . . .
> Withal, outside the gay and giddy whirl,
> *'Liza*'s a stupid, straight, hard-working girl.[2]

Although the initial idea for the "rapscallionly flower girl" appears to be Shaw's own, Henley's portrayal of a flower girl named "Liza," who "deems herself a perfect lady" despite her "shady" father, suggests itself as an early influence that, appearing while Shaw's idea was still fresh, may have helped reinforce and sharpen his characterization.

Although " 'Liza" stands out as the most suggestive of Henley's sonnets, two others in the same volume may also have been important to Shaw's imaginative processes: "Lady" and "Flower Girl." The first of these immediately follows " 'Liza" and describes the growing disorder in the social classes. It begins with a metaphor of neighborhoods invading each other:

> Time, the old humourist, has a trick today
> Of moving landmarks and of levelling down,
> Till into Town the Suburbs edge their way,
> And in the Suburbs you may scent the Town.

The "Lady" of the title is a house, personified as a

> . . . fair creature, pictured in The Row,
> As one of that "gay adulterous world," whose round
> Is by the Serpentine, as well would show,
> And might, I deem, as readily be found
>   On Streatham's Hill or Wimbledon's, or where
> Brixtonian kitchens lard the late-dining air.[3]

Although now only a social historian would understand the nuances of status associated with these neighborhoods in Henley's day, Shaw had been living in London for more than twenty years by this time and would have been almost as familiar with the caste system implied here as is his own Professor Higgins who, in the first scene of *Pygmalion*, jauntily claims

Fig.7. Liza "trapesing." From W. E. Henley, *London Types* (New York: R. H. Russell, 1898), courtesy of Rare Books Room, The Pennsylvania State University Libraries. I am grateful to Charles Mann and Sandra Stelts of Pattee Library for making this illustration available.

the ability to "place any man within six miles. . . . within two miles in London. Sometimes within two streets" simply by listening carefully to the person's particular dialect.[4] Like Henley, Higgins is aware that this caste system is not quite as iron-clad as it used to be. He explains to Pickering that "This is an age of upstarts. Men begin in Kentish Town with £80 a year, and end in Park Lane with a hundred thousand. They want to drop Kentish Town; but they give themselves away every time they open their mouths. Now I can teach them—" (4:679). The method whereby Higgins is able to defeat this "verbal class distinction" so that ambitious Londoners could cross social classes as easily as they could cross neighborhoods functions as the crux of the play.

So far Henley has presented a 'Liza who "deems herself a perfect lady," despite her "shady" class origins, and a "Lady" of a house that seems to suffer a similar class dislocation. The third poem that suggests itself as a possible influence on Shaw is the penultimate sonnet in Henley's series, "Flowergirl," which personifies London as a gentlewoman with dainty tastes who delights in every "delicate nurseling of the year. . . . / Her days to colour and make sweet her nights." Catering to this taste for posies is London's cheerfully shabby band of flower girls who venture

> . . . forth from *DRURY LANE*,
> Trapesing in any of her whirl of weathers,
> . . . foot it, honest and hoarse and vain,
> All boot and little shawl and wilted feathers:
>> Of populous corners right advantage taking,
>> And, where they squat, endlessly posy-making.[5]

Henley presents a far rosier picture of the flower girls' life than does Shaw since Henley has them "trapesing" rather than, say, "trudging" through London's "whirl of weathers," which Shaw presents in the first scene of *Pygmalion* as fairly miserable for the shabbily clad. But Shaw always delighted in lifting useful images from incongruous sources and exploiting them for his own artistic ends.

This sonnet may have set Shaw to thinking, not only by the rather stark contrast it presents between fashionable London with its delight in dainty flowers ("Her gaudies these!") and the poor wilted girls who minister to that taste, but also by the reference to Drury Lane and its associations with a certain famous orange girl. In the Epilogue to *Pygmalion*, Shaw refers to this mythic figure as a sort of Galatea: "Now, the history of Eliza Doolittle, though called a romance because the transfiguration it records seems exceedingly improbable, is common enough. Such transfigurations have been achieved by hundreds of resolutely ambitious young women since Nell Gwynne set them the example by playing queens and fascinating kings in the theatre in which she began by selling oranges" (4:782). Shaw uses a similar image of an actress learning to play a role that transcends her own class in the Preface to *Pygmalion*:

> Finally, and for the encouragement of people troubled with accents that cut them off from all high employment, I may add that

Fig. 8. Liza "endlessly posy making." From W. E. Henley, *London types* (New York: R. H. Russell, 1898), courtesy of Rare Books Room, The Pennsylvania State University Libraries. I am grateful to Charles Mann and Sandra Stelts of Pattee Library for making this illustration available.

the change wrought by Professor Higgins in the flower-girl is nei-ther impossible nor uncommon. The modern concierge's daugh-ter who fulfils her ambition by playing the Queen of Spain in Ruy Blas at the Théâtre Français is only one of many thousands who have sloughed off their native dialects and acquired a new tongue. Our West End shop assistants and domestic servants are bi-lingual. (4:664)

This brings us back to Shaw's initial ambition of seeing the elegant Mrs. Patrick Campbell learn a new language, the Cockney dialect, to prove her virtuosity in Nell Gwyn's line of work. If the orange-seller could play a queen, why not have this queen play a flower girl in a story that comments dramatically on the transformational process it makes necessary while exposing the hypocrisy and injustice of the social and economic caste systems that make that transformation seem so miraculous?

Suggestive as Henley's material is as a possible source of inspiration, it is only probable that Shaw read *London Types* when it came out in 1898. However, we do know that Shaw was aware of Henley's work. In 1888 he reviewed Henley's *Book of Verses* for the *Pall Mall Gazette*. Although he describes Henley as "a gentleman of respectable literary standing," the review is rather dismissive: "the book does not contain a scrap of evidence that the author could write prose if he tried."[6] Later in the review Shaw does cite some lines of poetry that are "finely struck," but his final line declares the book "horrible, fascinating, and wrong, yet rightly done . . . which no one should be advised to read, and which no one would be content to have missed."[7] This is more brutal than most scholars of Victorian verse would allow as reasonable. Shaw complains about Henley's "In Hospital" series, which is considered an admirable example of realism, and deprecates even "Invictus," the poem that has earned Henley immortality in anthologies of Victorian verse. Yet even Henley's biographer classes him as "admittedly a minor poet."[8] Despite the several collections of verses Henley published, including *The Song of the Sword* (1892), *London Voluntaries* (1893), *London Types* (1898), *For England's Sake* (1900), and *Hawthorn and Lavender* (1901), his importance to Victorian literature derives principally from his other literary activities—collaborating with R. L. Stevenson on plays, serving as editor for literary magazines (*London*, *The Magazine of Art*, and the *Scots Observer*, later called the *National Observer*), and writing essays on criticism, collected as *Views and Reviews* (1890). This wider influence allows one of his modern admirers to assert that "Henley's place in late-Victorian letters is certainly an important one: he crossed paths with almost all of the key literary figures of the era and . . . [t]he sphere of his influence will always be greater than his fame."[9]

Shaw was one of the "key literary figures" Henley "crossed paths with," personally as well as professionally, but the relationship was discordant. Shaw recorded in his diary entry for 24 April 1886 that William Archer introduced him to Henley that night after an evening at the theater, but the two had little contact until Shaw began contributing pieces to a magazine that Henley was editing. At that point the acquaintance was encouraged further by another mutual friend, James Runciman, the uncle of John F. Runciman, a music critic. In a letter to his biographer Archibald

Henderson dated 3 January 1905, Shaw explained that the elder Runciman "was a Cashel Byronite, and used to write me letters about Henley (among other subjects). He had known Henley and quarrelled with him; and what between Runciman & Cashel Byron, I got into correspondence with Henley." Soon Henley enlisted Shaw's musical expertise for his *Scots Observer* because, as Shaw explained to Henderson,

> among the various literary and artistic Dulcineas whose championship Henley mistook for criticism was Mozart. As I also knew Mozart's value, Henley induced me to write articles on music for his paper . . . and I did write some—not more than half a dozen— perhaps not so many. Henley was an impossible editor. He had no idea of criticism except to glorify the masters he liked, and pursue their rivals with spiteful jealousy. To appreciate Mozart without reviling Wagner was to Henley a black injustice to Mozart. Now he knew that I was what he called a Wagnerite, and that I thought his objections to Wagner *vieux jeu*, stupid, ignorant & common. Therefore he amused himself by interpolating abuse of Wagner into my articles over my signature. Naturally he lost his contributor; and it was highly characteristic of him that he did not understand why he could not get any more articles from me.[10]

The letter to which Shaw refers, dated 1 July 1890, was much more charming and diplomatic than this later account of it, even including an assurance that Shaw was "a great admirer" of Henley ("in a way"), so it is not very surprising that Henley did not feel rebuffed. However, Shaw did tell Henley plainly that "I had better not do the other articles for you. It is only trifling with the subject to get me to write for you if you are an anti-Wagnerite, or, for the matter of that, a Wagnerite either." Explaining his exasperation further, Shaw employed the same Quixote metaphor that he repeated in the letter to Henderson fifteen years later. He urged Henley to

> Let the Wagnerite get on his Rozinante (the critical essay) and make Wagner his Dulcinea to be tilted for with the old literary lances in the good old slashing style. Then you can get on your steed and tilt for Dulcinea Berlioz against him. You might as well tilt for Dulcinea Poe against Dulcinea Ibsen, as far as I am concerned; for the whole Dulcinea system only makes me laugh. . . . I have as much musical writing as I can stomach on the World; what I should like to do in my spare time is political writing.[11]

Since Shaw delivered the paper that would become *The Quintessence of Ibsenism* only seventeen days after he scoffed at this hypothetical match between Dulcinea Poe and Dulcinea Ibsen, the scorn seems unfair. Eight years later Shaw entered the lists for Wagner, presenting *The Perfect Wagnerite* in 1898. But perhaps Shaw's championship would be more justly compared with Ivanhoe's than with Quixote's since the writers he defends were genuinely worthy. In any case, Shaw decided to stop working under Henley's editing, which was conservative and procrustean enough to justify Shaw's sense that he was being stifled and ill-used.

Although the professional tie was severed, Shaw kept a balanced view of Henley. In his retrospective letter to Henderson after Henley's death, Shaw modulated his earlier exasperation with touches of respect: "Henley interested me as being what I call an Elizabethan, by which I mean a man with an extraordinary and imposing power of saying things, and with nothing whatever to say. . . . Give him the thing to be expressed, and he could find its expression wonderfully either in prose or verse. But beyond that he could not go."[12] He concludes his assessment of the man with ambiguous praise: "Henley, though a barren critic & poet, had enough talent and character to command plenty of consideration. A man cannot be everything."[13]

Despite this rather patronizing dismissal of Henley as a poet, Shaw retained an interest in the man even in Henley's later years, when he produced *London Types*. Shaw noted in the letter to Henderson that "[f]or a year before his death [in 1903] I had country quarters in Woking within three minutes walk of his house there; and I was slowly making up my mind to make his acquaintance seriously when he escaped me by dying."[14] We have no record that Shaw read *London Types* when it was published in 1898, but it seems likely that he would have. One of Henley's biographers describes the collection as "an ironic last commentary on life in the City" and reports that a contemporary critic judged them "capital photographs, which may be interesting a hundred years hence; but they are not pretty, and we are loth to call them art.' "[15] This mixed commendation sounds very much like the dubious compliment with which Shaw concluded his review of *A Book of Verses* in 1888. This later collection of Henley's verses may have struck Shaw as another book that he "would not be content to have missed."

In any case, the image of the "rapscallionly flower girl" would not leave Shaw alone. In 1901, four years after the reference in his letter to Ellen Terry and three years after Henley's " 'Liza" appeared in print, Shaw provided another glimpse of the flower-girl character that was taking shape in his imagination. The image reappears in an unlikely place, a passage of stage directions in *Man and Superman* introducing Ann Whitefield. Ann is a very different heroine from Eliza, but the resonance between the two stage directions that introduce them is unmistakable. In Ann's case, after describing the devastating effect that she produced on Octavius (a prototype for Freddy perhaps?), Shaw adds that such admiration was not *"ridiculous or discreditable, as Ann is a well formed creature as far as that goes; and she is perfectly ladylike, graceful, and comely, with ensnaring eyes and hair. . . . But all this is beside the point as an explanation of Ann's charm. Turn up her nose, give a cast to her eye, replace her black and violet confection by the apron and feathers of a flower girl, strike all the aitches out of her speech, and Ann would still make men dream"* (2:549). The stage direction introducing Eliza repeats not only the flower-girl image but the suggestion that her essence, her vitality—her genius, if you will—is totally unrelated to her place in the social order, and the apparent contrast between the elegant ladies in evening dress and her own bedraggled self is only superficial. Significantly, Eliza is introduced sitting physically at the feet of the ladies:

> *She sits down on the plinth of the column, sorting her flowers, on the lady's right. She is not at all a romantic figure. . . . She wears a little sailor hat of black straw that has long been exposed to the dust and soot of London and has seldom if ever been brushed. Her hair needs washing rather badly. . . . She is no doubt as clean as she can afford to be; but compared to the ladies she is very dirty. Her features are no worse than theirs; but their condition leaves something to be desired; and she needs the services of a dentist.* (4:671)

In this condition, she is practically invisible to Freddy (the Octavius figure), but he is immediately and irremediably smitten by her when she is presented to him washed, dressed genteely, and trained to speak elegantly. It is not these lady-like refinements, however, that strike Freddy, but her vitality, the quality that makes her different from the other young ladies of his acquaintance who are all equally well-scrubbed, well-dressed, and well-schooled in the usages of polite society, but not equally fascinating. Clearly Shaw had not backed down from his assertion about Ann: that essential magnetism would operate at any social level.

This may not have been the theme that Shaw meant to develop when he first conceived of his "east end dona" having an adventure of some kind with a "west end gentleman," but the image of the enchanting flower girl seems to have been associated in Shaw's mind rather early with the very insights about the illusions (and self-delusions) of social caste suggested in Henley's sonnets. We see the idea being worked out as early as 1901, when he created Ann, and we see another variation on the theme in *Major Barbara*, written in 1905. As it had in *Man and Superman*, the image appears here as a metaphor that suggests the essential irrelevance of social class in determining a person's real value. Again, the infatuation

of a young man for the vital heroine is a truer indication of that value
than what is suggested by her appearance. "She bought my soul like a
flower at a street corner," Cusins sighs, but he hastens to explain that the
Salvation Army rhetoric was lost on him: "[S]he bought it for herself. . . .
Dionysus and all the others are in herself. I adored what was divine in
her, and was therefore a true worshipper." Then came the ironic turn:
"But I was romantic about her too. I thought she was a woman of the
people, and that a marriage with a professor of Greek would be beyond
the wildest social ambitions of her rank. . . . When I learnt the horrible
truth—. . . . That she was enormously rich; that her grandfather was an
earl; that her father was the Prince of Darkness— . . .—and that I was
only an adventurer trying to catch a rich wife, then I stooped to deceive
her about my birth" (3:164). Describing how he first meets Barbara, Cusins sounds here like a more learned, intelligent version of Freddy, for he
is just as smitten by this earl's granddaughter disguised as a "salvation
lass" as Freddy had been with the flower girl disguised as a duchess. In
either case, it was the heroine's vital force that mattered.

   Major Barbara also prefigures a variation of the Galatea transformation
that Shaw develops from the idea of a "shady" father for the heroine, as
suggested by Henley's sonnet and fleshed out, finally, in Alfred Doolittle,
the dustman turned gentleman. Both "shady" fathers, Doolittle and Andrew Undershaft (alias the Prince of Darkness), are male Galateas who
undergo a similar miraculous change that vaults them from the slums
into a social class more appropriate to their natural gifts, and they become *better* (although certainly not saintly) as they grow richer. Undershaft asserts this himself when trying to explain to Barbara how such
transformations can be accomplished: "*I* was an east ender. I moralized
and starved until one day I swore that I would be a full-fed man at all
costs. . . . I was a dangerous man until I had my will: now I am a useful,
beneficent, kindly person. That is the history of most self-made million-
aires, I fancy" (3:173). Doolittle does not see his transformation as positive, nor does he admit that it makes him a better person, but Shaw
clearly expected us to see him as such: Doolittle is transformed from a
charming parasite, with nothing to expect in his future but the work-
house and a pauper's grave, into an equally charming rich eccentric who
is forced by his social position, as he dolefully explains, to "live for others
and not for myself: thats middle class morality" (4:762). Certainly the
Pygmalion in his case—Ezra D. Wannafeller, founder of the international
Moral Reform Societies—would be pleased with his work, for his religious
doctrine made the Christian philanthropist see Shaw's truth: that the artificial socio-economic caste system disguises more than it reveals about the
individual human souls that it classifies.

   We will never know whether this is the theme that Shaw meant to develop when he first conceived of his flower-girl role for Mrs. Patrick Campbell, nor can we know for certain that Henley's sonnets pointed Shaw's mind in that direction. However, considering the suggestive evidence, it seems only fair to recognize Henley for his possible influence on Shaw's Eliza Doolittle, even as we recognize Shaw's greater achievement in giving Henley's 'Liza a larger role, building a play around her that provides a profounder insight into the human condition than Henley's sonnets ever did.

Notes

1. Bernard Shaw, *Collected Letters 1874–1897*, ed. Dan H. Laurence (New York: Dodd, Mead, 1965), p. 803.

2. William Ernest Henley, *Poems* (London: David Nutt, 1908), 2:109.

3. Ibid., pp. 110–11.

4. Bernard Shaw, *Pygmalion*, in *Collected Plays with Their Prefaces*, ed. Dan H. Laurence (London: Max Reinhardt, 1970–74), 4:679. Subsequent references to Shaw's plays are to this edition and appear parenthetically in the text.

5. Henley, *Poems*, 2:117–18.

6. Bernard Shaw, *Bernard Shaw's Book Reviews*, ed. Brian Tyson (University Park: Penn State University Press, 1991), p. 416.

7. Ibid., p. 417.

8. Joseph M. Flora, *William Ernest Henley* (New York: Twayne, 1970), n.p.

9. Ibid.

10. Bernard Shaw, *Collected Letters 1898–1910*, ed. Dan H. Laurence (New York: Dodd, Mead, 1972), p. 481.

11. *Collected Letters 1874–1897*, p. 252.

12. *Collected Letters 1898–1910*, p. 482.

13. Ibid., p. 484.

14. Ibid., p. 481.

15. Jerome Hamilton Buckley, *William Ernest Henley: A Study in the "Counter-Decadence" of the 'Nineties* (Princeton, N.J.: Princeton University Press, 1945), p. 200.

Charles A. Carpenter

SHAW'S DRAMATIC REACTIONS TO THE BIRTH OF THE ATOMIC AGE

On 6 and 9 August 1945, the United States hastened the end of the war with Japan by dropping atom bombs on Hiroshima and Nagasaki. This turning point in world affairs and, potentially, in human destiny spawned what was readily termed the Atomic Age. Virtually every public figure in America and England responded somehow, eighty-nine-year-old Bernard Shaw among the first. From three days after the Nagasaki bomb to 6 August 1950, the fifth anniversary of Hiroshima, Shaw offered numerous reactions to the new era, some of them in dramatic form. Richard Nickson and Michael Holroyd have exposed us to most of Shaw's published journalism on the subject, and Alfred Turco has recently edited an unpublished item.[1] But no one has yet discussed his dramatic reactions, small segments of *Buoyant Billions* and *Farfetched Fables*, in the context of the Atomic Age. These bits of plays are unspectacular in themselves, but prove quite fascinating when set side by side and viewed in the light of his nondramatic comments, especially the late–1945 preface to *Geneva*.

After a false start on *Buoyant Billions* in 1936–37, Shaw restarted it on 2 August 1945. We can only imagine how his conception of it must have changed after he heard the news of Hiroshima four days later. In any event, he completed the play in 1947, and Act I now contains a brief argument conveying the positive implications of atomic discoveries.[2] This is not only Shaw's first dramatic treatment of the new era; it is the first one to be staged in England or Ireland.[3] His second play-segment also contains a brief discussion, this one weighted toward negative implications of atomic power. It appears in the first fable of the six in *Farfetched*

Fables, which he wrote in 1948.[4] (The second fable is indirectly relevant since it presents the plot dénouement of the first.) Since Shaw was in his nineties when he wrote these scenes, it is not surprising to find that the conceptions they embody are largely new applications of ideas that he had already formulated in essays and letters. But his mode of presenting them through the cut-and-thrust of debate emerging from real-life situations, with each point of view expressed in the character's own idiom but with heightened articulateness, is still distinctively Shavian.

Act I of *Buoyant Billions: A Comedy of No Manners* touches off from an all-too-familiar excuse for debate: a problematic son on the threshold of maturity confronts his prosperous, conventional father about his future. But Shavian twists keep the situation from being hackneyed: the young man, acknowledged by his father to be brilliant, declares his intention to pursue a career as "world betterer," which he considers all the more feasible with the advent of the Atomic Age. The father, who has long profited from the status quo, can see nothing but the dark side of the new era: soon not only America and England but many other nations will wield "irresistible" power simply because they "can afford to make atomic bombs, and wipe out a city and all its inhabitants in a thousandth of a second" (320). The son naïvely replies, "What does it matter if they can build it again in ten minutes? . . . Hiroshima and Nagasaki are already rebuilt; and Japan is all the better for the change." There is little rashness of youth, however, in his retorts that focus on the potentialities of atomic power to benefit mankind: "All the scientists in the world are at work finding out how to dilute and control and cheapen atomic power until it can be used to boil an egg or sharpen a lead pencil as easily as to destroy a city" (320). The son's Shavian propensity to exaggerate extends to following such ideas "as far as thought can reach." His rhetoric attains a glowing crescendo as a result: "When atom splitting makes it easy for us to support ourselves as well by two hours work as now by two years, we shall move mountains and straighten rivers in a hand's turn. Then the problem of what to do in our spare time will make life enormously more interesting. No more doubt as to whether life is worth living. Then the world betterers will come to their own" (320–21).[5] A sharp exchange of radically opposed views puts the cap on their argument:

> FATHER. Damn the atomic bomb!
> SON. Bless it say I. It will make world bettering possible. (322)

A reconciliation of sorts ensues when the son (rather absurdly) proposes that his father finance an around-the-world trip to investigate the chances of atomic science "ridding the world of the anopheles mosquito, the tsetse

fly, the white ant, and the locust" (322), and the father agrees—more to
get rid of him than anything else.[6]

The son's optimistic notions about what Shaw later labeled "atomic welfare"[7] had been in the air at least since the discovery of radioactivity.
Shaw himself attributed his early knowledge of atomic power to the writings of his friend H. G. Wells.[8] Wells's novel *The World Set Free*, published
in 1913, portrays a disastrous atomic world war but gives equal time, and
final victory, to the conceivable Utopian benefits of atomic energy. Both
possibilities were also heralded in a 1928 play that Shaw might have
known (especially since the hero is partly modeled on Eugene Marchbanks), Robert Nichols and Maurice Browne's *Wings Over Europe: A Dramatic Extravaganza on a Pressing Theme*.[9] The vein of extravagance in the
son's rhetoric is present in both these works. After Hiroshima, the promising side of atomic power was flaunted conspicuously in government
press releases and mass-circulation outlets as counters to the widespread
shock and horror the event produced.[10]

The tiny first scene of *Farfetched Fables* uses the pretext of a boy-meets-
girl situation to convey largely negative ideas about the Atomic Age. Here
the conflict that creates the few dramatic sparks does not arise from disagreement on the issues but from the impact of the new situation on the
male-female relationship. In a public park on a promising day, an attractive young man and woman meet for the first time. In the late Shavian
style, both fly in the face of convention by stating nakedly what they feel:

> YOUNG MAN. . . . I've got into this conversation with a view to our
> possible marriage.
> YOUNG WOMAN. Nothing doing. I'll not marry. (430)

We learn quickly that she equates marriage with bearing children and
that she will not "bring them into this wicked world to kill and be killed."
Later the young man argues that wars will not be fought with atomic
weapons because of their indiscriminate destructiveness (in his cockney
idiom he refers knowledgeably to the effects of their blasts, firestorms,
and radiation). He adds, pointedly, "Besides, bombs kill women. Killing
men does not matter: the women can replace them; but kill the women
and you kill the human race" (432).[11] This could be construed as a subtle
appeal to the maternal instinct. It is preceded by a startling event that
might also sway the woman: the United Nations countries have agreed to
abolish war and make the manufacture of atomic weapons a capital crime.
The newspaper extra announcing this development calls it "a new chapter in the history of the globe. The atomic bomb has reduced war to absurdity; for it threatens not only both victors and vanquished but the
whole neutral world. . . . [N]o nation will ever venture on atomic warfare

again" (431). Unfortunately, the young woman is skeptical that wars will cease to exist. She visualizes a further step in the evolution of genocidal weapons: a new kind of poison gas that is lighter than air so that it will disperse. "It may kill the inhabitants of a city," she says; "but it will leave the city standing and in working order" (432). The second startling turn in this eight-minute sketch occurs when the young man shows intense interest in the woman's idea—and no more in her. He reveals that he is a chemist in a chlorine gas factory and begins contemplating how to create the weapon she imagined. This settles the less-than-promising romance once and for all:

> YOUNG WOMAN [*rising wrathfully*] So that is what you are! One of these scientific devils who are destroying us! Well, you shall not sit next me again. Go where you belong: to hell. Good day to you.
>   *She goes away.*
> YOUNG MAN [*still thoughtful*] Lighter than air, eh? [*Slower*] Ligh—ter—than—air?
>   *The scene fades out.* (433)

The next scene in *Farfetched Fables* refers in no way to atomic power, but it completes the young man's story by fulfilling the young woman's prophecy. He invents the usable poison gas and sells it to a dictator, who destroys the population of the Isle of Wight to demonstrate its potency. Other countries who also got the formula (no doubt from the inventor) start a cataclysmic world war. After peddling his profitable commodity, we learn, the young man had moved to the Isle of Wight as a safety measure.

The connections between the subject matter in this little play and Shaw's published comments on the new Atomic Age in the aftermath of Hiroshima are remarkably close. His earliest articles in the press assert that the absurdity of the institution of world war was highlighted when the atomic bomb proved "too deadly to be used as a weapon, though it has had its momentary success by finishing the war with Japan."[12] A fortnight after Hiroshima he was prescient enough to raise the double specter of the proliferation of nuclear weapons and the invention of much more devastating ones: "What we have just succeeded in doing at enormous expense is making an ounce of uranium explode like [a supernova]. The process, no longer experimental, will certainly be cheapened; and at any moment heavier elements than uranium, as much more explosive than uranium as uranium than gunpowder, may be discovered."[13] By late 1945, when he composed his preface to *Geneva*, Shaw had refined these ideas markedly.[14] He states flatly that "if another world war be waged with this new weapon there may be an end of our civilization and its massed populations" (23). He now speaks of countries *consoling* them-selves "with the hope that the atomic bomb has made war impossible" (24) and shows little confidence in governments' being competent enough to forge international agreements banning the bomb and enforc-ing the ban. He echoes his fear that more devastating nuclear weapons may be devised (22), but goes far beyond this in his peroration:

> Meanwhile here we are, with our incompetence armed with atomic bombs. Now power civilizes and develops mankind, though not without having first been abused to the point of wiping out entire civilizations. If the atomic bomb wipes out ours we shall just have to begin again. We may agree on paper not to use it as it is too dangerous and destructive; but tomorrow may see the discovery of that poisonous gas lighter than air and capable . . . of killing all the inhabitants of a city without damaging its buildings or sewers or water supplies or railways or electric plants.[15] Victory might then win cities if it could repopulate them soon enough, whereas atomic bombing leaves nothing for anyone, victor or vanquished. It is conceivable even that the next great invention may create an overwhelming interest in pacific civilization and wipe out war.[16] You never can tell. (42–43)

The amusing tale of the young chemist is clearly a dramatically com-pressed equivalent, a "farfetched fable" or theatrical exemplar, of these grimly serious statements.

Neither *Buoyant Billions* nor *Farfetched Fables* is close to a full-fledged "drama of the Atomic Age." The Son's main objective in his argument with his father in the former play is not to convince him (or us) that world-betterment is more feasible than ever now that atomic power can be employed to that end, but to talk him into financing the first stage of his quest. The rest of the play, including the early part of the Act I argu-ment, focuses on the Son's pursuit of *financing*, not world-betterment. The new possibilities of the Atomic Age are never again mentioned. Simi-larly, the first two fables in the latter play show hypothetically that curb-ing the atom bomb will not necessarily prevent world destruction, but their main function is to establish the start-from-scratch situation for the ensuing futuristic episodes. These carry the chief thrust of the play, suc-cessively dramatizing the possible workings of Creative Evolution from restoring the human race (in amended form) to attaining the "vortex of pure thought" envisioned much earlier in *Back to Methuselah*. The sig-nificance and fascination of Shaw's varied reactions to the advent of a radically new stage in world history lie partly in their marked "Shavian-

ity," but also as phenomena of a still-fertile mind in its nineties. That they
exist at all is a farfetched fable in itself.

Notes

1. Richard Nickson's "Shaw on Nuclear War" (*Independent Shavian* 22:2–3 [1984]: 30–
33) quotes Shaw's journalism on the subject but does not discuss the plays or the preface to
Geneva. The third volume of Michael Holroyd's biography, *Bernard Shaw, 1918–1950: The
Lure of Fantasy* (New York: Random House, 1991), quotes a few relevant statements. The
previously unpublished article, printed under the heading "Bernard Shaw on Peace
(1950)," appears in *Unpublished Shaw* (*SHAW* 16), ed. Dan H. Laurence and Margot Peters
(University Park: Penn State University Press, 1996), pp. 185–93. It is remarkable for show-
ing that Shaw had kept up on the very latest development in the nuclear arms race, the
American decision to build a hydrogen bomb.

2. *Collected Plays with Their Prefaces*, ed. Dan H. Laurence (London: Reinhardt, 1974),
7:313–75. The play was substantially finished in 1947 but amended several times before its
first English performance at the Malvern Festival on 13 August 1949.

3. J. B. Priestley's *Summer Day's Dream*, which depicts conditions in the English country-
side fifteen years after an atomic war, was first performed one month after Shaw's play. A
few American plays preempted Shaw's, however; see my article, "American Dramatic Reactions to the Birth of the Atomic Age," *Journal of American Drama and Theatre* 7:3 (1995):
12–29.

4. *Collected Plays with Their Prefaces*, 7:429–33.

5. One of the most widely read early essays prompted by the atomic bomb, Norman
Cousins's *Modern Man Is Obsolete* (New York: Viking, 1945), gives the gist of this idea well
before Shaw: "The trend during the last fifty years toward shorter work weeks and shorter
hours will not only be continued but sharply accelerated" (p. 18).

6. In *Transformations and Texts: G. B. Shaw's* Buoyant Billions (Columbia, S. C.: Camden
House, 1992), Steven Joyce reveals that at one point in Shaw's process of composition the
atom bomb was discussed in Act III by members of the Buoyant family. (He does not say so
explicitly, but I think we can deduce that Mr. Smith and his son Junius do not bring up the
subject in Act I.) The Son—Ben in this version—claims to be a "professional revolutionist"
who, as a scientist, is well equipped for the job since science "is the only sphere in which we
can still hope for miracles" (pp. 50–51). It is The Youth, Fiffy, whom others recognize as
the budding world-betterer and who declares he will make beneficial use of the bomb: "Let
me get hold of it, and I'll start a war on the tsetse fly and make the deadly African bush
habitable. I will sweep away impenetrable jungles, irrigate barren deserts, and move mountains. Tigers and cobras, locusts and white ants, will become as legendary as dragons and
unicorns" (p. 55). Incidentally, Michael Holroyd errs in saying that the son leaves to investigate "the beneficial use of atomic *fusion*" (my italics; p. 486). At this time, it has to be atomic
fission.

7. In the London *Times* on the day before Christmas, 1949 (shortly after the Soviet
Union exploded an atomic device), Shaw urged a shift in attention from atomic warfare to
"the far more vital and pressing subject of atomic welfare" ("Atomic Welfare," repr. in
Shaw, *Agitations: Letters to the Press 1875–1950*, ed. Dan H. Laurence and James Rambeau
[New York: Ungar, 1985], p. 352).

8. Writing soon after Hiroshima, Shaw states: "From all over the world I have been asked what I have to say about the atomic bomb, about which H. G. Wells said all there is to say, and more, thirty years ago" ("The Atom Bomb," *New York Journal-American*, 19 August 1945, repr. in condensed form by Richard Nickson in *Independent Shavian*, 20:2–3 [1982]: 27. The substance of this article appeared a week earlier in England; Holroyd quotes brief excerpts of it from the *Sunday Express*, 12 August [*Bernard Shaw*, 3:482]).

9. The play was written in 1928 but not performed in London until 1932. See my article, "A 'Dramatic Extravaganza' of the Projected Atomic Age: *Wings Over Europe* (1928)," *Modern Drama* 35 (1992): 552–61.

10. Paul Boyer, in *By the Bomb's Early Light: American Thought and Culture at the Dawn of the Atomic Age* (New York: Pantheon Books, 1985), details what he calls "the search for a silver lining" in the immediate aftermath of Hiroshima (pp. 109–21).

11. A 1947 rehearsal edition of *Buoyant Billions* includes a passage, later omitted, in which a female member of the Buoyant family ("She") reminds the others that atomic bombs "kill women and children as well as men. Killing men didn't matter so long as women were left: we could keep the earth populated with five per cent of men or less; but wipe us out, and where are you?" (Joyce, p. 55).

12. "The Atom Bomb," p. 28. Interestingly, at this early date Shaw anticipates Orwell when he says that the wars that threaten us in the future are "civil wars" of many possible kinds, notably one in which Communists may drop atomic bombs on capitalists, capitalists on Communists, "and both of them on Fascists."

13. "The Atomic Bomb," London *Times*, 20 August 1945, repr. in *Agitations*, p. 337.

14. *Collected Plays with Their Prefaces*, 7:13–43.

15. Here as in *Farfetched Fables*, Shaw is echoing speculations dating from World War I on possible new forms of poison gas, but many contemporary readers would think of the neutron bomb, an atomic weapon that destroys mainly through radiation rather than blast and firestorm and thus has the effects he describes. The first successful test was held in 1962; the bomb became a center of controversy in the late 1970s when President Carter proposed to deploy it in European bases.

16. According to Sean O'Casey, Shaw died with the wish to end war virtually on his lips. On 10 November 1950 (eight days after Shaw's death), O'Casey informed the Secretary of the Sheffield Peace Congress of the British Peace Committee that "One of the last things, perhaps the very last thing, said by Bernard Shaw (unrecorded so far, but recorded now), before he sank into unconsciousness, was 'I hope the energy and time of the young wont [*sic*] be wasted in another war' " (*The Letters of Sean O'Casey*, 4 vols., ed. David Krause [New York: Macmillan, 1975–92], 2:754). Letters of 2 December 1952 and 19 January 1953 confirm this and reveal that his wife Eileen was with Shaw at the time (*Letters* 4:574, 576). Holroyd missed these letters and claims that Shaw's last words were "I want to die" (*Bernard Shaw*, 3:513).

Paul Bauschatz

THE UNEASY EVOLUTION OF *MY FAIR LADY* FROM *PYGMALION*

When Alan Jay Lerner and Frederick Loewe's *My Fair Lady* opened at the Mark Hellinger Theatre in New York on 15 March 1956, the musical achieved the first of its still-continuing successes. The popular press lauded the production, and there is no question that it was laudable for a variety of reasons. As Higgins, it starred Rex Harrison, who brought to his performance a wealth of experience playing Bernard Shaw's work on stage and screen, and, as Eliza, Julie Andrews, a singing actress with solid stage experience, but a relative newcomer to the New York stage. Her performance made her a star. The production was directed by Moss Hart and boasted costumes by Cecil Beaton. The whole was so well integrated that critics generally fell to listing its positive accomplishments. Out-of-town reports had predicted a success; all seven New York dailies fulfilled these expectations in their reviews of 16 March 1956.[1]

In their praise, few reviewers of *My Fair Lady* failed to credit Bernard Shaw, whose *Pygmalion* had supplied the text that Alan Jay Lerner had used to create the book of the musical. As many noticed, *My Fair Lady* claims a very close relation to its dramatic source. Brooks Atkinson, writing in the *New York Times*, noted that "Shaw's crackling mind is still the genius of [*My Fair Lady*]." As the musical opens, "the sly quips Shaw wrote for his [*Pygmalion*] begin to ripple along as before" (Walter Kerr, *New York Herald Tribune*). The production, "with breath-taking skill, has kept the essence of the original" (Robert Coleman, *Daily Mirror*); *My Fair Lady* "remains pure Shaw" (John Chapman, *Daily News*). Apart from its song lyrics, virtually all of *My Fair Lady*'s dialogue can be found in *Pygmalion*. Even the lyrics were credited with qualities appropriate to Shaw's dialogue. Robert Coleman noted that Alan Jay Lerner had "penned lyrics that beautifully complement the Shavian dialogue" (*Daily Mirror*). He had kept Shaw's "ironic point of view in his crisp adaptation and his sardonic lyrics" (Brooks Atkinson, *New York Times*). "Mr. Lerner's lyrics are witty, polished and intelligent, and they also have the great merit of sounding as if they belonged in a work stemming from the Master" (Richard Watts, Jr., *New York Post*).

This history, however, tells only part of a tale. *My Fair Lady* is not just *Pygmalion* with songs and dances. More fundamentally, *My Fair Lady* sets out to modify some of the peculiar structural aspects of its source. For example, much of *Pygmalion*'s more spectacular action occurs off stage. Eliza's phonetic training is not rehearsed for us, nor is her moment of triumph, which occurs off stage between Acts III and IV of the original version of the play. Surely, we should have some glimpse of these events. In addition, and more problematic all around, is the unresolved ending of the play, with Higgins left alone in his mother's flat while the rest of the characters go off to Doolittle's wedding. Conventional wisdom demands a closure that Shaw's text, subtitled with some irony "A Romance in Five Acts," denies us. The play does contain most of the conventional elements of the Romance genre: pastoral setting (Covent Garden, flowers, the garden party), change of social status, parental hindrance to the course of true love, characters of lower order revealed to have noble blood, a wedding at the conclusion, reaffirmation of the social order, etc., although these often show up in the wrong way with the wrong character at the wrong time (the father, not the daughter, gets married, for example). With such generic encouragement, it stands to reason that the "children" in the play (Eliza and Higgins) ought to become lovers. In fact, this conventional sense that the play needed a reconciliation, if not a real romantic ending, plagued it from its inception.

Pygmalion, in spite of its unconventional aspects, is not a play whose structure can be either adapted or altered easily. Early on, Eric Bentley had noticed how carefully the play had been constructed. He saw in Act I a prologue to Acts II and III, which formed the play's first unit, and Acts IV and V forming the second.[2] Whether Bentley is right about this is not really the point. (I, for example, see the play as being much more divided into units connecting Act I to Act II and Act IV to Act V and as pivoting them, as it were, around Act III, but *that* is not the point either.) What anyone closely observing *Pygmalion* comes to realize is that it *is* a very carefully constructed piece in spite of its peculiarities. Tampering anywhere simply creates unexpected difficulties elsewhere. *My Fair Lady*'s changes create new problems unknown in *Pygmalion*; some of these, it can neither control nor accommodate.

To say that *My Fair Lady* evolves from *Pygmalion* is overly simple. *Pygmalion* itself, at the time when *My Fair Lady* was conceived, existed in a number of forms. First, there was the original five-act play written in 1912. This play, which Shaw copyrighted in 1914 and 1916, was in its essentials the one that had been produced in London and directed by Shaw in 1914. The production featured Sir Herbert Beerbohm Tree as Higgins and Mrs. Patrick Campbell as Eliza. The play's checkered journey from page to performance was not easy.[3] By 1916, the printed version of the play had acquired its preface, "A Professor of Phonetics," and its sequel, "What Happened Afterwards," in which we are informed that Eliza marries Freddy.[4]

Second, there exists a series of scenarios toward potential film projects written during the 1930s. These were begun in 1934. There exists a final (last) screenplay, the 1938 revision, which was, in part, the one utilized for the 1938 film. Portions of these earlier scenarios had been used with varying faithfulness in two filmed versions of *Pygmalion* made prior to 1938. A German film (Berlin, 1935) used as its basis a translation of Shaw's 1934 screenplay but created a romantic ending for Higgins and Eliza. A Dutch film (Amsterdam, 1937) did likewise but departed even further from Shaw's original concept.[5]

Third, there was the film produced in 1938, the most successful cinematic adaptation of any work by Shaw.[6] It was not, however, identical to any of Shaw's extant scripts.[7] The film exists largely as a monument to the conviction and determination of Gabriel Pascal, who eventually produced it and who had earlier "charmed everyone in the Shaw household."[8] There is general agreement that, after Pascal, it was its director "Anthony Asquith who made *Pygmalion* a success," although he shares honors with Leslie Howard in the film's credits.[9] The acting in the film was of exceptionally high quality. "Wendy Hiller had been Shaw's choice for Eliza and he . . . had wanted Charles Laughton to play Higgins."[10] Wendy Hiller's performance as Eliza was universally praised. Pascal, who had brought Wendy Hiller to Shaw's notice, chose Leslie Howard, of whom Shaw disapproved, to play Higgins. Howard is likewise good in the role, but his impersonation shifts the events of the film in ways of which Shaw had been suspicious from the start. The film was a critical and popular success.[11] It won the Volpi Cup at the Venice Film Festival, and it won two academy awards, one ironically for Shaw, whose screenplay had been only partially utilized. Typically, Shaw referred to his award as "an insult."[12]

Finally, there is the script of the play, revised in the 1930s and copyrighted in 1941, still in five acts but with transitional scenes derived from and related to the additional material Shaw had produced while rethinking the play into cinematic terms. This version of the play is the one most

often now produced although portions of its "additional material" are
either played or left out, depending upon directorial whim or the techni-
cal capabilities of particular stages. This is the "Bodley Head" version of
the play.[13] It includes, in addition to the "Preface" and "Sequel" of the
original publication, a variety of other addenda: "A Note for Technicians," several comments by Shaw to newspapers on aspects of the first
production of the play, as well as some commentary related to the release
of the film. This version of the play is the one republished with the text
of *My Fair Lady* in 1975, without "Preface" or "Sequel," but with a portion
of the accompanying addenda.[14]

Although much of the basic plot line of *Pygmalion* remains unaltered in
revision and is well known, some specific instances of the variety mentioned above will prove helpful in seeing how the different versions, particularly the 1938 film, inform the creation of *My Fair Lady*. The action of
Act I of *Pygmalion* remains the same in all versions, although subsequent
revisions add material at the end involving Eliza's banter with a taxi man,
her departure from Covent Garden, and her arrival home. (All these variations are summarized in the Table on pp. 194–95.) Act II, in Higgins's
flat in Wimpole Street the following day, has Eliza come to have speech
lessons so that she can get work in a flower shop. Higgins makes a wager
with Pickering that he (or they) can pass her off as a duchess in six
months' time. Higgins and Pickering are then disturbed by the arrival of
Doolittle, Eliza's father, who "sells" his daughter to the two gentlemen
for five pounds—and no more! Too much money "makes a man feel prudent like: and then goodbye to happiness" (original *Pygmalion*, p. 151).
After Doolittle leaves, Higgins and Pickering realize that they "have taken
on a stiff job" (original *Pygmalion*, p. 156). All subsequent versions add a
scene in the middle of the act, where Mrs. Pearce bathes Eliza. Likewise,
there are at the end of the act, in varying degrees of complexity and
number, enactments of Eliza's phonetics lessons.

Act III of *Pygmalion* takes place in the drawing room of Mrs. Higgins's
flat on Chelsea Embankment some time prior to the six months specified
by the wager of Act II. Higgins wants to use his mother to test Eliza's new
English. Eliza tells a gruesome but well articulated story about her aunt,
her death, her hat, and her illnesses, after which she exits mid-act with
her famous "Walk! Not bloody likely. . . . I am going in a taxi" (original
Pygmalion, p. 167). After this, Higgins and Pickering attempt to explain
to Mrs. Higgins exactly what their relationship with Eliza *is* and what she
is being trained to do. They leave Mrs. Higgins to utter at the fall of the
curtain "Oh, men! men!! men!!!" (original *Pygmalion*, p. 174).

The filmed version reorganizes this material, placing the conversation
of Pickering and Higgins with his mother in the middle of the act. Eliza's
talk about her aunt and her exit then occur at the end of the scene. (No

version of Shaw's screenplay revises this order.) The film also adds more phonetics lessons at this point as well as preparation for the ambassador's reception. In addition, all later versions of *Pygmalion* offer at least one scene *at* the embassy where Eliza is passed off as a duchess. By the time of the screenplays, the event has become an indoor, formal ballroom reception.

In the original version of the play, there is no reference to its garden party's events prior to Act IV. That act begins with Pickering, Higgins, and Eliza returning to Higgins's flat. From the conversation between Pickering and Higgins, we learn that the bet has been won. (Subsequent versions delete as much of this dialogue as has been shown in the enacted transitional scenes.) Higgins and Eliza eventually fall into a long argument that ends with Higgins storming upstairs in high dudgeon and Eliza, emotionally spent, remaining on stage. The revisions leave this action pretty much alone, but all add additional transitional material toward the events the next day (in Act V) at Mrs. Higgins's flat. In both the screenplay and the revision of the stage play, we follow Eliza to her room; we watch her pack and leave Higgins's flat. We meet Freddy outside waiting for a glimpse of Eliza. (The film had edited scenes of Freddy attempting to meet Eliza into some of the phonetics lessons added *after* the debacle of Act III.) Freddy and Eliza decide to spend the night driving around in a taxi. In the screenplay, they are hassled by constables trying to get them off the street. In the film, they go back to Covent Garden where Eliza recognizes old friends, but they do not recognize her. The film also reintroduces Mrs. Pearce waking up Higgins, providing his first realization that Eliza has gone.

The original Act V has Higgins arriving with Pickering to confront his mother with Eliza's disappearance. Before his mother can calm him down, Doolittle appears, much changed and elegantly dressed. His moral stance on the danger of having too much money had led Higgins to recommend him to the late Ezra D. Wannafeller, an eccentric American millionaire, who subsequently left Doolittle a fortune to lecture for Moral Reform Societies. His happy days are over. He and his natural wife are now to be married—victims of middle class morality. Mrs. Higgins suggests that Eliza's father can now take care of her: "Yes, maam: I'm expected to provide for everyone now . . ." (original *Pygmalion*, p. 191). She also reveals that Eliza is present. Eliza and Higgins have another conversation, in which neither is willing to give ground to the other. Eliza clearly holds her own against Higgins, and the act ends in a stalemate, with Pickering, Mrs. Higgins, and Eliza getting ready to go off to Doolittle's wedding. Higgins is left on stage, alone and silent, as the curtain falls (original *Pygmalion*, p. 209).

In Shaw's revision of the play, the sequence of events is the same, but

Higgins, alone on stage at the end, has a final line: "She's going to marry Freddy. Ha ha! Freddy! Freddy!! Ha ha ha ha ha!!!!! [*He roars with laughter as the play ends*]" (Bodley Head *Pygmalion*, p. 782). The screenplay scenarios provide two possible endings: The first has Higgins alone (*no* final line), but he goes out onto the balcony and sees Freddy meet Eliza, Doolittle, and Mrs. Higgins below, about to go off to the wedding.[15] The second version has Higgins leave the flat with his mother. They discuss the possibility of a marriage between Freddy and Eliza prior to Mrs. Higgins's getting into her limousine and driving off with Freddy and Eliza to the wedding. After they leave, Higgins has two visions of Eliza: (1) He recalls his first meeting with her at Covent Garden, and (2) he visualizes her with Freddy running a flower shop. A policewoman disrupts his reverie and asks him if anything is wrong. "No," he replies, "A happy ending. A happy beginning," and he walks away.[16]

Needless to say, not one of these possible conclusions accounts for the ending of the film. True, Higgins does see Freddy and Eliza drive off in a taxi, but that is all. The camera watches him leave his mother's flat, walk along the embankment, and return home. He walks into his laboratory, and, sitting down, accidentally turns on his recording device. It has Eliza's voice: "I washed my face and hands before I come, I did." When Higgins turns off the recording, the voice continues. Eliza is at the door. Higgins looks at her but does not rise from his seat. Rather, he turns away, pulls his hat forward over his face, and asks, "Eliza? Where the devil are my slippers?" The theme music swells as the film ends.

The irresolute curtain of *Pygmalion*, even in its first production, had encouraged Beerbohm Tree to begin pantomiming reconciliatory endings. Tree had apparently suggested at rehearsals a gesture for Higgins at the end of Act V where he would go to the window of his mother's flat and throw "flowers to Eliza in the very brief interval between the end of the play and the fall of the curtain."[17] Shaw rejected the gesture outright.[18] It was only after the play's successful run was under way and Shaw had departed the scene that Tree moved to reincorporate the business. Shaw, informed of the state of affairs by Mrs. Patrick Campbell, once again insisted that the gesture be abandoned.[19]

Shaw's screenplays do nothing to encourage this reconciliation. "According to Anthony Asquith and his assistant Teddy Baird, the film makers shot three different endings. None was satisfied with the first, which conformed to Shaw's screenplay. The second, a compromise between Shaw's screenplay and a conclusion which has Higgins confident that Liza will return to him, . . . may have seemed too inconclusive for the movie makers."[20] The romantic ending of the film was created using only dialogue that Shaw had written since Gabriel Pascal had sworn to Shaw "adherence to every comma of the screenplay."[21] Shaw's lack of objection to the ending of the film seems to have resulted from his realization that protest would be useless since Pascal had, in effect, presented him "with a *fait accompli*."[22] Yet it is the film's ending of *Pygmalion* that most people now recall, not only because we recollect the film, but because many later stagings of the play have incorporated this ending. It is also, of course, the source of the entire substance of Act II, scenes 6 and 7 of *My Fair Lady*.[23]

The narrative sequence of scenes and just about all the dialogue of *My Fair Lady* derive from the filmed version of *Pygmalion*, not from the screenplay nor from those same scenes as they appear in the original and revised play scripts. It should not be a surprise that *My Fair Lady* was conceived in the image of the film of *Pygmalion* since negotiations for its creation were first begun by Gabriel Pascal in 1951. Pascal first made overtures to Rodgers and Hammerstein and Cole Porter, among others, before hitting upon Lerner and Loewe.[24] He also made the initial contact with Rex Harrison, for Higgins, with whom he had worked in the 1940 filming of *Major Barbara*. Pascal had originally tried to interest Mary Martin in the role of Eliza, but was unsuccessful. He then thought of Dolores Gray.[25] Although Pascal died in 1954, his concept and his film were never thereafter distant from the creation of the musical.

My Fair Lady divides *Pygmalion*'s original five acts into two: Act I's eleven scenes comprise Acts I, II, and III of *Pygmalion* with all the transitional material up through and including the ambassador's reception. Act II of *My Fair Lady* comprises Acts IV and V of *Pygmalion*: It is divided into seven scenes, of which scenes 6 and 7 are the equivalent of the film's romantic ending. (This scenario is summarized in the Table on pp. 194–95.) Although *My Fair Lady* is in some ways a faithful musical adaptation of the film of *Pygmalion*, it departs from it in two significant ways. These particular departures deeply disrupt the structural fabric not only of the film and its related screenplays but also of all the dramatic texts (original playscripts and revisions) that precede them.

The first problematic departure in *My Fair Lady* involves the play's subplot about Doolittle. Doolittle's two appearances in *Pygmalion* (in Acts II and V) provide shadow plots to the central relationship of Higgins and Eliza. Higgins is instrumental in controlling the affairs of both father and daughter. Higgins provides the wherewithal for Eliza's potential change in social status; likewise, he has inadvertently provided for the change in Doolittle's social status as well. Eliza desires the language to allow her to change from streetseller to clerk in a florist shop. Her aspirations toward lower-middle-class status are not shared by her father. However, Higgins's actions shift a good deal of money into Doolittle's hands. Even though Doolittle explicitly does not want to enter the middle class, his arrival at Mrs. Higgins's flat in Act V indicates clearly that he has done so. He is announced as "a gentleman" and is allowed easy access to the flat (original *Pygmailion*, p. 187). Doolittle's change of fortune calls into question Higgins's assertion to Eliza that her language can make her a "duchess"—or a shop girl.

An important aspect of the play turns on its association, at once, of language, clothes, and money to effect social change. Eliza acquires language and clothes; Doolittle acquires clothes and money. In spite of Higgins's blindness to the fact, money plays a central role here. Concern about money is a regular feature of the play from its beginning.[26] In Act I the Eynsford Hills consult about the amount of money to be given to Eliza to find out how she happened to know Freddy's name. Higgins throws his money at Eliza, who uses it to get a taxi home. She bickers with the taxi driver about the fare. Act II presents Eliza's concern about the cost of speech lessons, not to mention Doolittle's "selling" his daughter to Higgins and Pickering. The argument in Act IV comes eventually to turn on matters of cost about the rental of clothes and jewelry and the possibility of Eliza's being accused of stealing. Even Doolittle's reception by Mrs. Higgins and Colonel Pickering in Act V and their expressed willingness to attend his wedding occur after they learn of his windfall fortune. Doolittle's social acceptability, with its dependence upon monetary underpinning, provides a wry and ironic commentary on the play's main plot line.

When we turn to *My Fair Lady*, however, we observe something quite different. Instead of just two scenes, Doolittle appears in four: The first two (Act I, scenes 2 and 4) are not in any version of *Pygmalion*. In the first scene, Doolittle meets Eliza later during the same evening of Act I, after her first meeting with Higgins in Covent Garden. Doolittle borrows money from her. Then he and his pub-visiting friends sing "With a Little Bit of Luck," Doolittle's character-establishing song (*My Fair Lady*, pp. 37–40). It creates for us a man who is prepared to do as little as possible and to get for himself as much as his luck will allow. Act I, scene 4 takes place at Eliza's dwelling in Tottenham Court Road when Doolittle learns that Eliza has gone off to Higgins's flat. Doolittle sees the luck in this and sets off for Wimpole Street with a reprise of "With a Little Bit of Luck," in case we had missed its point earlier (*My Fair Lady*, pp. 62–63).

Act I, scene 5 is Doolittle's entrance into Higgins's flat, from Act II of *Pygmalion*. The scene is unsung. It is all Shaw's dialogue virtually intact, but notice the difference. Unlike the play, where this is our first look at Doolittle—we hadn't even known of his existence prior to this entrance—in *My Fair Lady* we know all about him, what he is like, what he has come for. Unlike the play, where this scene establishes him for Higgins and Pickering—and for us—here he is a known quantity. Unfortunately, the odd moral turn he must take in the dialogue—that is, he must through moral scruple refuse ten pounds because he understands the precariousness of having too much money—rings untrue. *My Fair Lady*'s Doolittle has already been established as a character who is out to get whatever he can, and there is not a reason in the world that he should balk at taking ten pounds.

Further changes are even more disturbing for Doolittle's characterization. His last scene, the one corresponding to his arrival at Mrs. Higgins's flat in Act V of *Pygmalion*, is drastically changed. To put it bluntly, Doolittle does not get anywhere near Mrs. Higgins throughout the whole of *My Fair Lady*. Rather, *My Fair Lady* uses the transitional material of the film of *Pygmalion* to maneuver Eliza back to Covent Garden. There, Eliza meets her father by chance. He is still in his old neighborhood at his old pub with his old companions, getting ready for an all-night fling before his impending wedding. Eliza is the *only* major character he meets. He sings here "Get Me to the Church on Time" (*My Fair Lady*, pp. 155–58). It is another rousing song, but it is a set piece, a music-hall song of the same kind as "With a Little Bit of Luck." Every aspect of *My Fair Lady* conspires to keep Doolittle at its conclusion in exactly the same social position he was in at the beginning. Because Doolittle, not Eliza, provides the most cogent social commentary in *Pygmalion*, his marginalization most firmly skews *My Fair Lady* away from *Pygmalion*'s central concerns with class, power, and money.

If *Pygmalion* is in large part about the power of money to determine social class, *My Fair Lady* is about falling in love. Now falling in love is not a bad narrative thread upon which to string the events of musical theater—it has been thought of before—but Shaw's *Pygmalion* does not lend itself easily to this kind of threading. The play necessitates that something must happen to and for Eliza. We should not ignore the fact that the play leaves Eliza, at the final curtain, with her question in Act IV still unanswered: "Whats to become of me?" (original *Pygmalion*, p. 179). The question had been raised in one form or another earlier: "Mrs. Higgins tries to make her son aware of the seriousness of the situation he is creating, and Mrs. Pearce . . . admonishes him of the need to think what he is about."[27] The women are much more aware of the reality of social position than either Higgins or Colonel Pickering. It is Mrs. Eynsford Hill and her daughter Clara who provide the most likely answer to Eliza's question: genteel poverty. Shaw's later assertions in his "Sequel" that Eliza will marry Freddy and into the social status of this family predict such an outcome. Even so, Eliza's question remains unanswered as the final curtain falls. The inconclusive nature of this ending moves us beyond the events of the play to ponder their implications.

The various alternative endings provided for the play try to knit up this rather stalemated situation. Shaw's own comments about the marriage to

Freddy attempt to forestall other solutions. The 1938 film-makers tried two alternate conclusions before hitting upon their romantic ending. Alan Jay Lerner agreed; he prefaces the text of *My Fair Lady* with his disclaimer that he is not convinced that Eliza should end up with Freddy.[28] True enough: *My Fair Lady* ends as the film of *Pygmalion* ended; Eliza returns to Higgins. This, however, is no real problem because the reconciliation at the end of *My Fair Lady* works quite well. The difficulties come earlier in the whole affair.

To get at this, we need to look at what happens in *My Fair Lady* to the material of Act II of the stage version of *Pygmalion*. This act began with Pickering and Higgins at Higgins's flat the day after their meeting at Covent Garden. Eliza arrives to have speech lessons. Higgins bullies her; Pickering interferes; the wager is established; Doolittle arrives and "sells" Eliza for five pounds; Higgins and Pickering realize that they have their work cut out for them. The play's revisions add to this Mrs. Pearce bathing Eliza and the following phonetics lessons. With the exception of the bathing scene, all this material, both original and subsequent, remains in *My Fair Lady*, in Act I, scenes 3 and 5. The whole of this, along with the additional interruption of Act I, scene 4—Doolittle's discovery that Eliza has moved to Higgins's flat—takes just about an hour to perform. It is quite a bit longer than the original Act II of *Pygmalion*. The added length derives in part from the additional phonetics lessons (all occurring in Act I, scene 5) and from the music. As it plays out, this section becomes the most fully articulated musical structure in the adaptation so far—and it will remain the most coherent and effective musical sequence in the whole of *My Fair Lady*.

In *My Fair Lady*, Eliza arrives at Higgins's flat at the beginning of Act I, scene 3, and her negotiation about the lessons begins. The dialogue is Shaw's. The scene comes almost to its close as Mrs. Pearce bundles Eliza off for her bath. At the end of Act I, scene 3, in the dialogue where Pickering asks Higgins if he is "a man of good character where women are concerned," Higgins sings the song "I'm an Ordinary Man" (*My Fair Lady*, pp. 56–59). It confirms that he is as much a curmudgeon about women as he is about the English language, a fact we had discovered earlier during the Covent Garden dialogue from *Pygmalion* and from Higgins's Act I, scene 1 song, "Why Can't the English?" (*My Fair Lady*, pp. 27–29).

Act I, scene 4 is the short Doolittle scene at Tottenham Court Road already noted. Then Act I, scene 5 returns to Higgins's study at just about the point of Doolittle's original entry into Act II of *Pygmalion*. After Doolittle's scene, however, Higgins begins to "teach" Eliza her phonetics. Very little of this appears in Shaw's screenplays. All these lessons come either from the film of *Pygmalion* or are additionally added to *My Fair*

Lady by Alan Jay Lerner. They begin with the vowels *A*, *E*, *I*, *O*, and *U*—all got wrong—resulting in petulant and antagonistic threats from Higgins. After the first lesson, Eliza sings "Just You Wait, 'Enry 'Iggins"—a fantasy of her having Higgins beheaded (*My Fair Lady*, pp. 76–77). Then, a return to more phonetics: She works on *H*, *G*, and "The rain in Spain stays mainly in the plain" (*My Fair Lady*, pp. 77–79). The phrase had appeared in the film of *Pygmalion* but not in any of Shaw's scripts. After this sequence, a chorus of servants sings a refrain about "Poor Professor Higgins." (*My Fair Lady* is considerably more upscale than *Pygmalion*, and one of the benefits of this shift in status is more servants, who provide choral background to the tension—both dramatic and narrative—that this sequence builds.) Then, more phonetics: "Cup of tea" is next (Shaw's idea) and a xylophone to demonstrate rise and fall of pitch and intonation (from the film of *Pygmalion*). After this, more "Poor Professor Higgins." Next lesson: Eliza is made to recite poetry with marbles in her mouth (from the filmed *Pygmalion*, originally in the German film).[29] One of these, Eliza swallows. More choral support: Now, rather than "Poor Professor Higgins," we get "Quit, Professor Higgins!" sung to the same music.

Tension has mounted rather noticeably through all these lessons. It has become very late. Higgins, about to give up, has Eliza try "The Rain in Spain" once more, and, "By George, she's got it!" (*My Fair Lady*, p. 87). The action evolves into the joyous "The Rain in Spain" trio, sung and danced by Pickering, Higgins, and Eliza (*My Fair Lady*, pp. 87–88). This concerted piece brings the phonetics lessons to a triumphant conclusion: It is the first and the *only* time in *My Fair Lady* that Eliza and Higgins join in song. The scene, however, is not over. As Higgins and Pickering decide to show Eliza off to Mrs. Higgins (not at home but at Ascot in *My Fair Lady*), Eliza is packed off to bed by Mrs. Pearce and the female servants. Eliza now sings "I Could Have Danced All Night," recalling the thrill of the preceding trio and expressing clearly her joy in having danced with Higgins. This stunning song is sung through three times before the scene's end, and it brings the whole of its preceding action to a sweeping, dramatic finish (*My Fair Lady*, pp. 91–94).

This scene should also bring down the Act I curtain. Half of *My Fair Lady*'s action is now over: Eliza knows she is in love; Act II need only provide Higgins his opportunity to come to the same conclusion. All factors point toward ending here, and it is easy to credit the following Ascot scene with "beginning the second act."[30] There is, however, no pause. *My Fair Lady* is committed to following the plot line and dialogue of *Pygmalion*, and *Pygmalion*'s Act III (Mrs. Higgins's at-home) now follows. In *Pygmalion*, the scene at Mrs. Higgins's flat, climaxing in Eliza's fantastic account of her aunt's demise and her shocking "bloody," provides a comic high point in the action. Shaw knew this and cautioned about not letting the success of this very funny scene disrupt the arc of the whole play. He refers to it memorably in his "FINAL ORDERS" given to Mrs. Patrick Campbell in a letter of 11 April 1914, just before the London opening. After a good deal of instruction about how this scene or that business should be played, Shaw concludes by noting, "The danger to-night will be a collapse of the play after the third act."[31]

It was not only the utterance of the forbidden word that concerned Shaw. The first two acts of the play as originally conceived pointed toward this moment, the first chance we have to see Eliza in the process of her transformation, the original version of the play having none of the phonetics lessons that all the later versions acquired. The scene of Mrs. Higgins's at-home, however, is constructed so that the "sensation" that Eliza's comment creates is not at its curtain. She leaves in mid-act, relinquishing the stage to Pickering, Higgins, and Mrs. Higgins, who re-establish the play's main plot line.

As originally conceived, the play resumes immediately with the action of Act IV: Pickering, Higgins, and Eliza return to Wimpole Street from the garden party. All the phonetics training after Act III's action, all the preparation for the garden party, all the events at the garden party itself take place off stage between these two acts. Act IV begins a new arc for the play, which Act V completes (or extends, should one find the ending inconclusive). The audiences at the first production must have been very interested in what had happened at the garden party when the curtain went up on Act IV since the events of Act III had not augured well for success. Although Shaw's revisions to the play (and his various screenplay versions) add some material from the ambassador's reception, all are un-resolved with respect to the degree of Eliza's triumph, and all lead directly into the events of Act IV in some way.

The film of *Pygmalion* changes this direction slightly. The events of the original ending of Act III are integrated back into its prior action rather awkwardly. Higgins and Pickering take Mrs. Higgins aside and discuss Eliza prior to her entrance to allow Eliza's utterance of "bloody" to end the scene. With the rest of the action of Act III gone, the connection to the events of Act IV is then facilitated with yet more phonetics and etiquette lessons and a great deal of scurry having to do with getting ready for the ambassador's reception. In the film, much is made of the elegance of the reception itself, and Eliza is allowed to dance with a young nobleman. Visually, her success is complete. Even so, the arc of the action of the first three acts of the play is, by this, merely extended. The plot problem of what is to become of Eliza still remains open and will still continue to focus the concluding events of the film.

My Fair Lady, making use of the film's sequence of events, works badly

against itself at this point. In *My Fair Lady*, the scene at Ascot, corresponding to Mrs. Higgins's at-home, is a dud, even though it does not always
appear to be as bad as it is. For example, the critics of the original New
York production remarked on the scene favorably: "The 'Ascot Gavotte'
at the races is a laconic satire of British reserve in the midst of excitement,
and very entertaining, too" (Brooks Atkinson, *New York Times*). Even more
laudatory is John Chapman's "the visual high spot of the evening is a
scene at the Ascot race track" (*Daily News*). Note, however, that Atkinson
is referring to the song that opens the scene, not to the dialogue that
follows, and that Chapman's adjective is *visual*. In performance, this scene
can be the most visually striking of the musical's first act. Cecil Beaton's
costumes for the original production were quite elegant, and the scene
provided the first opportunity in the show (except for its opening) to
offer real fashionable display. The visual effect wears off once the opening song is over, and the scene sinks or swims in its dialogue.

The dialogue, however, can no longer let us in on what Eliza is able to
do in the phonetics line since we have already discovered that in the previous scene, where she so effectively learned to utter "The Rain in Spain."
It is not intimate but public. Eliza's *faux pas* (no longer "bloody" but
"Move your bloomin' arse!!!") is uttered in front of a large contingent of
fashionable London society (*My Fair Lady*, p. 108). This creates a serious
logical problem for her following anonymity at the ambassador's reception. All that remains of Shaw's brilliantly constructed Act III is Eliza's
funny story about her aunt's death from influenza. It is still funny, but it
now has no point. We just have to wait through it until Eliza slips up
before we can move on to the ambassador's reception. This causes real
damage to the dramatic structure that Shaw had created and carefully
preserved in his revisions of the play.

The culmination of Act I, scene 5 of *My Fair Lady* is so powerful that
just about all the material from *Pygmalion*'s Act III, both original and
revisions, dutifully recounted to us in sequence in *My Fair Lady*, is extra-
neous to *My Fair Lady*'s natural resolution: Higgins's eventual realization
in Act II, scenes 6 and 7 that he can not get along without Eliza. To his
return home, which the musical appropriates from the film, is added
Higgins's final song, "I've Grown Accustomed to Her Face" (*My Fair Lady*,
pp. 181–83). It makes it clear to us, if not fully to him, that he has arrived
at an emotional point equivalent to the one that Eliza had articulated at
the end of Act I, scene 5. The conclusion of the film of *Pygmalion*, Eliza's
return to Higgins's flat, dissolved over Arthur Honegger's theme music,
which had helped "to guide the emotional reaction of the viewer."[32] This
is more than guidance; it is instruction. The significance of these carefully
placed effects was not lost on Lerner and Loewe, and it is no surprise that

TABLE: TABULAR HISTORY OF *PYGMALION* AND

PYGMALION	Act 1	and (Transitions)	Act 2	and (Transitions)	Act 3
Original 5-act play	Covent Garden, night) Higgins, Pickering, Eliza all meet for the first time.	X	(Higgins's flat, next day) Eliza arrives to have lessons; the wager is struck.	X	(Mrs. Higgins's at-home) 1.) Higgins tells his mother that Eliza will appear.
Revised play		Taxi to Eliza's room	BATHROOM SCENE — Doolittle arrives, gets 5 pounds, argues with Eliza, and leaves.	Phonetics Lessons	2.) Eliza arrives, converses, and shocks every-one. 3.) Higgins and Pickering try to explain to Mrs. Higgins about
Screenplay					Eliza.
Film				and more LESSONS	(same as above but with actions 2, and 3, reversed.)

MY FAIR LADY	Act I	X		X		X		X
	(Scene 1)	(Scene 2)	(Scene 3)	(Scene 4)	(Scene 5)	(Scenes 6&7)	(Scene 8)
		Doolittle introduced; he sings "With a little bit of luck."		DOOLITTLE AGAIN (Reprise of "luck" song)	Phonetics Lessons. These eventually conclude with "The rain in Spain" and with "I could have danced all night."	(At Ascot)	Freddy, outside Higgins's, sings "On the street where you live."

the last music (unsung) of *My Fair Lady* is a swell of "I Could Have Danced All Night" under its final tableau.

Shaw was always rightly suspicious of musical adaptation. He had been burned by Oscar Straus's version of *Arms and the Man* as *The Chocolate Soldier*. He said, in effect, that he would sue for infringement of copyright anyone ever mentioning, in connection with a production of that musical, that it was an adaptation of his play. In 1921, when he heard that Franz Lehár was interested in creating a musical version of *Pygmalion*, he nipped the project immediately in the bud.[33] Being intensely musical, Shaw understood instinctively the difference between a piece of dramatic literature and a libretto, and he knew his play to be an instance of the

MY FAIR LADY

and (Transitions)	Act 4	and (Transitions)	Act 5	(Various revised conclusions)
X	(At Higgins's flat after the garden party) Brief account of winning bet. Eliza and Higgins argue. They part angrily.	X Eliza leaves, meets Freddy. They declare their love and ride around London all night.	(At Mrs. Higgins's next day) Higgins arrives. Doolittle arrives to get married; Eliza appears. She and Higgins continue their previous conversation. All but Higgins leave for wedding. Higgins is alone on stage.	Higgins (alone on stage) concludes, "Marry Freddy, Ha! Ha!"
Departure for ambassador's reception. Higgins meets former student who discovers Eliza to be of royal Hungarian blood.				Higgins sees Eliza and Freddy leave. He has visions of Eliza first in Covent Garden, then with Freddy in a flower shop; he remarks, "A happy beginning, A happy ending."
More lessons (phonetics and etiquette); preparations for ambassador's reception. Freddy interrupts to see Eliza (sequence at reception as above).		Eliza leaves, meets Freddy, and they take a taxi to Covent Garden. Eliza is not recognized by old friends. Next day Higgins wakes up to find Eliza gone. He and Pickering try to find her.		Higgins sees Freddy and Eliza drive off from his mother's. He leaves, walks home. At home, he turns on recording of Eliza. She returns; he remarks, "Where the devil are my slippers?"

Act II

(Scene 9)	(Scenes 10&11)	(Scene 1)	(Scene 2)	(Scene 3)	(Scene 4)	(Scene 5)	(Scene 6)	(Scene 7)
Departure for reception.	Higgins meets former student who becomes suspicious of Eliza (transitional sequence not complete at curtain).	Details of incomplete scene at reception; "Hungarian and of royal blood" recounted here. Higgins and Eliza argue.	Eliza meets Freddy outside Higgins's.	(At Covent Garden) Eliza meets her father, who is now rich and will get married tomorrow. Doolittle sings "Get me to the church on time."	Pickering and Higgins try to locate Eliza.	(At Mrs. Higgins's) [Doolittle does not enter.] Higgins and Eliza continue their conversation.	Higgins walks home and sings "I've grown accustomed to her face."	Eliza returns.

former. He resolutely refused musical adaptation throughout his life. On 3 February 1948, Shaw wrote to E. A. Prentice, who wanted to set *Pygmalion* to music, "I absolutely forbid any such outrage."[34]

As it exists, *My Fair Lady* is structurally flawed. I have never seen a production of it where the audience did not groan audibly when the first act did not conclude after Eliza's triumphant "I Could Have Danced All Night" at the end scene 5 but kept trundling on toward scene 6 at Ascot. In spite of this, *My Fair Lady*'s well-deserved theatrical success continues. Its music is still stirring. It offers a fairy-tale story bound to please most viewers, and it retains its potential for compelling visual display. Yet *My Fair Lady* would probably have become an even stronger dramatic piece had it trimmed Shaw's play to its own musical ends. Now, just about forty

years after its original production, it appears that the portions of its text
that carry the most weight within *My Fair Lady*'s musical structure are
those that are least faithful to Shaw. Indeed, the scenes that provide *Pygmalion* with some of its greater dramatic punch—Doolittle's lament in Act
V and Eliza's recounting of her aunt's death in Act III—are stranded in
My Fair Lady by its focus on other issues. In spite of its public claims about
Shaw as its source, it is only uneasily that *My Fair Lady* reflects these connections. What this imperfect reflection does reveal, however, is how very
carefully constructed the events that constitute Shaw's *Pygmalion* are and
how they continue to render it a viable dramatic text.[35]

Notes

1. All seven of the New York reviews of *My Fair Lady* are included in *The New York Theatre Critics' Reviews for 1956* (*NYTCR* 17), pp. 345–48.

2. Eric Bentley, *Bernard Shaw* (New York: New Directions, 1947), pp. 119–20.

3. The history of the play's original production is reprinted in detail in Richard Huggett, *The Truth about Pygmalion* (New York: Random House, 1969). The production is reviewed from Tree's point of view in Hesketh Pearson, *Beerbohm Tree: His Life and Laughter* (New York: Harper & Brothers, 1956), pp. 172–82; and in Madeleine Bingham, *"The Great Lover": The Life and Art of Herbert Beerbohm Tree* (New York: Atheneum, 1979), pp. 215–31; for Mrs. Patrick Campbell's perspective, see Margot Peters, *Mrs. Pat: The Life of Mrs. Patrick Campbell* (New York: Alfred A. Knopf, 1984), pp. 336–44.

4. Quotations from this version of the play, hereafter called the original *Pygmalion*, are taken from Bernard Shaw, *Androcles and the Lion, Overruled, Pygmalion* (New York: Brentano's, 1916).

5. This material is detailed in Bernard F. Dukore's Introduction to *The Collected Screenplays of Bernard Shaw* (Athens: University of Georgia Press, 1980), pp. 40–49, 63–65.

6. The history of the making of the film is recounted in Donald P. Costello, *The Serpent's Eye: Shaw and the Cinema* (Notre Dame and London: University of Notre Dame Press, 1965), pp. 50–82; in Dukore's Introduction to the *Collected Screenplays*, pp. 59–63, 65–88; in Michael Holroyd, *Bernard Shaw, Vol. 3: The Lure of Fantasy, 1918–1950* (New York: Random House, 1991), pp. 386–93; and in the first twenty-three letters of *Bernard Shaw and Gabriel Pascal*, ed. Bernard F. Dukore (Toronto: University of Toronto Press, 1996), pp. 3–29.

7. An account of the shifts in the action of the original play's Act V from printed play to screenplay to the sound track of the film is given in Costello, *The Serpent's Eye*, pp. 165–88.

8. Dukore, Introduction, *Collected Screenplays*, p. 62.

9. Holroyd, *Bernard Shaw*, p. 391.

10. Ibid., p. 390.

11. Dukore, Introduction, *Collected Screenplays*, pp. 85–87.

12. Holroyd, *Bernard Shaw*, p. 392.

13. Quotations from this version of the play, hereafter called the Bodley Head *Pygmalion*, are taken from *The Bodley Head Bernard Shaw: Collected Plays with Their Prefaces, Vol. 4.* (London, Sydney, Toronto: Max Reinhardt, 1972), pp. 653–823.

14. Bernard Shaw, *Pygmalion*, and Alan Jay Lerner and Frederick Loewe, *My Fair Lady* (New York: New American Library, 1975).

15. Appendix F to *Collected Screenplays*, p. 482.

16. *Collected Screenplays*, p. 272.

17. Bernard Shaw, "H. Beerbohm Tree: From the Point of View of the Playwright," reprinted in the Bodley Head *Pygmalion*, p. 811.

18. Huggett, *The Truth about Pygmalion*, pp. 84–85.

19. Ibid., pp. 159–62; and Peters, *Mrs. Pat*, pp. 242–43.

20. Dukore, Introduction, *Collected Screenplays*, pp. 82–83.

21. Ibid., p. 82.

22. Louis Crompton, *Shaw the Dramatist* (Lincoln: University of Nebraska Press, 1969), p. 150.

23. Quotations from *My Fair Lady* are taken from Alan Jay Lerner and Frederick Loewe, *My Fair Lady: A Musical Play in Two Acts* (New York: Coward-McCann, 1956).

24. Valerie Pascal, *The Disciple and His Devil* (New York: McGraw-Hill Book Company, 1970), pp. 238–41.

25. Lawrence Langner, *G.B.S. and the Lunatic* (New York: Atheneum, 1963), pp. 242–57.

26. A different accounting of the role of money in the play occurs in Bernard F. Dukore, *Money & Politics in Ibsen, Shaw, and Brecht* (Columbia and London: University of Missouri Press, 1980), pp. 9–18.

27. Maurice Valency, *The Cart and the Trumpet: The Plays of George Bernard Shaw* (New York: Oxford University Press, 1973), p. 314.

28. *My Fair Lady*, p. [7].

29. Dukore, Introduction, *Collected Screenplays*, p. 46.

30. Gerald Bordman, *American Musical Theatre: A Chronicle* (New York: Oxford University Press, 1978), p. 597.

31. Bernard Shaw, *Collected Letters 1911–1925*, ed. Dan H. Laurence (New York: Viking, 1985), p. 225.

32. Costello, *The Serpent's Eye*, p. 72.

33. Shaw's reaction can be found in Bernard Shaw, *Bernard Shaw's Letters to Siegfried Trebitsch*, ed. Samuel A. Weiss (Stanford: Stanford University Press, 1986), pp. 224–25. Shaw's concerns about musical adaptation are discussed in Michael Holroyd, *Bernard Shaw, Vol. 4: The Last Laugh, 1950–1991* (New York: Random House, 1992), pp. 56–57.

34. Bernard Shaw, *Collected Letters 1926–1950*, ed. Dan H. Laurence (New York, Viking, 1988), p. 813.

35. An earlier version of this essay was given at the First International LYRICA Conference, The LYRICA Society for Word-music Relations, 4–6 November 1993, New Haven, Connecticut.

REVIEWS

Film-Plays by the Devil and His Director

Selected Correspondence of Bernard Shaw: Bernard Shaw and Gabriel Pascal. Edited by Bernard F. Dukore. Toronto, Buffalo, & London: University of Toronto Press, 1996. xl + 285 pp. Illus. Index. $40.00 (Canadian).

This is a sad book in many ways, tracing as it does by means of letters the trajectory of an artistic partnership between Bernard Shaw and Gabriel Pascal that shortly after its inception gave birth to its greatest success, the 1938 film of *Pygmalion*, only to be followed by two increasingly less successful film adaptations of Shaw plays, the 1941 *Major Barbara* and the 1945 *Caesar and Cleopatra*. Subsequently, over the last five years of Shaw's life, a series of fiascos and fiaschettos, as Pascal tried unfruitfully to arrange deals for the production of other Shaw plays as films, coincided with Shaw's growing ancientness and produced in him a certain impatience with Pascal. It ends on a rather bittersweet note with Pascal's declaring, as ever, his devotion to Shaw and promising that a new film deal is definitely in the works, and with Shaw's ordering Pascal to find himself artistic projects other than Shaw: "Devotion to an old crock like me is sentimental folly."

Reading the collection of letters straight through provides a dramatic experience on its own, for the two central characters, one a canny playwright-businessman, the other a roguish impresario, clearly charm and admire one another, yet each is a little wary of the other's ways. Shaw worries that Pascal for the sake of art will not pay attention to the number of pence in a pound, and Pascal worries that Shaw for the sake of his playwriting art will not agree to the necessary accommodations required by cinematic forms. The tensions arising out of these artistic and financial concerns provide much of the drama to be found in the letters, but not all of it, for the dance of Shaw's and Pascal's personal relations heightens the emotions of the drama.

Pascal takes the position early on in the relationship that Shaw is the greatest living dramatic artist, that only Pascal can bring Shaw's plays to the world through cinematic art, and that Pascal will therefore devote himself and his fortunes exclusively to the service of Shaw and his art. Shaw would be Pascal's Captain, master and friend, and Pascal would be the dedicated disciple. For Shaw's part, mistrusting, no, scorning the masters of Hollywood film form, he found the penniless Hungarian adventurer (therefore, like Shaw, a foreigner in England) the ideal interpreter of Shaw's plays. Pascal would not make the hated Hollywood accommodations and would be much more amenable to Shaw's strictures on how to adapt his plays. Also, Shaw liked Pascal.

A half-dozen letters here justify the expense of the whole book. They are those letters in which Shaw and Pascal exchange views on the playing of the film actors and on the interpretation of the characters. For they tell us in explicit detail how Shaw understood his own artistic purposes, how he meant specific characters to be played, and the effects he expected his works to achieve. As a rule, Shaw only communicated such things to artistic collaborators, for example, to actors during rehearsals, but seldom to interviewers, or non-artists. Also, Shaw rarely committed such revelations of his artistic intent to writing. The only other significant instance is the letters Shaw wrote to his Austrian translator, Siegfried Trebitsch. There, as here, Shaw was exceptionally candid about how he wanted his plays performed.

Let me give some examples. During the filming of *Major Barbara*, Shaw visited Denham studios and seems to have watched some scenes being shot and others in rushes; then in a letter dated 12 September 1940, Shaw writes to Pascal telling him what is right with the performances and what is wrong. Rex Harrison as Cusins speaks the verse assigned to him too colloquially; he should deliberately declaim the verse as such. Emlyn Williams makes Snobby Price "a smart cockney from beginning to end without the least variety. The acting value of the part lies in the contrast between the smart cockney talking honestly to Rummy, and the sniveling canting mock-pious hypocrite when the others are present." In other words, Snobby is Tartuffe, and Shaw has provided an invaluable texturing for the part ("sniveling canting mock-pious"). Shaw even proposes emendations in the directing and editing (done here by Pascal and David Lean, respectively): "When Lady B. calls them all names in the last act the whole effect is lost by her moving about from one to the other. She should stand like Jove hurling thunderbolts, only her eyes flashing in all directions—a close-up—and then turn her back and march away. A glimpse of the expressions of her victims may follow if you like. Lady B's explosions should be helped out by solo pictures close-up as much as possible." In response, Pascal promises to re-cut the scene according to Shaw's specifications, but as it exists now the sequence is a hybrid of Shaw's way and Pascal's way, but with half of Lady Britomart's thunderbolts from the screenplay left out so that neither Shaw's effect nor Pascal's prevails.

If Shaw won a half-victory in the battle over Lady Britomart's glances, he lost completely over Pascal's desire to bring Bill Walker back for the end of the film. In several letters, Shaw protested vigorously against Walker's reappearance, and, more importantly, he explained why: "To drag him back merely to give the actor another turn because he is so good is one of those weaknesses which an author must resist: to bring an actor on the stage with nothing to do after he has made his effect in scenes where he was all important is to spoil his part and make a disappointment of him instead of a success." Here we see both how conscientiously Shaw assumes authorial responsibility and how considerately he conceives roles for his actors. If Pascal wanted Bill to return, Shaw tells him the way he should have effected it: "You should have made him shadow Barbara until she threw herself into the river (instead of her hat) and then jump in and rescue her. . . ." For that would dramatize how Barbara's conversion of Bill affected him. As we know from the finished film, Pascal does indeed make Bill Walker return, but in a sentimental and unconvincing way at the end of the film.

In other letters, Shaw reveals how consciously he structured the action of his plays. For example, in rejecting Pascal's suggestion for a new way to begin *Major Barbara*, Shaw explains how he has built the first act upon the principle of increment and loss: "The play must begin with two people, rousing interest in two *new* couples, all six piling up the interest in Undershaft, the protagonist. Then they must go away one after the other until even Lady Britomart goes and leaves Stephen to finish the sequence *alone*." Such revelations of Shaw's aesthetic concerns are rare enough in Shaw's writing to make this collection of exceptional value to those interested generally in Shaw's art and specifically in the three plays turned into films by Pascal.

Shaw's sense of humor and comic inventiveness are in evidence here, as when Shaw suggests for the ball scene in *Pygmalion*, "Why not, by the way, a black princess talking Hottentot (all clicks) with Higgins following her and taking down the clicks frantically in his notebook?" When Pascal worries over the reception of a film of *Saint Joan* in America if the Catholic

Action boycotts it, Shaw responds: "When the Catholic Action can keep these Americans out of the saloons and gambling casinos and Ziegfeld Follies I shall believe in its power to keep them away from St Joan. Until then, we go ahead."

Lest I leave the impression that Pascal was not up to the task of transforming Shaw's plays into successful films, and if the cinematic adaptation of *Pygmalion* does not seem completely convincing proof of Pascal's skill, I must note that Pascal's understanding of Shaw's plays was often profound and his instincts for adjusting the plays to film requirements were sound. Of the latter, I offer as an example Pascal's suggested treatment of Barbara's conversion from despair back to hope, which results from her father's pointing out to her that she has set Bill Walker on the path to his own salvation. Pascal suggests that Barbara's "metamorphosis seems to be too abrupt," and he asks Shaw to provide "some supplementary lines for Barbara." Pascal's sense that Shaw's technique of sudden conversion did not work in this scene was correct, but even the additional lines could not quite save the scene from Wendy Hiller's artificiality in the moment.

Of Pascal's great admiration and love for Shaw's plays there can be no doubt, but he also grasped their more subtle meanings, and surely this is what struck a chord with Shaw and explains why Shaw should have assigned Pascal virtually the exclusive rights to film the plays. For example, of Dick Dudgeon's character in *The Devil's Disciple*, Pascal writes to Shaw, commenting on Robert Donat's interpretation of Dick, "It certainly takes away all the great tragical shadows behind him, without which spiritual background the dualistic character of Richard—who was certainly a 'Gemini'—is lost." Pascal here shows that he understood Shaw's intention to portray Dick Dudgeon as Anthony Anderson's psychological double and that Shaw meant Dick to have something of Hamlet, the alienated malcontent, in him, and not to be merely the wise-cracking picaro of melodrama.

For all his insight as an appreciator of Shaw's plays, Pascal did not have a sufficient cinematic imagination or assured enough style of his own as a film-maker to bring Shaw's plays strikingly to the screen with their special requirements. *Caesar and Cleopatra* (1945), the third of Shaw's and Pascal's collaborations (but without the editing art of David Lean), was not a success—neither was it a failure, but it felt like a failure. Looked at now, the film seems cinematically non-existent: that is, the camera does hardly anything. It looks like a transcription of an exceptionally expensive stage production with location settings. Some scenes as acting and as representations of Shaw's intentions succeed wonderfully well; others simply seem static. At first, Pascal tried to deceive Shaw about the success of the film, but finally in one of the saddest letters between them, Pascal acknowledges his sense of the film's failure: " 'Caesar & Cleopatra' was a bad picture because I was surrounded by saboteurs and I made it without joy and without inspiration. I hate the memory of it."

Thereafter, Pascal produces one plan on top of another to make Shaw adaptations: to build film studios in Ireland, to build them in the Bahamas, to make this film or that film, but nothing comes to fruition, and Shaw grows increasingly impatient with the collapses of Pascal's various projects until on 18 June 1950, a few months before his own death, Shaw writes to Pascal:

> I have been uneasy about you lately. You are laying out your life as if I were sure to live another fifty years, and putting all your eggs in that quite illusory basket accordingly. It is extremely unlikely that I shall live another three days; and when I die your connexion with me will have been a mere episode in your career. You will have half your life before you which you must fill up with new friendships and new interests and activities. Otherwise you will starve. Never forget that dealings with very old people can be only transient. Make young friends and young clients. Look for a young Shaw; for though Shaws do not grow on the gooseberry bushes there are as good fish in the sea as ever came out of it. Anyhow you must live in your own generation, not in mine.

Throughout the collection, much fun can be had considering the casting in films Pascal planned to do but did not: Marlene Dietrich as the Millionairess, Laurence Olivier as Dubedat, Ginger Rogers as Louka, Cary Grant as Bluntschli or Sergius, Spencer Tracy as Morell, Greer Garson as Saint Joan, and on and on, with roles re-assigned at a dizzying pace from letter to letter as plans for a particular film ebbed and flowed. Most fascinating of all projected castings, however, is the following: Pascal writes to Shaw of a lunch with Harley Granville-Barker during which Barker seemed to agree to perform the role of the Inquisitor in a film of *Saint Joan*. Shaw must have been quite shocked by this news since, several years before, Barker's wife had forbidden communication between her husband and his old friend. Whatever Shaw's reaction to this strange incident, it is not recorded in the present volume.

Also under the category of might-have-been belong distinguished composers who were considered by Shaw and Pascal: Shaw heard on the radio some incidental music by Benjamin Britten and suggested to Pascal that Britten should be enlisted to write the music for *Caesar and Cleopatra*: "He handled his trumpets beautifully; and his manner was not the lawless post-Wagnerianism that now sounds so tiresomely old-fashioned, but in the tradition of Gluck, Berlioz, and Chopin. It had the forgotten quality of elegance. And it was all original: he will not plant any ersatz Aida on us." Earlier Pascal had tried to get Toscanini to agree to compose the score for *Major Barbara*!

Bernard Dukore has discharged his editorial duties admirably here with helpful headnotes where they are needed and useful footnotes when they are required. His introduction is succinct and sufficient in its depiction of the relationship between Shaw and Pascal; it derives, as the editor acknowledges, from his more elaborate introduction to *The Collected Screenplays of Bernard Shaw*. (For those seeking a complete knowledge of the Shaw-Pascal alliance, Valerie Pascal's moving and entertaining memoir of her husband, *The Devil and His Disciple*, should be added along with Donald Costello's excellent *The Serpent's Eye* to the present volume of letters and the aforementioned collected screenplays.) Dukore is sympathetic to Pascal, as Shaw was, and for the same reasons: Pascal was a bit of a rogue, but an original, with considerable charm and flair. Professor Dukore's annotations require only one tiny addition: the identity of the actor who dubbed a few of Donald Calthrop's lines in *Major Barbara* (after the unfortunate man died during shooting); he was Felix Aylmer. I have no source for that additional information except my own ear.

John A. Bertolini

Arguments, Asides, Addenda: The Last Words

Bernard Shaw, *The Complete Prefaces, Vol. 3: 1930–1950*. Edited by Dan H. Laurence and Daniel J. Leary. London: Allen Lane, 197. x + 621 pp. Index. $75.00.

On 28 May 1948, a ninety-two-year-old Bernard Shaw wrote to Dean Inge, "I am very groggy on my legs, but I still have my wits about me." He recalled speaking to some centenarians, one of whom declared that old age is nothing but "buttoning and unbuttoning." In the third and final volume of the *Complete Prefaces*, it is an increasingly unbuttoned Shaw filling the more than 600-page volume. Edited and painstakingly annotated by Dan H. Laurence and Daniel J. Leary, the two scholar-editors in charge of all three volumes, this last is in many ways the most revealing. The essays range from pamphlet-length prefaces to his own work and the writing of others to brief and revealing notes. Lengthy introductions to *On the Rocks* and *Farfetched Fables* alternate with brief notes on the puppets in *Shakes versus Shav*. Along with such ephemera as spoken prefaces to the films of *Major Barbara* and *Pygmalion*, this final collection offers a potpourri of critical, personal, and analytical Shaviana. Some pieces are little more than curiosities. In this category falls a note "To the Intelligent Hebrew Woman," a species of addendum to the original *An Intelligent Woman's Guide to Socialism*. This is a last look at Shaw the quirky ("Hitler Has Won!"), the speculative ("The Miraculous Birth of Language"), and the self-referential ("Shaw Gives Himself Away"). Sometimes, he is satisfyingly informative, as he is in the Preface to *The Adventures of the Black Girl in Her Search for God*. To those readers who have been curious about the genesis of this uncharacteristic fable of a religious quest, Shaw uses the preface to give the reader his own account "for what it is worth." And it is worth a good deal, if only as a tongue-in-cheek disquisition on the uses of the knobkerry.

It is clear from the contents of this volume, which ends with a few invaluable "stragglers" in the Appendix that were unearthed after the manuscript had been completed, that the two editors were on an exhaustive treasure hunt. Some of the prefatory gems simply do not require the setting of the works they were appended to. They stand by themselves, ornamental and sparkling. A case in point is the "Note on Puppets," in which the author captures the essence of the craft in a few pithy paragraphs, citing the carver's art for its "mimicry," through which it suggests "human gesture in unearthly caricature." An aside about Jane Morris in a lengthy piece about her husband is a cameo within the full-scale portrait of William Morris. Shaw recounts with rueful relish an episode in which the "beautiful stately silent woman" slips some suet into his vegetarian menu and declares with satisfaction that it will do him some good. Another such insight is offered in the case of Florence Farr, whose "violent" reaction against Victorian morals was expressed in "a sort of Leporello list of a dozen adventures" of a highly sexual character. In "Pugilism," the Preface to a proposed but never-published volume on *Pugilism and Painting*, he defends his preoccupation with the manly art as just as acceptable as Lord Byron's boxing lessons. This particular mini-preface, incidentally, unearthed from the British Library and meticulously identified as to its genesis and destiny, is as much a tribute to its editors' sleuthing as to their subject's broad spectrum of enthusiasms.

Injecting himself into the Prefaces is a habit of a lifetime in Shaw's case. Even in the brief note on the film version of *Major Barbara* he reminisces about his first experience in reading about the evils of slavery in America and his subsequent determination to devote his own life to eradicating all white slavery everywhere. In "Days of Judgment," the Preface to *The Simpleton of the Unexpected Isles*, he reflects on some of the political offenses suffered through the ages from the crotchety point of view of an "old Irishman" too sensitized to Coercion Acts to ignore the universal assault

on "human worth." The "Preface on Bosses," his highly political introduction to *Misalliance*, offers an analysis of the phenomenon of despotism
from the point of view of a "bit of a psychologist," notably himself. And
"London Music in 1888–89," purportedly an overview of the subject, is
largely an account of the Svengali of his mother's career, the increasingly
disreputable Vandeleur Lee, who was to have so profound an influence
on Shaw's early career as a music critic. He also uses the framework of
the essay to expound on his own musical development. To a man who,
by his own account," had sung like a bird" through his childhood, the
advent of Lee is defined as a "meteoric impact . . . with his music, his
method, his impetuous enterprize [*sic*] and his magnetism." That he
never taught Shaw or any other member of his family anything worth
while, because like all artists he had "solely a working knowledge" of his
craft, is immaterial. He galvanized the entire household and propelled
the young G.B.S. into a frenzy of self-actualization. As late as 1937, Shaw
recalls that he was finally forced "to teach [himself] how to play written
music on the piano from a book with a diagram of the keyboard in it or
else be starved of music." An even later self-revelation, the Preface to
Buoyant Billions, reprinted in a limited edition in 1950, the year of his
death, stands as a mini-confessional more than a formal essay. Asked why
he has written the play so late in life, Shaw must reply that he does not
know. He apologizes ruefully for "perpetrating" yet another play and
"pontificating" at a time when he can scarcely walk through his garden
"without a tumble or two." Having admitted elsewhere that *Buoyant Billions* is only a bit of "tomfoolery," he uses the Preface for some more
fooling, warning the audience that it is about to see a "trivial" comedy, a
product of his "dotage" that should be regarded as a "comedietta" following a "prefacette."

The 1938 Preface to a new edition of Frank Harris's *Oscar Wilde*, first
published in 1916, is worth reading for two reasons. A series of detailed
editorial notes explains the complicated Shaw-Wilde relationship, while
the essay itself runs to more than forty pages and takes on a disputatious
Wilde biographer, Robert Hardborough Sherard. Somewhat uncharac-
teristically, Shaw comes to the defense of Frank Harris, in this instance
the underdog accused by Sherard of "habitual and malicious mendacity."
The characterization is Shaw's interpretation of Sherard's persistent ca-
lumniation of "poor" Frank, who draws some unprecedented sympathy
from Shaw. The latter, not always on record as Harris's champion, finds
himself entirely on Frank's side in this case. Citing as evidence Harris's
"transports of indignant scorn" that were always roused by "cruelty, injustice and oppression," Shaw took on Sherard as his own enemy, demol-
ishing his pretense of integrity point by point. The glee with which he
counterpunches, in a tongue-in-cheek strategy known euphemistically as

"preventive retaliation," is apparent in the eight points he sets up as Harris's moral failings from his interpretation of Sherard's snide accusations for the personal pleasure of disproving the spurious allegations.

If Wilde himself gets lost in the Harris-Sherard farrago, Shaw stands out sharp and clear against the background of infighting over poor Oscar's reputation. In tracing the history of the Wilde-Douglas sexual liaison and its unsavory fallout, he comes to a number of typically Shavian conclusions about the dangers of excess, in eating, drinking, and sexual indulgence alike, of which "all Wilde's set, Harris included," were guilty. In a "pox on all the houses" involved in the affair, Shaw first exonerates those involved as "remarkable specimens . . . distinctively supercharged," and above all, to his personal knowledge, just "human beings." That said, however, he proceeds to let them have it with both barrels: "They are monsters. Wilde is an angelic monster. Harris a diabolical one." As for the seductive and hapless Lord Alfred Douglas, he was "gifted or cursed with the degree of personal beauty" that draws men and women "indiscriminately." This observation in turn inspired a mini-essay on the history and dynamics of homosexuality and from a decidedly "unbuttoned" old Shaw a sympathetic review of the Wilde trial and its consequences.

The Preface to *Farfetched Fables* is a similarly lengthy and far-ranging essay in the mode of the earlier Prefaces to *Misalliance* and *Saint Joan* in Volume 2. This final Preface, written when Shaw was ninety-three and published posthumously in 1951, is the usual catch-all for all sorts of theories, opinions, and challenges to popular attitudes. One subsection is headed by the rhetorical "Am I a Pathological Liar?" Another, an impish mini-memoir, is given the tongue-in-cheek confessional title of "G.B.S. Miracle Faker." Speculative musings such as "Should I Be Shot in Russia?" abound for the purpose of typical political shock technique. The usual slap at the "schoolmasters" makes a return engagement along with the various genial challenges to the organized churches he decides to admonish in sections entitled "Catholicism Impracticable" and "A Hundred Religions and Only One Sauce." But in this late day, as Shaw himself said of so many of his own eccentric characters, there is not a bit of harm in him. Furthermore, the thirty-seven-page Preface has little, if anything, to do with the fables themselves, which bear more of a resemblance to James Thurber's *Fables for Our Time* than with the genre invented by Aesop and polished by La Fontaine. It is a jokey wizard spinning his wheels even as he waves his magic wand to give credence to the futurist predictions that dot the final essay. The nonagenarian concludes the rambling essays with some startling forecasts concerning the "brave new world" of the inevitable proliferation of nuclear weaponry. But it is a sanguine prophet who concludes by soothing our fear as he dismisses the danger of atomic annihilation as a serious threat exactly as the use of poison gas in the second World War failed to materialize.

The three volumes of the Prefaces really do not require the plays. They stand alone as witty essays, keys to a century's events and ideas, and an index to the writer's multi-faceted genius. They belong at the bedside of any reader who values the life of the mind and looks for clues to a century of change in Prefaces such as *Geneva* and "Days of Judgment." For literature enthusiasts there is the Preface to *Great Expectations* for a limited edition, and for sheer pleasure, the purely personal insights to the figures in Shaw's time, those whom he knew well ("Morris as I Knew Him") and those, such as Yeats, who floated in and out of his immediate field of vision. Whatever the subject—the origin of language or the history and function of the Royal Academy of Dramatic Arts, to whose graduates he offered some sober advice—the puckish oracle took on the challenge of peering into the future while recalling the past, all the while struggling in his own words to remain in tune with his times. To this end Laurence and Leary are to be further congratulated for tracing the evolution of significant Shavian principles and positions as formulated in the early Prefaces and adjusted to the changing scene through a long and vigilant career.

Rhoda Nathan

Shaw Reviews His World

Bernard Shaw's Book Reviews, Vol. 2: 1884–1950. Edited and with an Introduction by Brian Tyson. University Park: Penn State University Press, 1996. x + 588 pp. Index. $115.00.

This, the second volume of Brian Tyson's collection of book reviews by Shaw, takes off where its predecessor had contained him. That is to say, it lifts Shaw from the pages of the *Pall Mall Gazette* in the years 1885–88 and, stepping back a year or two the better to launch him into his career as a book reviewer, sends him whizzing through the 1880s, the '90s, the Edwardian years, and on until 1950—very nearly seventy years of writing about books by other people. There are more than seventy reviews, most of them re-published for the first time, ranging in length from a few hundred words to several thousand, making, all in all, a substantial collection. It is more strictly a selection because Professor Tyson has not included reviews of what he describes as the "special areas of art, music, theater and photographs." This is a disappointment. Still, Professor Tyson says that those special areas "might be expected to find a place in more specialized selections," and let us hope he will be proved right. Meanwhile we have seventy years of Shaw here reviewing books of verse, books on economic theory, books on ethics, books on and by eminent contemporaries—many of them, G.K. Chesterton and H. G. Wells, for example, close friends of his—biography, autobiography, history, and lest one forget his lifelong campaign against the"witchcraft" that masqueraded as modern medical practice, books on that subject as well. The selection is nothing if not comprehensive.

Book reviewing is a contemporary occupation, that is to say an exercise of the day for the day, fugitive columns in soon-discarded newspapers, more fugitive than the other occupations by which Shaw established his voice in London, music and theater criticism. The music or theater critic's views on works established in the canon—on Wagner or Beethoven, shall we say, or Shakespeare or Ibsen—are sustained by the works themselves, whereas with books, or at all events 999 out of 1,000 of them published in a given year, oblivion awaits within a twelve-month. Thus it is with practically all the titles Shaw reviews in these pages: the best one can say about most of them, if they are not instantly and utterly forgettable, is that they are interesting period pieces, even, very often, those by important figures of the day. Who today, apart from the specialist scholar, knows or cares about such works as the following, all of them paid the inestimable compliment in their time of considered attention by Shaw, many of them praised by him for this or that "important" or "enduring" quality: *The Historical Basis of Socialism* by H. M. Hyndman (1884), *A Minor Poet and Other Verse* by Amy Levy (1884), *The University Economics* by E. C. K. Gonner (1888), *A Publisher's Confessions* by Walter Hines Page (1905), *The Foundations of the Nineteenth Century* by Houston Stewart Chamberlain (1911), *What Is Coming?* by H. G. Wells (1916), *Herbert Spencer* by Hugh Elliott (1917), *Irish Impressions* by G. K. Chesterton (1919), *Outspoken Essays* by William Ralph Inge (1919), *A Constitution for the Socialist Commonwealth of Great Britain* by Sidney and Beatrice Webb (1920)? This short arbitrary list includes some of the most eminent names of the first half of the century, yet it makes the point: the book publishing industry and its corollary the book reviewing industry are founded in evanescence. The first is journalism in a hard cover, the second mere journalism.

Shaw was a journalist first and foremost, of course, totally contemporary, dedicated to the day, committed to evanescence, with this difference, that his commitment to the day was for the betterment of the day for the benefit of tomorrow—for the fulfillment of the Life Force. This was the criterion against which books were automatically measured. *All* books: the range of topics referred to above reminds one of the breadth of Shaw's mind and the stunning acuity with which he would range over the wide and variegated landscape of the contemporary world. It reminds one as well that his all-embracing mission could often turn the ephemerality of the topic into something rather more durable.

Not always. It has to be said that the encyclopedia of his mind as reflected in these reviews is dated in many respects, and often wrong. He could be and was talkative and opinionated. His aberrations were idiosyncratic and legion. As a professional controversialist, as these fugitive pieces all too palpably demonstrate, he has become the not infrequent victim of the historical process and its cruel way of turning the imperatives of one age into the errors of the next. For example: his sorties into Fabian economic theory may have been all very well for the 1880s and 1890s, but amount to gross error in the light of modern economic theory; socialism, the economic and moral pivot of so much of his career, seems now to have been rejected by history, or to be tolerated only in heavily diluted form; his tirades against aspects of medical science emerge now as the rather tiresome tirades of a faddist; his belief in the Life Force seems a quaint period aberration.

This introduces the question of style vis-à-vis utility. Shaw makes much of precisely this issue in "The Artstruck Englishman," his review of Dixon Scott's *Men of Letters* (1917), where Scott praises Shaw's style while ignoring the message. As Shaw says, "It was very much as if I had told him the house was on fire, and he had said, 'How admirably monosyllabic!' and left the nursery stairs burning unheeded." Quite so, but what if those nursery stairs turn out not to have been on fire; what if all that survives of the incident were those admirable monosyllables? What then? Then one gets splendid inutility, incandescent error.

What does this make of Professor Tyson's selection? A labor of love, certainly, and there will be occasion later in this review to comment on the dedicated scholarship that Professor Tyson has brought to his task. But also a largely inutile labor? To a certain extent, yes. Like the books they were responding to, the reviews amount to very little now, some fifty, sixty, seventy, and more years after the event. They add very little, if anything, to what one knows about Shaw, except, perversely and insistently, on how wrong time has proved him to have been in many of his observations. Should one therefore consign the book to oblivion, like the reviews themselves before Professor Tyson exhumed them?

Of course not. One can quite possibly argue that incandescent inutility has its utility, that Shaw extemporizing a few hundred words on a now-forgotten monograph on a totally obsolete subject will somehow rise above the immediate issue and make his report shine like an extravagant bauble. There could well be some (like Dixon Scott perhaps) to whom this would be quite enough. It is, however, better to see that the evanes-

cence Shaw was celebrating became something more permanent and relevant simply because he used the occasion to turn out a finely wrought
essay on the subject in hand, the better to serve him in his missions in
life. The review then became more than a mere report on this or that
book; it became an act of creation in its own right. That Shaw knew this
himself and saw many of his reviews as worthy of more than a twenty-
four-hour life—that they contributed to his stature as a critic of the contemporary scene and its eminent people—is evident from the number he
took up himself for inclusion in his *Pen Portraits and Reviews*. Here at least
he saw some more enduring form of life for them—for example, "The
Artstruck Englishman," already commented on, in which Shaw makes
the review the occasion for a cogent discussion of "literary voluptuous-
ness" *versus* "criticism of life;" "Samuel Butler: The New Life Reviewed"
(1919), in which Shaw insists, not for the first or last time, on Samuel
Butler's huge significance as a Victorian revolutionary and man of letters;
"Mr Frank Harris's Shakespear" (1910), a lovely example of Shaw putting down an opponent in controversy plus, as incidental bonus, an insight into Shaw's views on Shakespeare the man; "Tolstoy on Art" (1898),
which has him commenting on the great Russian with a perspicacity years
ahead of general appreciation. The list could be extended, but the point
is clear: *Pen Portraits* is itself nearly seventy years old since first publication
(although there have been a few reprintings), and the time is overdue for
some form of revival. Professor Tyson's selection does this admirably.

Pursuing the cause of "utility" as we are, one may note that this commodity does not stop short at the pickings from *Pen Portraits*. Professor
Tyson comments feelingly in his Introduction on "playing the resurrec-
tion man in the old newspaper rooms of our public libraries." A depressing business, he says. It certainly is, particularly if, as has been suggested,
one salvages largely inutile material from those moldering volumes, those
brittle film strips and un-cooperative microfiche. And yet it can happen
that the salvage operation yields nuggets of pure gold, a reward that has
come Professor Tyson's way more often than not. Once again, a short list
will have to suffice. There is Shaw in 1884, a stripling of twenty-some-
thing, untrained in the academic artifice of literary criticism, commenting
on "Recent Poetry" with the sure and certain (but never ostentatious)
criteria of a finely honed sensibility, while differentiating between "fancy"
and "experience" as though a second Coleridge had descended on the
age. We have him in 1892, not much older but greatly matured, reviewing "Mr Bernard Shaw's Works of Fiction" with an air of ironic gravity,
suggesting that the tolerably educated might derive something of value
from his novels, "in spite of their occasional vulgarity, puerility and folly."
Later, in 1909, when he had achieved the authority and the eminence to
pick and choose his books and to let rip as his inclination directed, we

have him on "Bernard Shaw on Shams of Rule and of Religion," his review of Hall Caine's *The White Prophet*, in which his polemic against literary censorship produces both a spirited defense of the novel and a swingeing attack on the narrow-mindedness that would want to see such works banned. Finally there is "The Case Against Chesterton" (1916) in which, in reviewing a critical work on Chesterton, he brings fresh perspectives to bear on the long and fruitful association in disagreement between him and G.K.C. This is an abysmally short list; it could easily be extended to include several dozen more displays of brilliance-plus-substance, more than enough to warrant the selection and the survival of these pieces.

The scholarship underpinning this collection is awe-inspiring. It represents years of meticulous research, as often as not into the murky catacombs of literary and social and political trivia of years gone by. Today's common currency is tomorrow's buried coin; the number of such coins Professor Tyson has dug out of the past century is beyond reckoning. Sometimes one wonders whether a coin or two had not better been left where it was—there is the danger of over-annotating—but on the whole one must record a vote of thanks and appreciation to Professor Tyson for his thoroughness and the luminous way the commentaries place these ephemera in the context of their period and Shaw's career.

Leon Hugo

Maturity: Shaw's Novels Revisited

Richard Farr Dietrich, *Bernard Shaw's Novels: Portraits of the Artist as Man and Superman*. Gainesville: University Press of Florida, 1996. xviii + 203 pp. Illus. Index. $39.95.

"The need for getting me to review my own works of fiction has arisen through the extreme difficulty of finding anyone else who has read them." So began Shaw's review of his five novels in 1892. The novels, written between 1878 and 1883, remain surprisingly neglected; except, that is, by Richard Dietrich, for whose time spent on these 'prentice works we should all be grateful. In *Portrait of the Artist as a Young Superman* (1969), Dietrich considered the five novels as controlled experiments in the creation of the Shavian personality and world view. That book, therefore, in addition to being a sensitive critique of Shaw's early fiction, was a kind of psychic biography of the young Bernard Shaw, and his progress through the persona of the insecure Robert Smith of *Immaturity* to that of the sensitive, yet comic, visionary Trefusis of *An Unsocial Socialist*. Now, thirty years on, in *Bernard Shaw's Novels*, Dietrich performs a typically Shavian exercise in revisiting, and revising, his own early work. His main thesis remains the same, namely, that Shaw "employ[ed] the novels for personal transmutation"; but the demonstration has deepened and widened, to prove that "evolutionary forces were at work pushing the realist element or type as the most desirable, the most highly evolved, the door to the future."

The book is divided into three parts. The first, an introduction to the novels, contains a most persuasive analysis of the pre-novel-writing Shaw, explains Dietrich's methodology, and both anticipates and undercuts possible postmodernist attacks on his "New Critical" approach by pointing out that discrediting New Critical theory does not discredit its chief method because "close reading" serves everybody's purpose and "few poststructuralist critics can do without it." Accordingly, Dietrich incorporates much of the relevant Shavian scholarship of the intervening thirty years, particularly Nicholas Grene's 1990 article "The Maturing of *Immaturity*," in which the manuscript of Shaw's first novel is compared with the published version.

This much-quoted article paves the way to Part 2 of Dietrich's book, "The Art of the Novels, or the Maturity of *Immaturity*," which contains an excellent exposition and brilliant analysis of that novel, whose excised portions occasionally read like the character assessments in Shaw's later stage directions, which describe motivation directly. With flashes of insight on nearly every page, Dietrich's detailed account of Shaw's writing makes fine reading, and he is at his very best when analyzing the Shaw sentence and picking out the subtleties of self-analysis in Shaw himself.

Part 3 of Dietrich's book, entitled "A Dialectical Portrait of an Emerging Superman," begins with a suggestive comparison of Joyce and Shaw (for Dietrich interestingly claims that Shaw antedates Joyce in writing his way through a psychic birth process) and reveals that Dietrich understands—as few others seem to—the spiritual side of Shaw, especially when he touches on the vexed connection between Shaw and Christianity. After he has given an excellent account of the nineteenth century's "scientific scepticism" which, having "emptied the skies of religion's God the Father," felt obliged to "fill the vacuum thus created by the invention of heroes and supermen," Dietrich plausibly explains the Shavian use of that term. He then proceeds to show in five chapters the transmutation of this concept through each of Shaw's novels. *Immaturity*, we are told, presents us with a proto-Shaw: a "Monster of Propriety" whose "extreme drive for correctness of behavior" sets up a comic tension with his view of the monstrosities of Victorian social and religious life. In *The Irrational*

Knot, says Dietrich, Shaw produces a "Monster of the Mind," focusing upon the conflict between Conolly's formidable intellect and monstrous self-control and the society in which he must live. Dietrich also traces the "familiar game of one-upmanship and Supermanship" in this novel as Conolly (Shaw) takes on the conventions of his day. However, the character of Sholto Douglas, seen by Dietrich as the "type of the perfect gentleman in conventional novels, who will talk Marian into running away with him, only to abandon her, pregnant, in New York," should more correctly be described as Zolaesque realism; for the infamous Langworthy Marriage was only a year or so away, in which a millionaire playboy seduced an Irish schoolteacher into a fake marriage, made her pregnant, and, in March 1883, actually did abandon her in Buenos Aires. *Love Among the Artists*, by contrast, according to Dietrich, presents us with a "Monster of the Body" in the person of Owen Jack, but we are reminded that "the mind, after all, *is* body," and so the novel deals more with the irrationality of physical existence in reaction against the extreme rationalism of its predecessor.

Not until *Cashel Byron's Profession*, it seems, does Shaw unite the mind *and* body of the Superman: Cashel Byron, the boxer, "thinks" with his body; Lydia Carew "feels" with her intellect; and the two marry, producing four (presumably synthetic) children. The final chapter in this section posits that Shaw's fifth novel, *An Unsocial Socialist*, is a less theoretical exposition of the same synthesis. The conclusion of Dietrich's book— although little more than a suggestive outline—reveals that just as Dietrich is sensitive to the spiritual side of Shaw, so also he shows an excellent understanding of Shaw's Donne-like synthesis of passion and reason.

All this is excellently done, and the disappointments I must record are small. First, considering that, according to Dietrich, "Of greatest relevance [to Shaw's becoming a novelist] was [Shaw's] wide reading of the English novel," it is perhaps surprising that he does not seem to have availed himself of Shaw's reviews of the genre in the pages of the *Pall Mall Gazette*, reviews that Shaw began while he himself was still attempting to write novels and that reveal what Shaw thought constituted a good novel, as well as his early thoughts on romance and realism. My second complaint is the thinness of the index. If one wishes to discover all the references to Shaw's characters Candida, or Ann Whitefield, for example, it is no use going to the index, which gives references to them only when the name of their play is mentioned.

My final cavil may be unfair, particularly since it is prompted by the very brilliance with which Dietrich analyzes Shaw's novels, but I wish more consideration could have been given to the reasons for their public failure. One motive for the publication of Dietrich's original 1969 study was to "get people to read the novels." Yet on page 7 of his most recent book on the subject, we are told that "they are seldom read and even more seldom criticized." After nearly thirty years, it seems, notwithstanding several dozen articles and even Dietrich's own edition of *An Unsocial Socialist*, little has changed. Shaw is still known only for his plays: his novels are merely his juvenilia. In consequence, although in *Bernard Shaw's Novels* Dietrich itemizes and answers well the six charges leveled against Shaw's fictions, namely that they are "unreal in their portrayal of life," "stilted and unnatural in their language," "plotless and disorganized," "inconsistent in their characterization," "propagandist and 'talky' in subordinating action to discussion of ideas," and "often irrelevant in their detail," one feels that such vindication prompts a greater question. After all, even if the above allegations were true, the same charges could be leveled at most of the major Victorian novelists, Dickens included. Dietrich does separate Shaw from other nineteenth-century writers by implying that we do not judge his novels as we judge others of the period, but by the degree to which they have "sloughed off" Victorian rhetoric. He suggests they should be seen instead as the work of a fabulist and fantasist, delighting in his language as one delights in Shakespearean blank verse. Perhaps they should. But why aren't they? Dietrich goes on immediately to say that *Immaturity* would have frustrated a Victorian reader by its decidedly un-Victorian hero and points out that Shaw's attempt "to open new channels for emotion" led the Victorians, "used to wallowing in the salt sea of Victorian sentimentalism," to find "normal emotion dry." But arguing that Victorian critics were incorrect in their assessment of Shaw does not indicate why their rejection of Shaw's novels was sufficient to consign them to permanent oblivion. Somewhere is missing the essential question of the relationship between publishing houses and works of art, common readers and critics, success and worth. Was Shaw a "mute Milton" in his novel-writing period? Dietrich's work seems to say so. But although Shaw's first novel hero Robert Smith may *be* a "gracehopper" [*sic*] of Joycean proportions, and the novel itself contain an Aldous Huxleyan discussion of art and life, both statements avoid the obvious truth that whereas Joyce and Huxley enjoy enormous reputations as writers of prose fiction, Shaw does not. To deepen the mystery, Dietrich establishes that Shaw's characterization and style in the unsuccessful novels are the same as in the successful plays (even to the extent of identifying a prototype Higgins—and perhaps a soupçon of Marchbanks—in Owen Jack, although he misses the prototype of Todger Fairmile in Cashel Byron).

Dietrich does at one point wonder aloud why Shaw abandoned the novel for the more public arrangement of the theater, agreeing with Bentley that one reason may have been a "craving for public participation in his private story," and he supplies another thought, namely that the novel lacks the persuasive magic of liturgical performance. Does that statement, I wonder, include a third possible reason for Shaw's abandonment of the novel for the stage, namely that the flesh and blood reality of the actor supplies human warmth and vulnerability, artistic components missing in Shaw's fiction?

In all five novels, it seems, the man-woman relationship rarely rises above the level of flirtation or physical attraction. Smith's attraction for Harriet Russell in the first novel is that of the artist/philosopher for a pretty Philistine who might prove a challenging pupil. In the second, Conolly's marriage to Maria is disastrous, and his "favorite type of holiday is one that involves . . . flirtation" (as witness his treatment of Mrs. Saunders and Mrs. Scott). In *Love Among the Artists* Shaw, according to Dietrich, is concerned with whether "artists should allow love to divert their energies," but the very form of Dietrich's sentence suggests a definition of love that makes it excrescential, rather than essential, and the book is more correctly concerned with whether geniuses should or should not submit to the institution of marriage. Notwithstanding the "concessions to popular taste" in Shaw's fourth novel, *Cashel Byron's Profession*, Lydia Carew's resolve to marry Byron is still "a plain proposition in eugenics," however ironic the outcome. Finally, in *An Unsocial Socialist*, Sidney Trefusis's marriage to Henrietta, "supported only by romance," causes him to run away from his new bride, and his scandalous behavior at her funeral is enough to justify the book's original title, *The Heartless Man*. Nor is his second marriage to Agatha grounded in love, but rather in their mutual disbelief in it, while his flirtations with Jane Carpenter and other women are a throw-back to the conduct of his earliest protagonist.

Shaw's desire to deepen the human element in his work may be found in his continuing consultation with friends, critics, actors, and actresses while his first plays were in process of being written. On the stage, living actors have to interact, to find human motivation for each move, thought, and speech, or they cannot perform it. Moreover theater, like love, is more a matter of show than tell. In addition to dialogue which, through tone of voice, can frequently imply something quite different from what the words are saying, actors offer the theatrical impact of their bodies, silence, colors, costumes, groupings, and relative positions on stage. In short, they present us with living people. Notwithstanding his proclaimed desire to make his plays "actor-proof," Shaw seems to have rejoiced in the flesh-and-blood reality of those who lent human warmth to his wit.

But that is a subject for a different study. *Bernard Shaw's Novels* is quite simply the best analysis of Shaw's novels in print and, as such, is invaluable to the serious Shavian. Moreover, steeped as it is in thirty or more years of Shavian rumination on the part of its author, it contains many

incidental truths. Says Dietrich, "It is the price of admission to Shaw studies that one has to enter the struggle with Shaw in order to understand
him." In *Bernard Shaw's Novels* he convinces us that it is a bargain.

Brian Tyson

Shaw As Spin Doctor

Charles A. Berst. *Pygmalion: Shaw's Spin on Myth and Cinderella.* New York:
Twayne Publishers, 1995. xiii + 158 pp. Illus. Index. $23.95 (cloth),
$13.95 (paper).

Shavians should not come to the above opus expecting that Charles A.
Berst will attempt to refine and deepen the definitive analysis already
provided of the play in his now classic study, *Bernard Shaw and the Art of
Drama* (1973). Written for Twayne's Masterwork Studies, *Shaw's Spin* (as
I hereby christen it) is rather a basic introduction and study guide for
which college undergraduates would seem the intended audience. Considered as such, the book succeeds—the more so because even initiated
readers of Shaw's drama will discover previously overlooked nuggets of
truth.

To be sure, Berst's audience imposes limits on his approach. Of *Pygmalion's* various mythic and fictional antecedents (from Prometheus to
Ibsen), overwhelming attention is given to the Cinderella story—less because it offers the most profound parallels than because it is the source
most readily familiar to the general reader. Moreover, Berst's method of
working through the play superdiligently line by line—while useful to
new readers—can at times devolve into bland exposition. At other times,
he pushes fine details too hard for significance. Is it really enlightening to
be told that the keys and small change that Higgins jiggles in his pockets
represent "keys to his way of life, along with the cash supporting it"?
Nonetheless, putting the text under the microscope can produce illumi-
nations. Quoting Higgins's boast, "By George, Eliza, I said I'd make a
woman of you; and I have. I like you like this," Berst shrewdly observes
that what Higgins actually promised was to make a *lady* of Eliza, and part
of his problem lies in his failure to recognize the distinction.

Every detail that Berst notes will be helpful to someone. While undergraduates need to be told exactly what Eliza means by "Theyll take away
my character," professors will equally appreciate being reminded (if we
ever knew) that "Monkey Brand" is a caustic cleanser with which Higgins

threatens to have Eliza scrubbed by Mrs. Pearce. The author is adept at showing how stage directions that the eye easily glides over (such as the striking of a church clock) are an integral part of Shaw's total dramatic effect. Even when making a well-established point, Berst puts his own "spin" on it: e.g., "Higgins fails to appreciate how his original boast that he could make Eliza a duchess or a shop assistant has led to the problem of the great disparity between the two."

Berst is also a considerate guide to the problem that *Pygmalion* exists in several versions; the "definitive text" is so designated only in the sense that it was the author's last. The issue is complicated by meddlings with the play itself (especially its ending), beginning with Beerbohm Tree as Higgins in the first London production and continuing into the post-Shavian age at least through *My Fair Lady*. Shaw himself was not guiltless of tampering with his own text. Berst judiciously weighs differences between the authorized version of 1941 (incorporating Shaw's additions from the screenplay of 1938 and other changes as well) with the first edition published in 1916. (*Pygmalion* actually had already been printed in German as well as in periodicals on both sides of the water.) Demonstrating subtle changes of emphasis and significant divagations in quality, Berst makes a persuasive case for the position that Shaw "got it right" the first time. Surprisingly, he defends the plausibility of Shaw's claim (in the afterword to the 1916 edition) that Eliza will marry Freddy. True enough, "Higgins avoids wedlock as if it were hemlock"; but Eliza's parting from him (assuming that it is final) hardly leaves the vacuous Freddy or necessarily *any* man as her sole alternative.

I gleaned much from this book besides the incidental fact (perhaps unknown only to me?) that Queen Victoria's native language was not English. For instance, I had never picked up sufficiently on hints in the text that the Eynesford Hills have recently declined on the social ladder—a fact useful for understanding the otherwise baffling behavior of (especially) Clara. It is of course not news that Eliza's own talents have as much to do with her success as Higgins's tutelage, but I was both surprised and convinced by Berst's showing that this young woman *also* has a taint of real snobbery and vanity that should work against our idealizing her. A more slight but intriguing observation is that the fourth act's opening stage direction indicating *"a summer night"* is a slip on Shaw's part because it is inconsistent with previous seasonal allusions in the play also designated as summer but necessarily taking place several months earlier.

Being the work of the author of perhaps the finest book we have on Shaw's plays *as* plays, yet intended primarily as a basic guide for those encountering *Pygmalion* for the first time, *Shaw's Spin* includes some observations that may annoy scholars for stating the self-evident, while other comments may strike neophytes as too esoteric to be worthy of notice. But this falling between two stools is forgivable and in any case unavoidable in a study of this kind. Whatever his or her level of sophistication, each reader of Berst's opus will be enlightened, even if not in the same way. For an undergraduate audience, the book is a trustworthy Baedecker; for critics and scholars, it offers a chance to experience *Pygmalion* again—in some ways anew.

Alfred Turco, Jr.

John R. Pfeiffer*

A CONTINUING CHECKLIST OF SHAVIANA

I. Works by Shaw

Shaw, Bernard. *"The Adventures of the Black Girl in Her Search for God,* Inscribed Presentation Copy." Sale listing of *Black Girl*. London: Constable, 1932. Reprint, original black and white pictorial boards, octavo. Inscription: "To Vera Noble, from Bernard Shaw 14th. Dec. 1932"; together with "ten autograph letters and cards, 1930–1934, signed by Charlotte Shaw, to Vera Noble dealing with various domestic matters, holiday arrangements and clothing, also commenting on Cape Town, the success of Shaw's play at Malvern," Shaw's breakdown through overwork, and congratulating her on her baby. Seventeen pages, octavo, envelopes. *Sotheby's* LN7412 "Jack" (17 July 1997), item 350. £400–500.

———. *Arms and the Man.* In *Literature: Reading Fiction, Poetry, Drama, and the Essay.* Fourth Edition. New York: McGraw-Hill, 1997. Not seen. An ancillary section, "The Interpretation of Drama," furnishes an analysis of Act II of *Arms.* Not seen.

———. "Four autograph cards signed, one with a typed and corrected memorandum for a letter to the press on behalf of the Society of Authors, to Lord Gorell about meetings and issues concerning the Soci-

*Thanks to Richard E. Winslow III for discovering and supplying page copies for a number of entries in this list. Professor Pfeiffer, *Shaw* Bibliographer, welcomes information about new or forthcoming Shaviana: books, articles, pamphlets, monographs, dissertations, films, videos, reprints, and the like, citations of which may be sent to him at the Department of English, Central Michigan University, Mt. Pleasant, MI 48859.

ety." Four cards and two quarto pages, three autograph address panels, stamped and postmarked Istria, London, Buxton, and Ayot St. Lawrence, 1929–34. *Sotheby's* LN7412 "Jack" (17 July 1997), item 446. Asking price: £600–800.

———. "The King, the Constitution and the Lady: Another Fictitious Dialogue." In Dennis Griffiths, *Plant Here the [London Evening] Standard*. London: Macmillan, 1996; p. 265. Reprint of Shaw's story of 5 December 1936 in the *Evening Standard*, p. 7, which parodies the affair of Mrs. Wallis Simpson and Edward VIII.

———. Letter of 17 October 1915 to Lee Shubert. See McNamara, Brooks, in Books and Pamphlets, below.

———. "Utopias." *SHAW: The Annual of Bernard Shaw Studies*. Volume Seventeen. University Park: Penn State University Press, 1997.

Shaw, Bernard, and Dorothy R. Bates. *The George Bernard Shaw Vegetarian Cookbook, Revised Ed.* Summertown, Tenn.: Book Publishing Company, 1995; paper $8.95. Not seen. Other electronic listings provide "The Book Publishing Company presents the George Bernard Shaw Vegetarian Cookbook in Six Acts: Based on George Bernard Shaw's Favorite Recipes," as revised in 1987 by Dorothy R. Bates.

Shaw, Bernard, and Robert Donat. "Collection of material relating to Shaw." Five letters and cards, chiefly autograph, signed by Shaw, a retained autograph draft letter by Donat, and carbon copies of four other letters by him to Shaw. Eighteen pages, chiefly quarto, 14 February 1940 to 20 August 1943. Content relates to the actor Donat's connection with production and tour of *Devil's Disciple* and *Heartbreak House*. Also included is a marked-up script for Donat's radio broadcast of *Dark Lady of the Sonnets*. *Sotheby's* LN7412 "Jack" (17 July 1997), item 175. £1,500–2,000.

II. Books and Pamphlets

Bailey, Peter. See *The Chocolate Soldier*, below.

Barnes, John. "Tropics of a Desirable Oxymoron: The Radical Superman in *Back to Methuselah*." *SHAW: The Annual of Bernard Shaw Studies*. Volume Seventeen. University Park: Penn State University Press, 1997.

Bogdanovich, Peter. *Who the Devil Made It: Conversations with Robert Aldrich . . . Raoul Walsh* (subtitle includes sixteen names). New York: Alfred A. Knopf, 1997. Edgar G. Ulmer speaks about his direction of *Damaged Goods* (1933), a film based on a Eugène Brieux play translated by Charlotte Shaw (not by G.B.S. as the text states). Otto Preminger speaks about his Jean Seberg film of *Saint Joan*, which was a great popular and commercial success contrary to Preminger's statement that Shaw's play "was never a popular success."

Bonham Carter, Violet. *Lantern Slides. The Diaries and Letters of Violet Bonham Carter, 1904–1914*. Eds. Mark Bonham Carter and Mark Pottle. London: Weidenfeld and Nicolson, 1996. Violet was a daughter of Prime Minister Asquith by his first wife. References in the letters are to G.B.S. at his apogee as seen by a young woman who knows everybody and goes everywhere. Quotes Beatrice Webb that Shaw "is a gambler—he gambles in many ideas but invests in none." Quotes her stepmother Margot that Shaw's sense of humor is "destructive." She is unhappy at the allegation by Margot that Shaw did not take Father Keegan, his creation in *John Bull's Other Island*, seriously: "I am sorry as I loved the mad parson & can't bear to see him degraded by his creator. To me there is something wrong and unnatural about this cuckoo-like indifference and lack of tenderness for your own creations." Violet wrote that when eighteen (in 1905).

Booth, Michael R., and Joel H. Kaplan, eds. *The Edwardian Theatre: Essays on Performance and the Stage*. Cambridge: Cambridge University Press, 1996. Includes a number of references to Shaw and mentions *Androcles*, *Major Barbara*, *Press Cuttings*, and *Plays for Puritans*.

Bradbury, Ray. "G.B.S.: Refurbishing the Tin Woodman: Science Fiction with a Heart, a Brain, and the Nerve!" *SHAW: The Annual of Bernard Shaw Studies*. Volume Seventeen. University Park: Penn State University Press, 1997.

Bryden, Ronald. See *Mrs Warren's Profession*, below.

Burrell, Brian. *The Words We Live By: The Creeds, Mottoes, and Pledges That Have Shaped America*. New York: Free Press, 1997. Naturally, Shaw is tapped for samples. One is, "Do not [do] unto others as you would that they should do unto you; their tastes may not be the same."

The Chocolate Soldier: Shaw Festival 1997 (Shaw Festival production program). Includes "Director's Notes" by David Latham and "Boudoirs and Battlefields" by Peter Bailey, describing something of the history of the reception of *Soldier* along with G.B.S.'s ambivalence about the content (highly displeased) and the popular/box-office success (he approved and was later disappointed that he had not secured more of the royalties).

Cole, Lloyd. *Philosophy of George Bernard Shaw*. Concord, Mass.: Paul, 1995. Not seen.

Cypess, Sandra M. "Spanish American Theatre in the Twentieth Century." *The Cambridge History of Latin American Literature, Volume 2: The Twentieth Century*. Eds. Roberto González Echevarría and Enrique Pupo-Walker. Cambridge: Cambridge University Press, 1996. Among others, describes Rodolfo Usigli (1905–79) who, in the 1950s, became one of the most active dramatists in Spanish America. His work is associated with Shaw, whom he knew and with whom he corresponded.

Like Shaw, Usigli wrote comedies and historical plays and used satire to censure sociopolitical and sexual hypocrisy.

Deane, Seamus. *Strange Country: Modernity and Nationhood in Irish Writing Since 1790*. Oxford: Clarendon Press, 1997. Among several references, Deane observes that Ireland created a national literature that was also a colonial one, only lately recognized, and the tensions are interesting. The position of exile occupied by Dubliners like Shaw, Wilde, O'Casey, Beckett, Moore, and Joyce was the "high art and form of emigration . . . a form of dispossession that retained—imaginatively—the claim to possession." A later comment: "Occultism, theosophy, Gothic fiction, the twilight of the Celtic gods, are all recognizable antidotes to the despiritualized Fabianism that Yeats always recognized as the domain of Bernard Shaw."

Dietrich, Richard F. Review of *Shaw's People: Victoria to Churchill* by Stanley Weintraub. *Biography* 20:4 (Fall 1997): 489–92.

———. "The War of the World-Betterers" (review of *Correspondence of Bernard Shaw: Bernard Shaw and H. G. Wells*, edited by J. Percy Smith). *SHAW: The Annual of Bernard Shaw Studies*. Volume Seventeen. University Park: Penn State University Press, 1997.

Douglas, Kirk. *Climbing the Mountain: My Search for Meaning*. New York: Simon & Schuster, 1997. Douglas: "We started our own production companies . . . I worked for his [Burt Lancaster's] in *The Devil's Disciple*. We were reaching out to do more than just action pictures or westerns. *The Devil's Disciple*, a play by George Bernard Shaw, would never have been made into a movie if the two of us didn't take cuts in our salaries to get it done. But we wanted to do something deeper, something worthwhile."

Eliot, T. S. *Inventions of the March Hare: Poems 1909–1917*. Ed. Christopher Ricks. New York: Harcourt Brace, 1996. Eliot in a 3 May 1957 letter to Henry Sherek: "I sometimes think that Shaw is best at musical comedy for *The Chocolate Soldier* and *My Fair Lady* are the only two of his works which I should like to see again and again."

Emeljanow, Victor. "The Nineteenth Century: Victorian Period: Victorian Drama and Theatre." In *The Year's Work in English Studies*, Volume 75 (1994). Oxford: Blackwell, 1997. Notices of three pieces about Shaw, including a substantial discussion of *George Bernard Shaw and the Socialist Theatre* by Tracy C. Davis (1994). See also Griffiths, Trevor, below.

Evans, T. F., ed. *George Bernard Shaw: The Critical Heritage*. New York: Routledge, 1997. A reissue of *Shaw: The Critical Heritage* (1976) at $135.

Fadiman, Clifton, and John S. Major. *The New Lifetime Reading Plan*. Fourth edition. New York: HarperCollins, 1997. Lists 133 authors from the anonymous writers of *Gilgamesh* to Chinua Achebe. The Shaw works mentioned are *Selected Plays and Prefaces*, *Superman*, *Androcles*,

Arms, Candida, Disciple, Caesar, Major Barbara, Pygmalion, Heartbreak, Methuselah, and *Saint Joan.* Also comments that Shaw's stock has slipped a few points in the last fifty years.

Ferguson, Ann L. *"The Instinct of an Artist": Shaw and the Theatre: An Exhibition from the Bernard F. Burgunder Collection of George Bernard Shaw.* Ithaca, N.Y.: Cornell University Library, 1997. Burgunder was keenly interested in Shaw's involvement in theatrical production, which accounts for the collection's rich assortment of rehearsal notes, theater programs, prompt books, and production photos. This generously illustrated pamphlet describes about 100 items in twelve cases of the exhibition. To be reviewed in *SHAW* 19.

Ferguson, Robert. *Henrik Ibsen.* London: Cohen, 1996. Not seen. The review essay by David Edgar, "Which Is the Hero?" *London Review of Books* (20 March 1997), pp. 10–11, is as much about Shaw on Ibsen as a review of Ferguson's book. Edgar sees Shaw's *Quintessence of Ibsenism* as "certainly the best essay by one playwright about another and one of the best pieces of sustained dramatic criticism ever written."

Foltz, William. "The Year in Literary Biography." *Dictionary of Literary Biography Yearbook: 1996.* Detroit: Gale Research, 1997; pp. 63–64. Includes a review of Stanley Weintraub's *Shaw's People: Victoria to Churchill.*

Frankfurter, Felix. See Holmes, Oliver Wendell, Jr., below.

Gahan, Peter. *"Back to Methuselah:* An Exercise of Imagination." *SHAW: The Annual of Bernard Shaw Studies.* Volume Seventeen. University Park: Penn State University Press, 1997.

Grange, William. *Comedy in the Weimar Republic: A Chronicle of Incongruous Laughter.* Westport, Conn.: Greenwood, 1996. Refers to a number of G.B.S. productions in Germany from 1919 to 1933, saying almost nothing but place and date of performances. For *The Apple Cart* more information is given, but it is wrong. King Magnus does not abdicate in favor of his son: he only threatens to do so, which is sufficient to cow the British Cabinet.

Grene, Nicholas. "The Edwardian Shaw, or the Modernist That Never Was." *Low and High Moderns: Literature and Culture, 1889–1939.* Eds. Maria DiBattista and Lucy McDiarmid. New York: Oxford University Press, 1996. Grene argues that Shaw "vehemently denied that he was a rationalist; he saw himself as a prophetic visionary," but the irrationalism of the Edwardian plays implies a greater future rationalism: "Visionary dreams thus prefigure a literal reality to come, unlike the nonrational associative forms of modernist writing which uncover truths buried in the unconscious of the past." Shaw believed that history was a comedy whose happy ending for the human race we all are striving to attain. "The modern for Shaw was not something incomparably new and different in essence; it was just one more installment of futurity."

Griffiths, Trevor. "The Twentieth Century: 3 Drama." In *The Year's Work in English Studies*. Volume 75 (1994). Oxford: Blackwell, 1997. Notices two articles on Shaw. See also Emeljanow, Victor, above.

Grossman, Elwira M. "Witkacy and Shaw's Stage Statues." *SHAW: The Annual of Bernard Shaw Studies*. Volume Seventeen. University Park: Penn State University Press, 1997.

Grunwald, Henry. *One Man's America: A Journalist's Search for the Heart of His Country*. New York: Doubleday, 1997. Grunwald begins Chapter Thirteen with extracts from *Man and Superman*'s "The Revolutionist's Handbook," ending with "AND YET Revolutions have never lightened the burden of tyranny: they have only shifted it to another shoulder." He uses this reference to explain his perception of the similarity between Nazism and Communism.

Gyorgyey, Clara. "Hay, Julius (Gyula)." *Literary Exile in the Twentieth Century: An Analysis and Biographical Dictionary*. Ed. Martin Tucker. New York: Greenwood, 1991; pp. 305–6. Hay (1900–1975) was "The only internationally known Hungarian playwright of communist persuasion"; his earlier plays "emulated the rational irony of G. B. Shaw."

Haddad, Rosalie Rahal. *Gorge Bernard Shaw e a renovação do teatro inglês* [George Bernard Shaw and the renewal of the English theater]. São Paulo: Olarobrás/ABEI, 1997; 134 pp.; paper. Not seen.

Holmes, Oliver Wendell, Jr., and Felix Frankfurter. *Holmes and Frankfurter: Their Correspondence, 1912–1934*. Eds. Robert M. Mennel and Christine L. Compston. Hanover, N. H.: University Press of New England, 1996. Holmes mentions G.B.S. twice: "I have just read Bernard Shaw's article in a late *New Republic* [9 (6 January 1917); a review of Chesterton's *The Perils of Peace*; C2106] with much pleasure at what seemed to me its wisdom and wit" (13 January 1917); "Shaw's *Back to Methuselah*, which I think a failure, shows the tendency you observe but riles me by bringing literary gifts to aid a dogmatic attitude to which, so far as I can see, he is not entitled" (25 July 1921).

Holroyd, Michael. "Appeasement and Equality: Bernard Shaw's Utopia." *Hailing Heaney: Lectures for a Nineties Nobel*. Eds. Rosa González and Jacqueline A. Hurtley. Barcelona: PPU, 1996; pp. 55–69. Discusses Shaw's neglected identity as an *Irish* Nobel Prize winner, noting that he "had kept up connections with his native country far more assiduously than most people realised" and had accepted the Honorary Freedom of Dublin in his old age "although, the Nobel Prize excepted, he refused almost all public honours elsewhere." Although he lived most of his life in England, he regarded himself as a foreigner there and took pride in being an Irishman. He became "an Irish fifth column agent within the

English ranks" in his lifelong literary and political efforts to improve the world. Shaw's dreams of utopian society had their origins in Ireland.

―――. *Bernard Shaw: The One-Volume Definitive Edition*. London: Chatto & Windus, 1997. Not seen. Reviewed in *TLS* (17 October 1997), p. 34.

Hugo, Leon H. "Indefatigable!" (review of *Bernard Shaw: Theatrics*, edited by Dan H. Laurence). *SHAW: The Annual of Bernard Shaw Studies*. Volume Seventeen. University Park: Penn State University Press, 1997.

―――. "Shavian Studies in North America: A Glut on the Market?" (review of *Bernard Shaw: Theatrics*, edited by Dan H. Laurence; *Bernard Shaw and H. G. Wells*, edited by J. Percy Smith; *Shaw's People: Victoria to Churchill* by Stanley Weintraub; *Bernard Shaw: The Ascent of the Superman* by Sally Peters; *Shaw and Joyce: "The Last Word in Stolentelling"* by Martha Fodaski Black; and *Bernard Shaw's Novels: Portraits of the Artist as Man and Superman* by Richard Farr Dietrich). *Review* 19 (1997): 1–21.

Hull, Elizabeth Anne. "On His Shoulders: Shaw's Influence on Clarke's *Childhood's End*." *SHAW: The Annual of Bernard Shaw Studies*. Volume Seventeen. University Park: Penn State University Press, 1997.

"In Good King Charles's Golden Days": Shaw Festival 1997 (Shaw Festival production program, 1997). Includes "Director's Notes" by Allen MacInnis and "Shaw's Seventeenth-century Einsteinian Universe" by J. L. Wisenthal, who sees the play as Shaw's conflation of the "curvilinear universe" of Einstein, which so delighted G.B.S. with its implications of the "unexpected" and "wilful," with the views of the "seventeenth-century figures who ought to have met, whether or not the mere facts of history indicate that they actually did so."

Indick, Ben P. "Shaw's Science Fiction on the Boards." *SHAW: The Annual of Bernard Shaw Studies*. Volume Seventeen. University Park: Penn State University Press, 1997.

Jameson, Fredric. "Longevity as Class Struggle." In *Immortal Engines: Life Extension and Immortality in Science Fiction and Fantasy*. Eds. George Slusser, Gary Westfahy, and Eric S. Rabin. Athens: University of Georgia Press, 1996; pp. 24–42. *Back to Methuselah* is mentioned. Not seen.

Kaplan, Joel H. See Booth, Michael R., above.

Kelly, Linda. "*Richard Brinsley Sheridan: A Life*. London: Sinclair-Stevenson, 1997. Not seen. The *TLS* review by David Nokes (18 April 1997, p. 32) says that Shaw was among those recruited to provide puffs for *School for Scandal*.

Knowlson, James. *Damned to Fame: The Life of Samuel Beckett*. New York: Simon & Schuster, 1996. One of several Shaw references: Beckett saw a lot of Captain Alan Duncan and his Rathmines-born wife, Belinda (*née* Atkinson) in Paris and was "irritated by Duncan's avid hero-worship of George Bernard Shaw as an essayist and a playwright."

Lahr, John. *Light Fantastic: Adventures in Theatre*. London: Bloomsbury, 1996; paper, 1997. Offers several references to G.B.S., including a chapter, "Lerner and Loewe: Shaw Business," a review of the Howard Davies production of *My Fair Lady* at the Virginia Theatre (no date provided), first published, as were virtually all the pieces in the volume, in the *New Yorker*.

Lindemann, Albert S. *Esau's Tears: Modern Anti-Semitism and the Rise of the Jews*. Cambridge: Cambridge University Press, 1997. Shaw is cited for his statement in "The Sanity of Art" that "Jews from Moses to Marx and Lassalle have inspired all the revolutions" and for his praise of Houston Stewart Chamberlain's anti-Semitic *The Foundations of the Twentieth Century* (1899).

Lodge, David. *The Practice of Writing*. New York: Allen Lane the Penguin Press, 1997. Shaw is used to keynote a chapter entitled "Playback: Extracts from a Writer's Diary": "A perfectly adequate and successful stage representation of a play requires a combination of circumstances so extraordinarily fortunate that I doubt whether it has ever occurred in the history of the world."

Louvish, Simon. *Man on the Flying Trapeze: The Life and Times of W. C. Fields*. New York: W. W. Norton, 1997. One reference to Shaw's plays, as starred in by "Grace George" (1879–1961), one of seven women named by Fields's wife Hattie when she sued him in 1947 for having given away a half million dollars to lady friends.

Lynn, Kenneth S. *Charlie Chaplin and His Times*. New York: Simon & Schuster, 1997. The first London entertainment bid that Chaplin accepted was at Lady Astor's. "Words failed him upon being introduced to Bernard Shaw." Shaw was a Chaplin fan. Chaplin "was startled" to find Shaw "among the flower-shirted tourists" in Hawaii in 1936.

Major, John S. See, Fadiman, Clifton, above.

McDowell, Frederick P.W. "The Latest Biography of Shaw" (review of *Bernard Shaw: The Ascent of the Superman* by Sally Peters). *SHAW: The Annual of Bernard Shaw Studies*. Volume Seventeen. University Park: Penn State University Press, 1997.

McNamara, Brooks. *The Shuberts of Broadway: A History Drawn from the Collections of the Shubert Archive*. New York: Oxford University Press, 1990. Three pages describe the relationship of Lee Shubert and Shaw. Shubert produced *Widowers' Houses*, *Fanny's First Play*, and *Jitta's Atonement*. He tried but failed to produce *Philanderer*, *Great Catherine*, and *Pygmalion*. Included are a photocopy of a 27 October 1915 Shaw letter to Shubert on engaging the actress Gertrude Kingston to play in *Great Catherine* and *The Inca of Perusalem* and a reproduction of the program for the 16 September 1912 production of *Fanny*.

Morris, Sylvia Jukes. *Rage for Fame: The Ascent of Clare Boothe Luce*. New

York: Random House, 1997. Luce kept Shaw's photograph beside her bed for inspiration. She met her "literary hero" at his flat in London on 16 June 1939. She liked *Saint Joan* the best of the plays.

Mrs Warren's Profession: Shaw Festival 1997 (Shaw Festival production program, 1997). Includes "Director's Notes" by Tadeusz Bradecki and "Mrs. Warren's Home Address" by Ronald Bryden, offering an account of Shaw's most direct knowledge of prostitution, including the large extent of it that one encountered as a pedestrian in late nineteenth-century London. Bryden also speculates that among possible sources for the name "Mrs. Warren" was perhaps Warren Street, which closed the north side of Fitzroy Square where Shaw lived at number 29 with his mother until he was 42. The Crawford divorce case of 1885 had ruined the statesman Sir Charles Dilke when Mrs. Crawford testified that Sir Charles had taken her for seduction to 65 Warren Street.

Niven, Penelope. *Steichen: A Biography*. New York: Clarkson Potter, 1997. Steichen, photographer and painter, called G.B.S. his best model, although at first he felt that Shaw was almost impossible to photograph. His chance came when he wanted to try the new color photographic plates, which naturally interested Shaw, a talented amateur photographer. Impressed with Steichen's results, Stieglitz asked to print his superb color photos of Shaw in *Camera Work*.

Obraztsova, Anna. "Bernard Shaw's Dialogue with Chekhov." *Chekhov on the British Stage*. Ed. and trans. Patrick Miles. Cambridge: Cambridge University Press, 1993; pp. 43–53. No literal "dialogue" is provided here. Shaw's influence in having Chekhov performed in England is reported, along with similarities between Chekhov and G.B.S., including "But both the Russian and the English writer needed the traditions of vaudeville and the farce to give fresh edge to their comic writing, and to consolidate their artistic positions."

O'Toole, Peter. *Loitering with Intent: The Apprentice*. Westport, Conn.: Hyperion, 1997. Not seen. The *Washington Post Book World* review by Jonathan Yardley (2 February 1997, p. 3), provides O'Toole's description of that "rich communion in the trinity of author, actor and audience" in a performance of *You Never Can Tell* by O'Toole and his classmates for their teachers at the Royal Academy of Dramatic Art.

Peters, Margot. "Intersections" (review of *Shaw's People: Victoria to Churchill* by Stanley Weintraub). *SHAW: The Annual of Bernard Shaw Studies*. Volume Seventeen. University Park: Penn State University Press, 1997.

———. *May Sarton: A Biography*. New York: Alfred A. Knopf, 1997. During her theater years, Sarton played the role of Dolly in *You Never Can Tell* (p. 123).

Peters, Sally. "Wit, Common Sense, and Prophetic Vision" (review of *The Complete Prefaces, Vol. 2: 1914–1929*, edited by Dan H. Laurence and

Daniel J. Leary). *SHAW: The Annual of Bernard Shaw Studies*. Volume Seventeen. University Park: Penn State University Press, 1997.

Pfeiffer, John R. "Ray Bradbury's Bernard Shaw." *SHAW: The Annual of Bernard Shaw Studies*. Volume Seventeen. University Park: Penn State University Press, 1997.

Salter, James. *Burning the Days: Recollections*. New York: Random House, 1997. Salter recalls that he once wrote a script for a play when "only the seed of a story was provided," a romance between "a reclusive star" who grants an interview "to a very private, literary writer": "I prepared myself—why, I cannot remember—by reading Bernard Shaw's *Man and Superman*, and . . . I wrote the script. Something might have come of it but never did."

Sarton, May. *May Sarton: Selected Letters, 1916–1954*. Ed. Susan Sherman. New York: W. W. Norton, 1997. At least seven references to G.B.S. Sarton liked the Shaw/Terry letters very much. In addition she played Joan, directed the play, and had a part in *You Never Can Tell*. In 1947 she wrote of Shaw's "desert," perhaps referring to *Doctor's Dilemma*, and that "the trouble is there is never any mystery, any *silence* in Shaw."

Sheehy, Helen. *Eva Le Gallienne: A Biography*. New York: Alfred A. Knopf, 1996. Le Gallienne's reading in 1921 included Shaw's *Methuselah*.

Shippey, Tom. "Skeptical Speculation and *Back to Methuselah*." *SHAW: The Annual of Bernard Shaw Studies*. Volume Seventeen. University Park: Penn State University Press, 1997.

Slusser, George. "Last Men and First Women: The Dynamics of Life Extension in Shaw and Heinlein." *SHAW: The Annual of Bernard Shaw Studies*. Volume Seventeen. University Park: Penn State University Press, 1997.

Sparks, Julie A. "Shaw for the Utopians, Čapek for the Anti-Utopians." *SHAW: The Annual of Bernard Shaw Studies*. Volume Seventeen. University Park: Penn State University Press, 1997.

Spoto, Donald. *Notorious: The Life of Ingrid Bergman*. New York: Harper-Collins, 1997. Two Shaw/Bergman connections are described. The first is of her meeting with G.B.S. when he was 93. Questioned by Shaw about why she had not done *Saint Joan*, she responded, with a smile, "I didn't like it." In 1971 she played Lady Cicely Waynflete in a London production of *Captain Brassbound's Conversion*.

Stone-Blackburn, Susan. "Science and Spirituality in *Back to Methuselah* and *Last and First Men*." *SHAW: The Annual of Bernard Shaw Studies*. Volume Seventeen. University Park: Penn State University Press, 1997.

Thompson, Hunter S. *The Proud Highway: Saga of Desperate Southern Gentleman, 1955–1967: The Fear and Loathing Letters, Volume I*. Ed. Douglas Brinkley. New York: Villard, 1997. A 14 December 1957 letter to George Logan, son of an eminent Kentucky judge, relates a Thompson dream vision of himself on a cloud of smog overlooking Jersey Shore, Pennsylvania, with H. L. Mencken on his left and G.B.S. on his right, and preacher Billy Graham. Shaw says, "Nobody with a grain of sense, would live in that place for more than a month." Thompson lived in Jersey Shore from 29 November to 24 December in 1957.

Toland, John. *Captured by History: One Man's Vision of Our Tumultuous Century*. New York: St. Martin's Press, 1997. Toland, the Pulitzer Prize-winning cultural historian, interviewed the "most dangerous Nazi," S.S. Lt.-Colonel Otto Skorzeny, who had in fact saved the lives of a number of American prisoners at Rupp's Inn. Skorzeny told of the kidnapping of the Hungarian Admiral Miklós Horthy's son when Horthy was planning to deal with the Russians. The method of kidnapping young Horthy had been partly inspired by Shaw's play, *Caesar and Cleopatra*, in which young Cleopatra escaped capture by being wrapped in a carpet. At the Citadel, Skorzeny wrapped young Horthy in a carpet and took him to the airfield. The ransom demanded was to let Skorzeny take the Citadel, the seat of Hungarian government. Horthy caved in. Skorzeny's troops took the Citadel with loss of only seven lives.

Turner, Tramble T. "George Bernard Shaw (1856–1950)." *British Playwrights, 1860–1956: A Research and Production Sourcebook*. Westport, Conn.: Greenwood, 1996; pp. 364–80. A reference-work article on G.B.S. Not seen.

Wallmann, Jeffrey M. "Evolutionary Machinery: Foreshadowings of Science Fiction in Bernard Shaw's Dramas." *SHAW: The Annual of Bernard Shaw Studies*. Volume Seventeen. University Park: Penn State University Press, 1997.

Wansell, Geoffrey. *Terence Rattigan*. New York: St. Martin's Press, 1997. Shaw and Rattigan are connected in at least two references. Dr. Keith Newman, a psychiatrist, watched all the performances of Jack Watling, an actor in Rattigan's *Flare Path*, during Newman's London R.A.F. assignment, from which he wrote a book, *250 Times I Saw a Play*. He sent the manuscript to Shaw. Shaw commented that the experience would have driven him mad and that he thought that the author might not have come out of it without a slight derangement. Also, several pages are given to the Rattigan/Shaw controversy in the pages of the *New Statesman* in which Rattigan favored the theater of character over theater of ideas. Rattigan's reputation as a serious dramatist suffered in the event, which was not Shaw's intention.

Weintraub, Rodelle. "Bernard Shaw's Fantasy Island: *Simpleton of the Unexpected Isles*." *SHAW: The Annual of Bernard Shaw Studies*. Volume Seventeen. University Park: Penn State University Press, 1997.

Whelan, Richard. *Alfred Stieglitz: A Biography*. Boston: Little, Brown,

1995. Five indexed references. Stieglitz admired Shaw. He missed one chance to meet him when, because he had lost his voice, he had to break a lunch date and could not reschedule. Later, in 1908, Agnes Ernst, the first female reporter of the *New York Morning Sun*, quoted him in part: "We have no formulated theories, like George Bernard Shaw's, because we believe that a formulated theory is a narrowing thing, lacking in that perfect freedom which we are looking for. . . ."

Wisenthal, J. L. "Shards of Shaw" (review of *Shaw and Joyce: "The Last Word in Stolentelling"* by Martha Fodaski Black). *SHAW: The Annual of Bernard Shaw Studies*. Volume Seventeen. University Park: Penn State University Press, 1997.

———. "Shaw's Utopias." *SHAW: The Annual of Bernard Shaw Studies*. Volume Seventeen. University Park: Penn State University Press, 1997.

———. See *"In Good King Charles's Golden Days"*, above.

Wolf, Milton T. "Foreword: Shaw and Science Fiction." *SHAW: The Annual of Bernard Shaw Studies*. Volume Seventeen. University Park: Penn State University Press, 1997.

III. Periodicals

Adams, Elsie B. "A Portrait of Shaw" (review of Stanley Weintraub's *Shaw's People: Victoria to Churchill*. *ELT* 40:2 (1997): 203–6.

Alberge, Dalya. "Fair Lady Deal Boosts Royalties for Shaw Estate." London *Times* (6 February 1997), p. 5. Settlement of a dispute over royalties from *My Fair Lady* will divide proceeds of nearly two million dollars among the British Museum, the Royal Academy of Dramatic Art, and the National Gallery of Ireland. Since 1956 the share to the Gallery alone has been £3,000,000, mostly from *My Fair Lady* royalties.

Albert, Elaine. "How Does It Feel to Begin to Learn to Read?" *Education Database (ERIC)*, 1994; AN# ED377446; CLH# CS011908; 8 pp. (microfiche). The abstract describes an exercise of reading *Androcles* in "Shavian Alphabet," suggesting that the result supports using the "i/t/a—Initial Teaching Alphabet" for beginning readers.

Allett, John. "Bernard Shaw and Dirty Hands Politics: A Comparison of *Mrs Warren's Profession* and *Major Barbara*." *Journal of Social Philosophy* 28:2 (Fall 1995): 32–45. "It is not easy to imagine the kind of person who would willing[ly] undertake the burden of politics in such circumstances—to wear 'a hair shirt beneath the motley,' to use J. Percy Smith's phrase, but for present purposes it suffices that such a 'superman' would, at least, do what is necessary and then seek not only understanding but also forgiveness." Undershaft is "just this sort of moralizer," while Mrs. Warren "comes closer to the Catholic 'ideal' identified by Walzer ('continuously questioning the worthiness of what they do even as they do it. Furthermore, there is an expectation that those who engage in dirty hands politics will do penance no matter how justified are their actions.')"

Bemrose, John. "Mrs. Warren's Profession" (review). *Mclean's* (9 June 1997), p. 82.

———. "Passion for the Past: The Shaw Festival's Leader Hunts Down Drama." *Maclean's* (9 June 1997), p. 79. Christopher Newton has been the artistic director of Ontario's Shaw Festival for eighteen years. Newton is a history buff who enjoys tracking down little-known works and period details.

Bridges, Linda. "Directors on the Loose." *National Review* (15 September 1997), pp. 80, 82. In part a review of the 1997 Shaw Festival production of *Mrs Warren*.

Buckley, Christopher. "Want to Send a Witty E-mail? Pretend It's a Telegram—In Its Day, the Soul of Wit." *Forbes* (10 March 1997), p. S15. A disadvantage of E-mail is that it can be too wordy. A model of succinctness was Shaw to Winston Churchill: "Have reserved two tickets for my first night. Come and bring a friend if you have one." Not seen.

Cohen, Edward H. "Shaw." In "Victorian Bibliography for 1995." *Victorian Studies* 39:4 (Summer 1996): 737–38. Seventeen entries, retrospective to 1993.

Coleby, John. "GBS's Classics." London *Times* (30 April 1997), p. 23. Writing as the Clerk for the Society of Authors (1970–76) and the Rights Manager for the National Theatre (1976–80), Coleby suggests that Shaw's good plays would be produced if people sublicensed the rights from Duncan Weldon. See Hall, Peter; Simon, Charles; and Smoker, Barbara, below.

Conlon, John J. "Shaw & Lady Gregory" (review of *Shaw, Lady Gregory and the Abbey: A Correspondence and a Record*, edited by Dan H. Laurence and Nicholas Grene). *ELT* 40:3 (1997): 45–47.

"D. T." Review of Michael Holroyd's *Bernard Shaw: The One-Volume Definitive Edition*. *TLS* (17 October 1997), p. 34.

Dallat, C. L. "After the Censor Had Gone." *TLS* (27 September 1996), p. 21. The 1929 Irish statute for the Censorship of Publications is still on the books. It was used to prevent reading of Wells, Zola, Hemingway, and Shaw. Not seen.

D'Aquila, Ulysses. "Gay Men's Biography" (review of *Bernard Shaw: The Ascent of the Superman* by Sally Peters). *Lambda Book Report* 21 (January 1997): 21–22.

Edgar, David. See Ferguson, Robert, under "Books and Pamphlets," above.

Einsohn, H. I. "Bernard Shaw and Gabriel Pascal" (review of *Bernard*

Shaw and Gabriel Pascal, edited by Bernard F. Dukore). *Choice* 34:6 (February 1997): 968–69.

———. "Bernard Shaw's Book Reviews" (review of *Bernard Shaw's Book Reviews, Volume 2, 1884–1950*, edited by Brian Tyson). *Choice* 34:8 (April 1997): 1333.

Farrell, Elizabeth. "Literary Treks through Ireland." *Europe* (October 1996), p. 34. Notes the tree in Lady Gregory's garden in Dublin with carved initials of G.B.S., among others. Not seen.

Feingold, Michael. "*Misalliance*" (review of the Roundabout/Laura Pels Theatre production). *Village Voice* (2 September 1997), p. 91.

Foster, R. F. *W. B. Yeats: A Life, I: The Apprentice Mage, 1865–1914*. Oxford: Oxford University Press, 1997. Many references to G.B.S., including pages on *Arms*, *John Bull*, and *Blanco Posnet*.

Franklin, Nancy. "American Gladiators" (review in part of the Roundabout/Laura Pels Theatre production of *Misalliance*). *New Yorker* 73:26 (8 September 1997): 93–94.

Front and Center (September 1997). Roundabout Theatre Company (New York) subscriber magazine. Features a photo of Shaw for its cover and a one-page "Profile" of Shaw in connection with the production of *Misalliance*.

Ganz, Arthur. " 'Don Giovanni' Shavianized: 'Man and Superman' as Mozartean Commentary." *Opera Quarterly* 13 (Autumn 1996): 21–28. From an abstract: *Superman* was inspired by and a tribute to *Don Giovanni*. The *Superman* characters are modern, darker versions of those in *Giovanni*, with much of Shaw's personal philosophy on romance, sex, and morality clearly evident. Even so, Shaw displays understanding and sensitivity to the complexities of Mozart's story and the beauty of his music. Not seen.

Garebian, Keith. "Retheatricalizing Theatre: The 1996 Shaw and Stratford Festivals." *Journal of Canadian Studies* 31:4 (Winter 1996–97): 164–75. Not seen.

Gaunt, Philip. "Birmingham Revisited: Cultural Studies in a Post-Soviet World." *Journal of Popular Culture* 30 (Summer 1996): 91. From an abstract: A renewed interest in the early studies of the Birmingham Centre for Contemporary Cultural Studies (BCCCS) and its ideas derived from Fabianism will help cultural studies in a post-Soviet world of "localisms." Fabianism, a form of evolutionary socialism "developed in the UK by George Bernard Shaw and Sydney Webb[,] advocated gradualism rather than revolution." The later studies of the BCCCS moved toward totalitarian Marxism, but with the end of the Soviet system, there could come a revival of the essentially British brand of socialism. Not seen.

Gee, Maggie. "Waiting for the Bomb to Drop" (review of the Almeida

Theatre production of *Heartbreak House*). *TLS* (19 September 1997), p. 20.

Gibbs, A. M. "Bernard Shaw's Family Skeletons: A New Look." *Bullán: An Irish Studies Journal* 3 (Spring 1997): 57–74. Shaw's parents were likely very much in love in the early years of their marriage. George Carr was not as thoroughgoing an alcoholic as alleged, was probably a very attentive father, and was a reasonably "convivial" person. The Carr Shaws were not poverty-stricken. Shaw's family was not dysfunctional. His sister Lucy was a warm friend to G.B.S. Shaw's treatment of class issues was ambiguous because "he himself was a member of the class he was so often attacking."

Goreau, Angeline. "The Round Room Comes to an End." *New York Times Book Review* (2 November 1997), p. 39. An elegiac essay on the closing of the British Library (Museum) Reading Room that mentions that G.B.S. "taught himself to write here." See also Lyall, Sarah, below.

Grant, Robert. "Who's Sorry Now?" *TLS* (3 October 1997), p. 36. This review of Paul Oppenheimer, *An Intelligent Person's Guide to Modern Guilt* (London: Duckworth, 1997), informs readers that Shaw "started it with the *Intelligent Woman's Guide to Socialism and Capitalism*. Then came the first in this Duckworth series, John Vincent's *Intelligent Person's Guide to History*, followed by Roger Scruton's *IPG to Philosophy* (the switch to 'person' was presumably a tongue-in-cheek dig at Shaw and feminism)."

Hall, Peter. "Shaw's Classics 'in the Doldrums.' " London *Times* (21 April 1997), p. 23. A complaint that Shaw's major works will not be much performed because Duncan Weldon owns the rights and is likely not to produce more than one a year with a suggestion that the Society of Authors who sold him the rights should reconsider how it administers the Shaw estate. See Coleby, John, above; Simon, Charles; and Smoker, Barbara, below.

"Heroes and Humans" (in part a review of *Bernard Shaw: The Ascent of the Superman* by Sally Peters). *Economist* (18 May 1996), pp. S13–14.

Holland, Merlin. "Not Unkind and Not Untrue: Looking Again at Frank Harris's 'Technicolour' Life of Wilde." *TLS* (24 October 1997), p. 17. This essay includes a description of Shaw's significant role in countering the reputation for unreliability of Harris's *Oscar Wilde: His Life and Confessions*, which tackles Wilde's homosexuality. Shaw felt that Harris's account was about right. Robert Sherard, Wilde's loyal friend and first biographer, attacked Harris's *Wilde* in *Oscar Wilde Twice Defended* (1934) and *Bernard Shaw, Frank Harris and Oscar Wilde* (1937). Based on another Harris claim, Shaw's characterization of Wilde as a "swindler" for allegedly selling the same play scenario, "Mr. and Mrs. Daventry," to several parties for £100 each, turns out to be, in the light of surviving correspondence, "distressingly close to the truth." In Shaw's words, this was "a very serious fraud, to be dismissed goodnaturedly with a laugh only because it was such a transparent excuse for begging." Merlin Holland is Wilde's grandson.

Holroyd, Michael. "The Political Philosophy of Bernard Shaw and the St. Pancras Vestry," *Camden History Review* 21 (1997): 2–6. Analyzes Shaw's political philosophy and traces his successes and failures as a member of the St. Pancras Vestry and then the St. Pancras Borough Council between 1897 and 1906. Reproduces the galley proof, corrected and amended in Shaw's hand in 1947, for "A Socrates in Fitzroy Square" (C3725).

————. "Shaw's Corner." *Royal Oak Newsletter* (Fall 1997), p. 3. Discussion of Shaw's library at Ayot St. Lawrence, commenting on the general contents of the collection in the (T. E.) Lawrence Room at Shaw's Corner, the way that "His library reflects the extraordinary width of his interests," and his "Shavian" attitudes toward books and book production.

Hornby, Richard. "California Theatre: Four New Plays and a Revival" (in part a review of the Pacific Resident Theatre, Venice, California, 1996/97 production of *Mrs Warren's Profession*). *Hudson Review* 50:2 (Summer 1997): 298–304.

Kanfer, Stefan. "Kidding the Pants Off Broadway" (in part a review of Donal Donnelly's *My Astonishing Self* at the Irish Repertory Theater in New York). *New Leader* (10 February 1997), pp. 22–23. Not seen.

Kauffmann, Stanley. "Gabriel Blew His Horn" (review of *Bernard Shaw and Gabriel Pascal*, edited by Bernard F. Dukore). *Theater* 27:2–3 (1997): 159–61.

Kiberd, Declan. "The Periphery and the Center: How Ireland's False Rural Ideal Arose in the Early 1900s." *South Atlantic Quarterly* 95 (Winter 1996): 5–22. From an abstract: The false image of rural Ireland fed a sense of national identity that masked real class divisions and harsh living conditions. Instead of a pastoral society dominated by cities, Ireland in reality saw new rural landowners immigrate to and shape urban centers. Writers such as Synge and Shaw perceived the paradox. Not seen.

Klein, Scott W. "The Subaltern 'Ulysses': Shaw and Joyce" (in part a review of *Shaw and Joyce: "The Last Word in Stolentelling"* by Martha Fodaski Black). *Modern Fiction Studies* 42 (Winter 1996): 883–87. Not seen.

Lennon, Peter. "My Heart Belongs to Da." *Guardian* (22 May 1996), p. 10. An interview of Shivaun, daughter of Sean O'Casey, in which she mentions the £50 sterling that Shaw sent to her parents at her birth. Not seen.

Long, Tom. "Edwin B. Pettet, 81; Taught Theater at Brandeis, Did Show about Shaw." *Boston Globe* (15 May 1997), p. D151. Theater professor Pettet retired from Brandeis University in 1968. He was devoted to Shaw, former president of the Shavian Society of New York City, and, in his retirement, the performer of "My Specialty Is Being Right When Other People Are Wrong," a one-man show based on Shaw's writings.

Lyall, Sarah. "In Hallowed Reading Room, Last Page Is Turned." *New York Times International* (25 October 1997), p. A4. This article on the closing of the Round Reading Room at the British Library (Museum) after 140 years mentions Shaw among the famous people who used it. See also Goreau, Angeline, above.

Lyons, Donald. *"Major Barbara"* (review of the Jean Cocteau Repertory production). *Wall Street Journal* (26 January 1996), p. A8. Not seen.

———. Review of Pearl Theatre New York production of *Misalliance*. *Wall Street Journal* (18 September 1996), p. A16.

———. "Saucy Shaw; Singing Expats" (review of the Roundabout Theatre New York production of *Misalliance*). *Wall Street Journal* (8 August 1997), p. A11.

Marks, Peter. *"My Astonishing Self"* (review of Donal Donnelly's Irish Repertory Theater performance in New York). *New York Times* (24 January 1997), p. B3.

Marx, Bill. "Lyric Stage Looks on the Light Side of *Pygmalion*" (review of the Lyric Stage production). *Boston Globe* (27 September 1997), p. C7.

Morley, Sheridan. "A Waspish World" (in part a review of a touring production of *Mrs Warren* in England). *Spectator* (31 May 1997), pp. 50–51. Not seen.

Newey, Glen. "Balked Scraps from the Farmyard" (review of the Old Vic Theatre production of Harley Granville Barker's *Waste*). *TLS* (4 April 1997), p. 32.

O'Casey, Shivaun. See Lennon, Peter, above.

Omasreiter-Blaicher, Ria. "Die gescheiterte Emanzipation der Frauen im feministischen Drama der Gegenwart" [the failed emancipation of women in contemporary feminist drama]. *Anglia* 112:3–4 (1994): 390–410. Not seen.

Orchard, Andy. "A Long Way from Amoral to Amorous" (review of the Albery Theatre production of *Pygmalion*). *TLS* (15 August 1997), p. 20.

Parker, Stephen. "On Peter Huchel's Adaptation of Shaw's 'Denshawai Horror' and Related Matters." *Neophilologus* (Dordrecht, Netherlands) 79:2 (April 1995): 295–306. Not seen.

Peters, Susan L. Review of *Bernard Shaw: The Ascent of the Superman* by Sally Peters. *Library Journal* (15 March 1996). Not seen.

Pharand, Michel. "Shaw & Freudian Games" (review of *Bernard Shaw: The Ascent of the Superman* by Sally Peters). *ELT* 40:1 (1997): 72–77.

Pope, Laura. *"Mrs Warren's Profession* Revisits Old-Time Controversy" (review of the Peterborough Players, Manchester, New Hampshire, production). *Union Leader* (7 August 1997), p. B4.

Pottie, Lisa M. "Shaw, George Bernard." In "Modern Drama Studies: An Annual Bibliography." *Modern Drama* 39:2 (Summer 1996): 276–77. Sixteen items from 1992 to 1995.

———. "Shaw, George Bernard." In "Modern Drama Studies: An Annual Bibliography." *Modern Drama* 40:2 (Summer 1997): 215. Eight items from 1994 to 1996.

Rae, Lisbie. Review of *Bernard Shaw: The Ascent of the Superman* by Sally Peters. *Modern Drama* 40:2 (Summer 1997): 298–99.

Ramsden, Timothy. "Queen of 'Earts" (review of Royal Lyceum Theatre, Edinburgh, production of *Pygmalion*). *Times Educational Supplement* (26 April 1996), p. SS7. Not seen.

Review of *SHAW* 16: *Unpublished Shaw*, edited by Dan H. Laurence and Margot Peters. *Nineteenth-Century Literature* 51:4 (March 1997): 559.

Russo, Francine. "Point Man" (review of Pearl Theatre, New York, production of *Misalliance*). *Village Voice* (17 September 1996), p. 90. Not seen.

Shaw, Charlotte. See *Adventures of the Black Girl* in "Works by Shaw," above.

"Shaw's Corner." *In Britain* 3 (March 1997): 18–21. A generously illustrated account of the house and environs at Ayot St. Lawrence, Hertfordshire, anchors a thumbnail sketch of Shaw in his retreat from London and includes an account of the surrounding villages and major buildings. Charlotte is erroneously called "Florence, his wife" (perhaps confused with Hardy's second wife from research for a similar feature on Max Gate?). Copy of article supplied by Nedra McCloud.

Siegel, Ed. "ART's *Man and Superman* Is a Devil of a Good Time" (review of the American Repertory Theatre production). *Boston Globe* (16 May 1997), pp. D1, D4.

Simon, John. "*My Astonishing Self*" (review of Donal Donnelly's Irish Repertory Theatre performance in New York). *New York* (17 February 1997), p. 57. Not seen.

———. "Shaw Copyright." London *Times* (19 May 1997), p. 21. Testifies that Shaw told him in 1938 that he preferred having his plays performed to being paid or preserving the script (at least of *Methuselah*) intact. See Colbey, John; and Hall, Peter, above; and Smoker, Barbara, below.

Smoker, Barbara. "'Outrageous' Suppression of Shaw." London *Times* (24 April 1997), p. 23. Writing as Secretary of the Shaw Society, Smoker supports Hall's anger at the suppression of Shaw's best plays and relates the history of the Society of Authors' banning for ten years the production of *Pygmalion* to give *My Fair Lady* a clear run. Shaw had not intended such practice, and E. M. Forster, T. S. Eliot, and Graham Greene opposed the ban in 1956, Greene going so far as to announce his resignation from the Society of Authors in protest. See also Coleby, John; Hall, Peter; and Simon, Charles, above.

Solomonson, Michael. "*Man and Superman*: The Shavianizing of Friedrich Nietzsche." *Independent Shavian* 34:3 (1996): 54–59. "The evidence clearly suggests that Shaw was actually one of the early voices calling for a critical reexamination of Nietzsche's elevation as an original thinker. Shaw's writings and his manipulation of Nietzschean ideas, as demonstrated in *Man and Superman*, further indicate his interest in debunking the idolization of the philosopher and his views. By doing so, he attempted to put Nietzsche in a revised critical context while also calling attention to his own strongly held feminist and socialist agenda."

Sommers, Michael. "Let's Have More Bernard Shaw: *Misalliance* Is Brainy Banter Lit by Slavic Virago's Biplane" (review of the Roundabout Theatre production). *Birmingham News* (10 August 1997), p. F2.

Sterritt, David. "*Misalliance* and *1776* Signal Strong Fall Season" (in part a review of the Roundabout Theatre production of *Misalliance*). *Christian Science Monitor* (19 August 1997), p. 15.

Sutherland, Donald. "Breakfast at Ayot (An Imaginary Conversation)." *Shavian* 8:2 (Spring 1997): 8–10. A short humorous script of G.B.S. and Charlotte discussing where they might go for summer vacation, with intimations of how the onset of World War II touched Shaw in July 1939. The two actually went to Frinton-on-Sea, Essex, in August/September.

Tanitch, Robert. "All Talk and No Action (But What Talk)" (review of the 1997 Shaw Festival production of "*In Good King Charles's Golden Days*"). *TLS* (10 October 1997), p. 21.

Taylor, Markland. "*Jitta's Atonement*" (review of the Berkshire Theater Festival, Stockbridge, Massachusetts, production). *Variety* (12 August 1996), p. 42.

Walshe, Eibhear. " 'Angels of Death': Wilde's *Salomé* and Shaw's *Saint Joan*." *Irish University Review* 27 (Spring/Summer 1997): 24–32. "Despite many differences in terms of self-construction, both Shaw and Wilde share an imaginative interest in the transgressive girl [Salomé and Joan] but both find themselves unable to sustain these 'angels of death.' Thus, to leave off female dress is, for both artists, to shed protection from the murderous rage of a discomforted patriarchal world."

On page 26, Walshe credits Wilde with sending Shaw a copy of *De Profundis*, the prison-written "letter" to Alfred Douglas. Wilde did not do this, nor could Shaw have commented upon it in Wilde's lifetime. The text that Shaw read was Robert Ross's expurgated version, published five years after Wilde's death.

Weales, Gerald. "Shaws for All Seasons" (review of *SHAW* 14; *SHAW* 15; *Shaw:Interviews and Recollections*, edited by A. M. Gibbs; *Bernard Shaw: The Ascent of the Superman* by Sally Peters; and *Bernard Shaw and H. G. Wells*, edited by J. Percy Smith). *Sewanee Review* 105:2 (April/June 1997): 273–81.

Wearing, J. P. "Shaw's Novels" (review of *Bernard Shaw's Novels: Portraits of the Artist as Man and Superman* by Richard Farr Dietrich). *ELT* 40:4 (1997): 501–3.

Weintraub, Stanley. "Who's Afraid of Virginia Woolf?: Virginia and G.B.S." *Charleston Magazine* (Autumn/Winter 1997), pp. 29–39. The intriguingly tensioned connection between Woolf and Shaw began as early as 1898 and progressed until shortly before her death in 1941, "and it would take Virginia all her life to discover that he really did like her." The high point of the relationship came in an exchange of letters in 1940 wherein Shaw connects meeting her with his writing of *Heartbreak House* "because I conceived it in that house somewhere in Sussex where I first met you and, of course, fell in love with you. I suppose every man did." Woolf replied in kind: "As for the falling in love, it was not, let me confess, one-sided. . . . Indeed you have acted a lover's part in my life for the past thirty years; and though I daresay it's not much to boast of, I should have been a worser woman without Bernard Shaw."

Winter, Elizabeth. "Gained in Translation." *TLS* (17 October 1997), p. 31. Commentary on four 1997 translation prizes, including the Bernard Shaw Translation Prize, which is "awarded every three years for translation from the Swedish and Finland-Swedish. The prize money is put up by the Anglo-Swedish Literary Foundation, endowed by George Bernard Shaw from his Nobel Prize." In 1997 the prize went to Michael Robinson for *The Selected Essays of August Strindberg* (Cambridge: Cambridge University Press, 1997).

Wisenthal, J. L. Review of Stanley Weintraub's *Shaw's People: Victoria to Churchill. Modern Drama* 40:1 (Spring 1997): 165–66.

Independent Shavian 34:3 (1996). Journal of the Bernard Shaw Society. Includes "Shaw and Telepathy" by Jan Ehrenwald, "As Sure as Shaw" by David Blum, "*Man and Superman*: The Shavianizing of Friedrich Nietzsche" by Michael Solomonson, "Max Nordau Redivivus?" "Letter from England" by T. F. Evans, "Michael Collins and Bernard Shaw," review of *SHAW* 16 by Sally Peters, review of Richard Farr Dietrich's *Bernard Shaw's Novels* by John Koontz, "News about Our Members," "Society Activities," and "Our Cover." See also Solomonson, Michael, above.

Independent Shavian 35:1 (1997). Journal of the Bernard Shaw Society. Includes "Officers of the Bernard Shaw Society Salute Richard Nick-

son," "Salute to Nickson" by Dan H. Laurence, "Poisoning the Prole-
tariat" by Bernard Shaw, "An Unusual Master's Thesis on Shaw,"
"Shaw in Ezra's Dog Pound," "No More Reading in Shaw's Favorite
Reading Room," "Manhattan Postscript," "Eliza Doolittle as a Belly
Dancer," "GBS: Marianne Moore's 'Colossal Bird'," "B. H. Haggin on
GBS," "Daly's One Night Stand," "Letter from England" by T. F.
Evans, "Theater by the Blind Presents Shaw," "Nothing But Shaw" by
Richard Nickson, "To Err is Shavian: *Re* Brahms," "Shaw in a Speaking
Part," "Shaw Materials at Museum of the City of New York," "The As-
tonishing Donal Donnelly" by Daniel Leary, "Corrigenda," "Obituar-
ies," "News about Our Members," "Society Activities," "Addendum,"
and "Our Cover."

Shavian 8:2 (Spring 1997). The Journal of the Shaw Society. Includes
"Editorial," "Obituary," "Breakfast at Ayot" by Donald Sutherland,
"Our Theatres in the Nineteen-Nineties," "Book Reviews," "Unpub-
lished" by Penny Griffin (review of *SHAW* 16), "The Whirlwind and
the Rock" by Janet Moat (review of *Bernard Shaw and Gabriel Pascal*,
edited by Bernard F. Dukore), "More Reviews" by T. F. Evans (review
of *Bernard Shaw's Book Reviews, Vol. 2*, edited by Brian Tyson), "Further
Thoughts on Literacy" by Donald Sutherland (review of *The Way We
Live Now* by Richard Hoggart), "Questions on Chesterton" by Patrick
Heron (review of *Wisdom and Innocence: A Life of G. K. Chesterton* by
Joseph Pearce), "Literary Survey," "Scraps and Shavings," and "Notes
of Meetings." See also under Sutherland, Donald, above.

IV. Dissertations

Coppa, Francesca. "Blood and Aphorism: Joe Orton, Theatre, and the
New Aristocracy in Great Britain." New York University, 1997. *Dissertation Abstracts Online* 58–14A: 1153. From the abstract: "Orton gained
entrance to the British intelligentsia by performing the position of
'angry young playwright,' appropriating and subverting the post-1956
dramatists as those dramatists had previously appropriated and subverted the British dramatic canon as derived from Oscar Wilde and
George Bernard Shaw, who had themselves consciously appropriated
and subverted the conventions of 19th century theatre. . . . Orton was
marginalized by both his class and sexuality, and by creating the persona of 'Joe Orton,' and developing a reasonable, assured epigram-
matic tone, he, like Wilde and Shaw before him, attempted to move
from margin to center."

Haverkorn, Monique A. "A Theatrical History of the Houston Shaw Festival, 1979–1992." M. A. Thesis, University of Houston, 1993. *Dissertation
Abstracts Online* (*MAI* 31–04: 1428). "The Houston Shaw Festival (HSF),

which began in 1979, was an annual theatrical event produced by the University of Houston-Clear Lake (UHCL) in Texas for 14 years. HSF was the only festival of its kind, in the United States, dedicated to producing George Bernard Shaw's works."

Holmes, Catherine Denham. "Annotations to William Faulkner's 'The Hamlet.' " University of South Carolina, 1994. *Dissertation Abstracts Online* 55–11A: 3512. References suggest analogues and sources for episodes or passages in the novel from Faulkner's wide reading, including works by Shaw.

Keats, Patrick Henry. "G. K. Chesterton and the Victorians: Dialogue, Dialecti, and Synthesis." Catholic University of America, 1994. *Dissertation Abstracts Online* 55–02A: 0284. In his critical biographies, including the one on Bernard Shaw, Chesterton developed the central tenets of his "theories regarding literature." Chapter two focuses on Dickens, Browning, Stevenson, and Shaw, each of whom, according to Chesterton, provided "antidotes" against the more pernicious ideologies pervading the late nineteenth and early twentieth centuries. Chesterton "praises them for their honesty and seriousness of purpose; their belief in truth; their optimistic world views; their salutary use of humor."

Koehler, Kristen Jean. "Comparison of Plot and Characters in Bernard Shaw's 1912 'Pygmalion' and Its Screenplay in 1938." M. A. Thesis, Michigan State University, 1994. *Dissertation Abstracts Online* 33–03: 0698. Conclusions concern the changes in plot and character development from play to screenplay and the effects on the overall dramatic concept of the screenplay.

Rae, Margaret Elizabeth. "The Christopher Newton Years at the Shaw Festival." University of Toronto, 1995. "Newton set the Festival on a new course, radically transforming both playbill and approach to staging. . . . Central to Newton's approach is the ensemble. He built a flexible, loyal group of actors and designers who staged highly acclaimed spectacular productions such as *Cavalcade*. Refining the mandate to plays about the beginning of the modern world sharpened the playbill's focus; an eclectic mixture of contemporaries, both provocative and popular, joined Shaw in the Festival's three theatres. . . . Newton transformed the Shaw Festival from lavish summer stock to an internationally recognised company: from a budget of $2 million to $10 million; a season of 278 performances to 706; a narrow range of playwrights to a wide choice of exciting and seldom performed European and American contemporaries."

Rijnbout, Frans A. "The 'New Woman' in Plays by Harley Granville Barker and His Contemporaries" New York University, 1997. *Dissertation Abstracts Online* 58–01A: 0031. *Getting Married* and *Misalliance* are among the plays examined to identify female stage characters who can be defined as "New Women." Harley Granville Barker's portrayal of the "New Woman" is more honest and inclusive than those by Shaw, John Galsworthy, and Elizabeth Robins. These latter use their plays and stage characters as mouthpieces for their socio-political beliefs while "Barker illuminates the lives of his characters by allowing them to speak with their own, complex voices."

V. Recordings

Caesar and Cleopatra ([1945] film starring Vivian Leigh, Claude Rains, 129 minutes), #11464DB, $19.98. Filmic Archives, The Cinema Center, Botsford, CT 06404–0386. Telephone: 1–800–366–1920.

———. #AUHMK020053, $14.95. The Movie Book (Critics' Choice Video), P.O. Box 749, Itasca, IL 60143–0749. Telephone: 1–800–367–7765. Lists also *My Fair Lady* (1964 film starring Audrey Hepburn and Rex Harrison, 190 minutes, remastered), #ARFOX000974/5, $14.77.

Candida (one scene), with teacher's guide and script. In *For the Director, Blocking a Scene*. Ninety minutes, color. #V182, $148.00 (plus $17.00 shipping). *Performing Arts Buyers Guide 1997*. Stagestep, 200 Hamilton Street, Suite C200, Philadelphia, PA 19130. Telephone: 1–800–523–0960. Works with two student directors as they begin their first directing project, a scene from *Candida*. Not seen.

The Design of Modern Theatre: Adolphe Appia's Innovations (50 minutes), #AYM3366, $149.00. Films for the Humanities and Sciences, P.O. Box 2053, Princeton, NJ 08543–2053. Telephone: 1–800–257–5126. "His designs for Ibsen and Shaw productions link 20th-century theater to the freedoms of ancient Greek drama and mark Appia as the father of modern theatrical design." Not seen.

G. B. Shaw/Eugene O'Neill. One hour/two cassettes. #E8332, $39.95 (plus $5.95 shipping) [1997]. Wellspring Media Inc., 65 Bleecker Street, New York, NY 10012. Telephone: 1–800–538–5856. "Passionate about social reform, George Bernard Shaw and Eugene O'Neill used their critically-acclaimed plays to voice controversial ideas." Part of "Famous Authors Series" that includes Dickens, Twain, Steinbeck, and Hemingway. Not seen.

My Fair Lady (1964 film starring Rex Harrison and Audrey Hepburn, 171 minutes), #7572, $19.98. Fusion International, 17311 Fusion Way, Country Club Hills, IL 60478. Telephone: 1–800–959–0061. Lists also *My Fair Lady Soundtrack*, CD #11358, $16.98; cassette #11721, $9.98.

———. See *Caesar and Cleopatra*, second entry, above.

My Fair Lady Remastered Edition (starring Rex Harrison and Audrey Hepburn), #1 VHS (529335), $19.98. Quality Paperback Book Club, Camp Hill, PA 17012–0001. Telephone: 1–800–998–1979.

My Fair Lady Soundtrack. See *My Fair Lady*, above.

Pygmalion (cassette tape of radio premiere starring Alfred Lunt and Lynne Fontaine, approximately one hour), #RB-31, $4.98. Radio Yesteryear, Box C, Sandy Hook, CT 06482–0847. Telephone: 1–800–243–0987.

VI. Other Media

"M. E." "Shaw (G.B.) Portrait miniature of Shaw." Head and shoulders, with white hair, beard, and moustache, wearing a brown coat and a white shirt, on a blue background, gold frame, oval, $2^{3/4}'' \times 2^{1/2}''$, n.d. *Sotheby's* LN7412 "Jack" (17 July 1997), item 349. £300–500.

CONTRIBUTORS

Paul Bauschatz is Associate Professor of English at the University of Maine. He is currently engaged in research on language in the visual and temporal arts.

John A. Bertolini, Professor of English and Film at Middlebury College, Vermont, and member of the *SHAW* Editorial Board, is author of *The Playwrighting Self of Bernard Shaw* and editor of *SHAW* 13: *Shaw and Other Playwrights*.

Charles A. Carpenter is Professor Emeritus of English at Binghamton University. He is the author of *Bernard Shaw & the Art of Destroying Ideals: The Early Plays* and *Modern Drama Scholarship and Criticism 1966–1990: An International Bibliography* (2 vols.). His latest book, *Dramatists and the Bomb: American and British Playwrights Confront the Nuclear Age, 1945–1964*, will be published this year.

Fred D. Crawford, *SHAW* General Editor, is Associate Professor of English at Central Michigan University. He has written several books and articles on modern British literature, most recently *Richard Aldington and Lawrence of Arabia: A Cautionary Tale*, and is completing a biography of the American news broadcaster Lowell Thomas and an edition of Thomas's letters.

Bernard F. Dukore, University Distinguished Professor Emeritus of Theatre Arts and Humanities at Virginia Tech, has written numerous books and articles, chiefly on modern drama and theater. His most recent Shavian works are *The Drama Observed*, *Bernard Shaw and Gabriel Pascal*, and *Bernard Shaw on Cinema*.

Robert G. Everding is Professor of Theatre and Dean of the College of Fine Arts and Communication at the University of Central Arkansas.

He was the founder and initial artistic director of the Houston Shaw Festival as well as a past contributor to *SHAW*.

Leon H. Hugo is Professor Emeritus of English at the University of South Africa and a member of the *SHAW* Editorial Board. He has contributed several articles and reviews to the *SHAW* and is the author of *Bernard Shaw: Playwright and Preacher* and *Edwardian Shaw: The Writer and His Age*, to be published in 1998.

Dan H. Laurence, author of *Bernard Shaw: A Bibliography* and editor of Shaw's *Collected Letters* and *Shaw's Music*, was Literary and Dramatic Advisor to the Shaw Estate from 1973 to 1990 and is an Associate Director of the Shaw Festival, Ontario. His latest publications are *Theatrics* and, with Daniel J. Leary, the third and last volume of Shaw's *Complete Prefaces*.

Rhoda Nathan, President of the Bernard Shaw Society, teaches English at Hofstra University. In addition to writing about Shaw, she has published extensively on American literature and is author of a critical biography of the New Zealand writer Katherine Mansfield. She is a 1997–98 Everett Helm Visiting Fellow at Indiana University Lilly Library.

John R. Pfeiffer is Professor of English at Central Michigan University and Bibliographer of *SHAW*. His most recent articles are on Richard Francis Burton, Octavia Butler, John Christopher, and Etheridge Knight.

Michel W. Pharand has taught in universities in North America, Iraq, and Japan, and is currently a visiting research scholar at the University of Georgia. He has published on Robert Graves, Lawrence Durrell, and on Shaw's affinities with Eugène Brieux, Henri Bergson, and Romain Rolland.

Julie A. Sparks is a doctoral candidate at the Pennsylvania State University specializing in Shaw and utopian studies.

Mark H. Sterner is a theater historian currently teaching at Illinois Central College in East Peoria. In addition to writing about Shaw, he has published articles on method acting, nineteenth-century British dramatists, and the evolution of American burlesque.

Alfred Turco, Jr., is Professor of English at Wesleyan University and a member of the *SHAW* Editorial Board. He is author of *Shaw's Moral Vision* and editor of *SHAW* 7: *Shaw: The Neglected Plays*.

Brian Tyson, English Professor Emeritus at the University of Lethbridge, Alberta, is author of *The Story of Shaw's "Saint Joan"* and editor of *Bernard Shaw's Book Reviews in the "Pall Mall Gazette" from 1885 to 1888* and *Bernard Shaw's Book Reviews, Volume 2: 1884 to 1950*.

Jeffrey M. Wallmann is an instructor in the English Department at the University of Nevada, Reno. He has published more than 200 novels under 22 pseudonyms in several genres, including mystery, science fiction, western, and historical romance, in addition to more than 100 short stories, novelettes, and articles. His work has appeared in numerous anthologies in six languages and has been adapted for television and movies.

Rodelle Weintraub has edited *Fabian Feminist*, *Shaw Abroad* (*SHAW* 5), and the Garland *Captain Brassbound's Conversion*. She has also co-edited, with Stanley Weintraub, two Bantam volumes of Shaw's plays: *Arms and the Man & John Bull's Other Island* and *Heartbreak House & Misalliance*.

Stanley Weintraub, Evan Pugh Professor of Arts and Humanities at Penn State, edited the *Shaw Review* and *SHAW* from 1956 through 1990. He has written or edited more than forty books on Shaw and his times, most recently *Shaw's People: Victoria to Churchill* and *Albert: Uncrowned King*.